Pride of Baltimore

The Story of the Baltimore Clippers 1800–1990

Thomas C. Gillmer

INTERNATIONAL MARINE

Camden, Maine

Published by International Marine

10 9 8 7 6 5 4 3 2 1

Library of Congress Cataloging-in-Publication Data

Gillmer, Thomas Charles, 1911-
    Pride of Baltimore : the story of the Baltimore Clippers,
1800-1990 / Thomas C. Gillmer.
        p.   cm.
    Includes bibliographical references and index.
    ISBN 0-87742-309-1
    1. Baltimore clippers—History.   2. United States—
History—War of 1812—Naval operations, American.
3. Privateering—Maryland—Baltimore Region—History—
19th century.   4. Pride of Baltimore
(Ship)   I. Title.
VM311.F7G55   1992
387.2′24′0973—dc20   91-44196
                                                                          CIP

Questions regarding the content of this book should be
addressed to:

International Marine
P.O. Box 220
Camden, ME 04843

Typeset by A & B Typesetters, Bow, NH
Printed by Arcata Graphics, Fairfield, PA
Design by Joyce C. Weston
Illustrations on pages 8, 9, 31, 35, 89, 93, 112 by Tom Price
Edited by J.R. Babb, Jane Crosen, Thomas P. McCarthy
Production by Janet Robbins

Contents

Baltimore; the revival of old construction techniques; launching, ballasting, and rigging; broad horizons; sailing characteristics and performance; a tragic destiny

The official investigation of the *Pride*'s loss; the conclusion: "a sudden and extreme wind"; designing a replacement ship, the *Pride of Baltimore II*; improving on authenticity; sources of quality wood; construction, launching, rigging; a fast passagemaker; the new ship's performance and promise; the total archaeological experiment

Appendices

Acknowledgments

Writing a book is not like designing a ship or an antique topsail schooner, except that in each case some outside help is needed.

The book-writing process, far more than ship design, needs outside help like a seed needs water and rich soil and sunshine. It was my association with the research involved in replicating two Baltimore Clippers, in the beginning, from which the seed for this book germinated. It did take root, but the ground was not very fertile. For it to grow, encouragement was important, together with recognition of the historic story. I would like to name several people to whom I am especially indebted, not only for their special skills, but for their enthusiastic help and cooperation.

Accomplished historian/archivist Jane Wilson McWilliams was an unlimited source of knowledge of archives related to the neglected phase of American history I was trying to piece together, of where else I could find confirmation and evidence for apparent happenings and trends. She was of immeasurable energy and patience, and I am as much indebted to her for this as for her knowledge.

Next there is Tom Price and his pen. With his knowledge of sailing and watercraft, he was able to realistically put wind and motion into the sails of schooners and other vessels that he drew for my requirements. A skilled craftsman regularly employed in the Naval Academy's Ship's Hydrodynamics Laboratory and part of its support staff, Tom knows the form and way of a ship in the water.

There were also many cooperative museum coordinators and staff, such as Kathy Flynn, with the Peabody Museum in Salem, Massachusetts; Richard Dodds, Curator of the Chesapeake Bay Maritime Museum in St. Michaels, Maryland; the very helpful and knowledgeable John Vandereedt of the National Archives in Washington, D.C.; Jeff Goldman of the Maryland Historical Society in Baltimore; Dr. Paul F. Johnston, Curator of Transportation at the National Museum of American History, Smithsonian Institution; as well as many others.

And, of course, I cannot fail to express my appreciation for and praise of the building crews of both *Prides* of Baltimore. Without the unique skills and dedication of these individuals, it would not have been possible to translate architectural concepts into fully operational sailing vessels. It is unlikely that their kind will ever assemble again for such an enterprise.

To gather the documentation and support for this historical narrative requires many months of continuous search—much of it unfruitful, digressive, or wasteful. The rewarding part, when completed, is most satisfying, and I cannot complete my grateful acknowledgments without a special thank you to my most diligent, capable, knowledgeable, and patient secretary, Joyce Valiukonis.

Thomas C. Gillmer
Annapolis, Maryland
1991

Preface

Baltimore Clippers, as we now call them, developed in the Chesapeake in the late 18th and early 19th centuries according to a simple, urgent formula: speed combined with exceptional performance under sail.

Speed, of course, is a relative thing. There has always been a quest for speed, particularly in waterborne craft, but most often it has been subordinated to other interests. In the late 18th century, fast fishing vessels operated from both sides of the English Channel to speed the fresh catch to market. Fast and maneuverable vessels operated under lateen sails in the Mediterranean—mostly in the hands of Arab pirates. But in Europe and America, the concerns of high-seas commerce subordinated speed in favor of enhanced ability to transport cargo—or heavy weapons.

The average speed of sailing ships had changed little in nearly half a millennium. Medieval cogs of the Hanseatic League, the ships of Columbus, Magellan, or James Cook—all averaged, under good sailing weather, only six-and-one-half or at best seven knots.

In 1492, Columbus's *Santa Maria* crossed the Atlantic in 32 days, sailing in the easterly tradewinds. One-and-a-half centuries later, the *Mayflower*, in Atlantic winter gales, took more than two months. The *Santa Maria* was a slow sailer and so was the *Mayflower*. According to their logs and journals, neither could sail much better than five-and-one-half knots—average performance for a merchant vessel of their day.

John Paul Jones, as an aggressive naval officer, pleaded, "Give me a fast ship, for I intend to go in harm's way." Instead, the Continental Congress gave him an old but renovated French East Indiaman, a large and heavily armed (but slow) sailing fortress, the famous *Bonne Homme Richard*. Jones's log reveals daily speeds of five, six, or seven knots, and an occasional (and highly exceptional) eight—a result of Jones's tendency to carry sail even in gale-force winds that often carried away spars. Speed was relative. All these monuments to sea power and workhorse commerce moved slowly, their holds full and their decks heavy with guns.

By the late 18th century, shipwrights in the Chesapeake Bay region had begun to build seagoing vessels in their own way, discarding the shipping-board rules and the bureaucratic and Admiralty thinking that had so long guided shipbuilders abroad and in most of the developing American colonies.

The world into which these Chesapeake Bay builders were moving their product was hostile and ruthless. America had no credible naval strength or effective protection of commerce. The Baltimore-built schooners were built to survive—or blunt the effect of a blockaded coast, if it came to that—through superior sailing performance.

Maintaining the European trade was the underlying financial force that fueled the growing shipyards at Fells Point. But at the same time, the Royal Navy's bullying and illegal tactics, stopping and searching American ships and kidnapping American sailors for British naval service, was becoming intolerable. The smell of armed conflict was heavy in the air along the almost defenseless American coast. Consequently, by the early 1800s a new type of relatively small seagoing vessel, generally of square topsail schooner rig and able to outsail most any vessel wherever encountered, began to appear in the Chesapeake Bay. The Chesapeake builders introduced state-of-the-art topsail schooners and brigs of up to 200 tons, with astonishingly better sailing performance—performance encompassing not only raw speed through the water, but an ability to sail closer to the wind. The new vessels made way upwind at unprecedented rates, and in adversarial meetings at sea could take the weather gauge and hold it, or cut out merchant ships from an enemy convoy, or slip through enemy blockades almost at will. A Baltimore Clipper could accelerate rapidly, and easily reach and cruise at speeds up to 11 and 12 knots.

During the War of 1812, the Baltimore Clippers reflected their brightest image, but alas received little credit for it. It is hoped that the following pages will redress that, and substantiate their deserved importance in bringing the war with England to an honorable end. Their history also has a brief dark side, but their heritage prevailed and influenced watercraft design universally. Indeed, they must be credited as the ancestor of the great clipper ships of the mid-19th century.

This narrative intends to present an accurate account of the exceptional sharp-built vessels of the upper Chesapeake, derived from designing, building, and operating the re-created *Prides* of Baltimore. I hope that it makes their importance in our early history apparent, and brings to light their exploits, their beauty, and their unique heritage. They were truly the first all-American contribution to shipbuilding and design.

Thomas C. Gillmer

Introduction

This is the story of a long-neglected part of American maritime history. Like many stories of past endeavors, more has been forgotten or plowed under than has been given notice or credit where due. Our story is of the creation, growth, and impact of a simple type of sailing vessel, nurtured on the Chesapeake Bay. The impact of these remarkable fast-sailing schooners and brigs on our country's conflicts and growth was somehow, unhappily, lost to history. Perhaps it is because during their first and only great public exposure, as privateer schooners in the War of 1812, they were not part of the government establishment. Their decks were not trodden by upwardly mobile young naval officers. They took no part in historically noted naval engagements, even though precious few naval engagements in that war resulted in victorious applause or had an impact on the war's conclusion.

I am aware of the sensitivity of many patrons and followers of traditional naval history, and I do not mean to belittle United States naval activity in the War of 1812. Win or lose, in battles or single-ship engagements, that activity was heroic. The Battle of Lake Erie, the only fleet engagement, was a singular success and a strategic national victory. The few frigate-to-frigate and ship-to-ship engagements ending in British defeat or withdrawal were notable occasions, resulting in much lifting of public spirit.

But the activities of the small, fast, topsail schooners of the Chesapeake were not of the type given to public attention. Their victories were not the spectacular and celebrated surrenders after day-long battles; rather, their victories and successes were hidden by the very nature of their service. Their successes were strategical rather than tactical, and involved a war of attrition against the English economy — preying on English merchant ships and transports, running enemy blockades, passing unseen in the dark of the moon through shrouded seas. When discovered, they could outsail their opponents, and so the privateers followed regular and consistent schedules. Ultimately, they brought this audacious effrontery to the very waters and shores of Great Britain, and there was nothing the Royal Navy could do about it. The British merchant ship convoys were only marginally effective; the privateer schooners from the Chesapeake could cut out the stragglers and, one at a time, take them captive, transfer cargo, and sink them.

The vast and much-heralded naval superiority of Great Britain was helpless against these frequent raids, and the constant drain on their supply lines continued. War on the Continent persisted, and Napoleon's troops remained England's greatest threat. England could little stand this additional frustration and cost. At one point, commerce was brought to a mere trickle because of American privateers, mostly Baltimore-built schooners. British marine insurance rates rose to intolerable levels, despite the fact that nearly all United States naval frigates were bottled up by the British blockade.

In America, private investors of Baltimore and elsewhere found privateering profitable; the clippers were popular investments throughout the 15 states. When Captain Thomas Boyle of the Baltimore Clipper *Chasseur* posted on the front door of Lloyd's of London a notice that Great Britain was under a state of total blockade, it was considered a boastful presumption. It was not taken as such by the marine insurers within. Finally, the enemy's frustrations ran their course, and in 1815, with the Treaty of Ghent, the British government came to terms, satisfying complaints that had brought our young, struggling democracy to the desperation of war. The War of 1812 has been called the second American Revolution, and perhaps it was. It restored American self-esteem, it created a peace at home and a freedom on the seas and abroad to build a solid and dependable trade. America finally earned respect among world nations.

The Baltimore Clipper was soon forgotten by the public, but not by those who needed fast vessels. After 1815 these remarkable sailing machines fell into disrepute. The majority were sold by their owners and investors into South American and Caribbean ownership, where they found new employment in South American insurrections and revolutionary wars and conflicts. Some were resold into the slave trade—a terrible business in which they proved only marginally profitable. Their speed meant they often could outrun their naval pursuers, but their small holds limited their capacity for human cargo. Later, naval patrol vessels of similar design made evasion more difficult, and their careers as slavers ended.

Although these hastily built wartime vessels did not enjoy long lives, their style, sailing performance, and unique design lived on. Large pilot boats of the Atlantic Coast adopted their style. Baltimore Clippers were studied in England as early as the 1812 conflict, and their style was later copied and built there. Most important, it is believed now that, despite some previous claims to the contrary, the Baltimore Clipper design spawned the great Clipper Ship Era of the 1850s. This heritage, together with the remarkable 1812 wartime record of these plain, "sharp-built" schooners of Baltimore, is significant enough to give belated recognition of their unparalleled contributions to American history and maritime development.

Lately, two well-constructed, late-20th-century examples of 1810-type square-topsail Baltimore Clipper schooners have substantiated the reputation for speed and mobility that was so well advanced by the clippers of 175 years ago. The design, construction, and operational experience of each of these living representatives of sailing archaeology are relevant to the Baltimore Clipper story, and told on the following pages. Even the tragic loss of *Pride of Baltimore* in 1986 did nothing to diminish her performance and reputable history of nearly 10 years and 150,000 nautical miles at sea. Her successful mission had won such broad support that there was a spontaneous mandate for replacement. The second *Pride of Baltimore* followed and was afloat and at sea in October 1988.

The story goes on. . . .

CHAPTER ONE

Origins: Fast Schooners
of America and Europe

Some time during 1974, the city officials of Baltimore began to inquire about the feasibility of re-creating a Baltimore Clipper as a center of attraction for the reawakening waterfront. The city had two requirements: the ship must be an authentic replication of an early-19th-century Baltimore Clipper, and it must be built on location—on the waterfront of the newly developing Inner Harbor.

A representative of the Charles Center-Inner Harbor Management visited me at the time, but after duly considering the matter, I rejected it, at least temporarily. Those two requirements—authenticity and building it in Center City, where no shipyard existed or should properly exist within two or three blocks of the business district of downtown Baltimore—needed more time and study.

Few replica ships or re-creations of this sort were being or had been built elsewhere, perhaps not since *Mayflower II*. She had been built in 1953, in Devonshire, England, for the historical group now known as "Plimoth Plantation." She was designed by the well-known architect and historian William Baker of Boston and based on very sparse documentation.

There had been, of course, the HMS *Bounty*, built in Lunenburg, Nova Scotia, in 1961 for filming the well-known story on the mutiny. There was also a re-creation in 1970 of Sir Francis Drake's *Golden Hinde* of 1577 which, like *Mayflower II*, was built in Devonshire without much to go by but Elizabethan-style, non-technical, general-

◀ 1

ized ship rendering and tonnage measurements. These were all good ships and served historical purposes, but close authenticity was not a prime requirement.

In the case of more recent vessels such as the Baltimore schooners of the first decade of the 19th century, there is considerably more information. More, but still not enough: no design plans, few contemporary pictures, some British dockyard plans of specific vessels, which were invaluable, but for the most part vast, empty volumes of knowledge.

The place to begin the study of these intriguing vessels was their beginnings, their origins, if such could be found. So, in mid-1975, before the construction had been fully agreed upon and certainly before a design had been drafted, I undertook research that led me first to recall the maritime environment of the Chesapeake Bay in the colonial and post-colonial periods.

The origins

During this early time, the shores of the Chesapeake, for the most part, were in the same primeval state as Captain John Smith found them in 1608. There were several colonial settlements and towns on the Eastern and Western shores. Between these towns, communication and transport were essentially waterborne. The few roads frequently led to ferry landings. Because of wind and tide and winter weather, sailing ferries were not entirely dependable nor, even at their best, very swift. As the country developed to the west of the Chesapeake Bay, the Eastern Shore in particular gradually became isolated and insular. Indeed, less than 50 years ago travelers and shipments of produce to Baltimore and Annapolis from various destinations on the Eastern Shore depended largely upon the ferries.

It was this isolation, as well as the natural resources, that undoubtedly contributed to the creativity of Maryland and Virginia shipbuilders living on both shores of this great primordial sunken estuary. The Bay's shoreline is almost impossible to measure, so penetrated is it by tidal rivers, genuine rivers, creeks, coves, and tidal inlets. It divides and subdivides, erodes, shifts, and rebuilds as the ocean tides flood up from the south and ebb with the freshwater drainage from the surrounding country. The great Potomac and greater Susquehanna spill their constant flow from what are now six sovereign states.

The resources discovered by the first 17th-century settlers were not gold or easy living, but wooded land and extensive seafood-laden waters and shores with natural harbors with minimal change in tidal level. The land on the western shore was rich for crops, but the eastern shores were not as well suited for contemporary cash crops such as tobacco. The trees were tall, however, and oak and pine grew in abundance.

In this great natural domain, people naturally turned to their resources, most settlers being dependent on the water and waterborne craft and trade. The first boats were built primitively; in more populated centers they were built on styles and rules already imported from Europe.

The indigenous watercraft began in most lowly form, the same as in any primitive country anywhere. It was, of course, a style adopted from the land's own native Americans—the dugout log canoe, a sturdy, dependable craft, but with severe limitations. The log canoe seems to endear itself to people who are isolated, clinging to the tried and true and ancestral ways. But it must be noted that the residents of the eastern shores of the Chesapeake Bay had, over the 350 years after the first English settlements, refined the log canoe to a higher state of the art than any other maritime people.

It began, of course, with a single log, as was used by resident natives. As demand for travel and exploitation of marine life grew, the log-bottomed watercraft became larger and more complex. First two logs were fastened together, then three, then five. In the middle to late 19th century, the log canoe had developed about as far as it could go. By that time it had formed the foundation of the Bay's most efficient and ubiquitous sailing oyster-gathering boats. The Chesapeake Bugeye, with its two raked masts, broad deck, and clipper bow, could outsail any other fishing rig on the Bay. It was powerful enough under sail to drag its heavy iron dredge over an oyster bed, and when its hold was full and its decks nearly awash, it could sail quickly to the markets of Baltimore or Annapolis to unload its precious living cargo. These boats, nearly 20 registered tons, 60 feet long, and schooner rigged, were direct descendants of dugout log canoes. Indeed, mid-19th-century builders on the Eastern Shore who were not adequately learned to loft keel patterns and frames built their hulls with seven to nine logs. (The still-surviving racing log canoe is built of five logs.) These shapely sailing bottoms were literally sculpted by the skillful builder's adze — a tool so old that it was used by the Egyptians and early Aegeans to build their boats in the Bronze Age, nearly 4,000 years ago. The adze is still used in wooden ship building and in other wood construction where heavy timbers must be shaped on site.

The last surviving working bugeye — the *Edna E. Lockwood*, built on the Chesapeake's Eastern Shore in 1889 — is now owned, maintained, and sailed by the Chesapeake Bay Maritime Museum in St. Michaels, Maryland. She has a bottom of nine logs.

I mention the Chesapeake log canoe not in connection to the origins of the first Baltimore Clippers or the larger schooners, but to focus on the importance and significance of the skill of the native, isolated Chesapeake boatbuilders. The men who built the Chesapeake Bay log canoes were from the same families as the builders of the great sharp-built schooners, the ultimate Baltimore Clippers of the first years of the 19th century. The inherent creative skills of these builders are apparent in the illustrations of the log canoe *Jay Dee* under construction (Figures 1-1 through 1-3) and sailing (Figure 1-4).

During the pre–Revolutionary War and colonial years, Chesapeake builders constructed vessels that were more sophisticated than the log canoes, and closely related to the later fast, seagoing craft and the larger schooners. It is best to begin with the boats of the American colonial period.

Colonial shipbuilding

The first colonial shipbuilders came to America from European shipyards, in response to demand from the New World. Their ships, especially the larger merchant ships and smaller war vessels, were also in demand back in Europe. Frequently, ships built in the Chesapeake region were delivered to England with a hold full of Virginia or Maryland tobacco (Figure 1-5); no doubt the ships built in New England also took this same advantage with their export goods. For the colonials owed their loyalty to their homelands and governments, be it England, Holland, France, or elsewhere. Colonial ships, sold

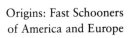

Figure 1-1. Center log of the log canoe roughed out. Note center-board bossing.

Figure 1-2. Roughed-out starboard side logs of canoe. Two wing logs attached to center log.

abroad, had been built according to European standards and shipping rules—old rules, traditional and rigorous.

Sometime in the mid-17th century, smaller coastwise vessels began to appear whose sails hung no more from the long, awkward sprits or squareyards, but from gaffs pivoted aloft at the mast. This evolution of rig, probably born in Holland, became the true fore-and-aft sail. It was an invention of liberation. These first gaff-rigged *fore-and-afters* were seen on small one- and two-masted open boats (Figure 1-6). Their quick maneuvering in going to windward must have attracted amazement and envy, and larger coastwise boats soon began to use this style of sail. The *gaff*—the spar at the top of the sail angled to the mast with open jaws—moved port-to-starboard, holding the sail laced or hooped to the mast and along its luff. The *boom*—the horizontal base spar—controlled the sail's radial movement at the deck level. A boat of this rig with two or more masts became known as a *schooner* (Figure 1-7).

This sort of rig was not an American invention. It began in Holland for inland and harbor craft and quickly spread in northern Europe and then to America, where conditions for its exploitation were ripe.

Figure 1-3. Log hull completely adzed, exterior and interior smoothly sculpted.

Here we are concerned with the schooner because it originated from a growing sloop—a sloop of a single mast carrying a gaff-rigged mainsail and a jib with also, perhaps, several outer jibs. Let us take another look at this *sloop* of the mid-18th century.

During this time, some very large sloops were sailing in many countries, perhaps most commonly in northern Europe. In Holland, this type was known as a *sloep*; in Sweden, a *slup*; in France, a *chaloupe*; in Spain and in the Basque region, a *chalupa*. The English

Figure 1-4. The resulting five-log canoe of Figures 1-1, 1-2, and 1-3: The famous racing canoe of Maryland's Eastern Shore, Jay Dee.

word, *shallop*, was more ambiguous. True, a shallop was often a small, single-masted fore-and-aft-rigged boat, but the term was also used more loosely to describe various small open boats. The British ultimately became deferential and described a sloop as a single-masted craft with a gaff sail and a fixed bowsprit for several triangular headsails. A similar craft was identified as a *cutter* if the bowsprit was not fixed but could be withdrawn inboard for shortening the rig; the mast was accordingly a bit farther aft, to balance the flexible head

Figure 1-5. Colonial Chesapeake-built brig of 1778, Middleton, *shown resting against stone quay at low tide.*

rig. To add to the confusion, the British and their New England colonies regionally referred to some working sloops as *smacks*.

But in developing pre-Revolution America and during the whole 18th century, sloops were most abundant as coastwise and estuarine transport. They were vessels of up to 80 or more feet in length. Some naval sloops were armed with eight or ten guns, as on John Paul Jones's first navy command, *Providence*.

The schooner's definition does not indicate what use the vessel was put to, and rightly so. There were fast schooners, slow schooners, lumber schooners, fishing schooners, topsail schooners, privateer schooners, schooner-yachts—these were the most familiar ones. We will be interested in fast privateer schooners and from whence they came. But, for now, let us look at the descriptive and deceptive word *fast* as applied to sailing vessels.

◀ 9

Origins: Fast Schooners
of America and Europe

Figure 1-6. Typical 17th-century Dutch schooner, circa 1650.

Pride of Baltimore

Speed on the water

Fast is a relative term, and when applied to waterborne craft in terms of speed or rate of motion, it seems unimpressive. With our media reporting sailing yachts breaking records held for 135 years by some of the great Yankee Clippers, and with multihull *America*'s Cup defenders being challenged in court because they exceed intended speeds, we must speak only of traditional, monohull, displacement-type vessels. These are the historical watercraft of a very simple concept of unknown age.

The speed of a traditional waterborne craft is limited almost entirely by its length on the waterline: its flotation length. The formula, developed according to hydrodynamics experimentation in the mid-19th century and still holding, states that this speed is *limited by the speed on the wave train the vessel is generating in going through the water and in the same direction.* As a vessel goes faster, the length between ship-generated wave crests that are running with the vessel becomes greater. When this wave length, beginning with the first crest under the bow, becomes longer than the vessel's waterline, the stern

Figure 1-7. Chesapeake schooner 1750, after HMS Berbice.

will fall and the bow will rise, and then begins a generally impossible uphill climb. Expressing the simple relationship of speed and length in knots and feet, is a generally useful ratio called the *speed/length ratio*, the ship's speed in knots divided by the square root of its water-line length. For most sailing displacement hulls, the speed/length ratio is close to a limiting constant value of 1.34. It can easily be seen that the natural law indicates increased length means greater speed.

A sailing vessel, in order to be fast, has two fundamental resources: its hull shape must be moved easily through the layer of water in which it floats, and it must have the power in its sail plan to overcome the hull's water resistance up to the optimum speed. We are concerned primarily with the hull shape, although the sail plan is not unimportant.

It has been said often by writers and historians of the early Baltimore schooners (who share each other's opinions) that the fast, sharp-built hulls were inspired by Bermuda sloops (Figure 1-8) of the

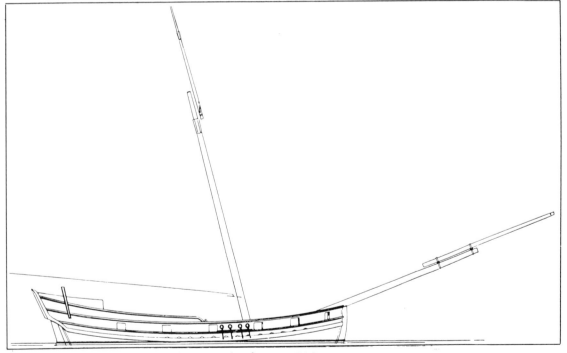

Figure 1-8. Profile of typical Bermuda sloop, 1780.

mid- and late 18th century, whose characteristics were in turn descended from the Jamaican pirate vessel of the 17th century. There is no better response to this than "Poppycock!" There is absolutely no evidence for this sort of ancestry. In the first place, the hulls of Bermuda sloops are well documented from contemporary illustrations and the fine design drawings in Chapman's *Architectura Navalis Mercatoria* of 1760. The Bermuda sloops show no similarity to the sharper Chesapeake types of the same period. Rather, they were of high freeboard, full and chunky bows, and generally similar to British fishing and Channel craft of the same period. Further, the alleged ancestry to Jamaican pirate craft is entirely incredible. Like all pirates, those from Jamaica used whatever craft they could steal!

The creation of a *low-drag* form is not something that can be credited to any specific origin. It was not created or invented by anyone from any particular land or chronological frame. Perhaps it was earlier applied or adapted, but such first use would be unknown. The ideas and examples of form related to low fluid resistance exist in nature and can be applied by any interested observer. The shape of islands in a river, the form of wind-eroded sand on a beach, the shape of fish and water mammals—all are graphic proof of optimal low fluid drag.

The true origins of the sharper, faster sailing craft that influenced the Chesapeake builders came from old and basic sources, seen in the experience and skill of the builders of watercraft. These fine craftsmen, through the ages, left no documents but their work—their beautiful and graceful boats—and their knowledge existed more than 24 centuries ago in the eastern Mediterranean and 11 or more centuries ago among the fjords in Scandinavia; this we know from archaeological finds still being uncovered. These skills were alive in the ancient Aegean islands, on the Scandinavian fjords and islands, and on the Mediterranean coasts of Tuscany and Aquitaine, Algiers and Morocco, and still later in the colonies of America, in the Chesapeake and northern New England—and innumerable places in between. Design for speed is as instinctive as it is hereditary; it is the sum of both.

I am aware that this line of thought does not entirely follow the writings of past historical traditionalists on Baltimore Clippers, and I expect there will be some objection. In any case, we can no longer indulge the common illogical and unsubstantiated stories of ancestral origins. Let me offer some early examples of fast, seagoing hulls created for specific applications, as were the "sharp-built" schooners of Baltimore.

Historical precedence

The wealthy 15th-century Mediterranean maritime states of Genoa and Venice built very fast war galleys to protect and advance their interests. The hulls of these vessels were descendants of earlier craft showing the results of rational design for speed. Long and shallow, with low freeboard for the rowing crew, these galleys were narrow in the immersed body but with flare above to support the oarlocks far outboard. The vessels were basically for oar propulsion but had auxiliary sails (Figure 1-9).

The hull form of these Mediterranean galleys, when the extravagant use of human power became impractical, was preserved among some of the states along the African coast. The Moslem pirates gave their long, lightly constructed *xebecs* (Figure 1-10) a form similar to that of the older galleys. The xebecs were slightly deeper for sailing and of greater beam, but their *entry* (immersed form forward) was fine and knifelike. The after underbody, or *run*, was flattened out in the quarters that rose from amidships in a deep, fin-like after end. The keel was deeper aft than forward, a feature now called *drag* — relatively justified as a name, but drag provided the lateral resistance that made these boats capable of going to windward. The sailing rig of the xebec was generally one or two masted, with lateen sails on long yards. These early hull features of Mediterranean craft, contributing to low water resistance and thus speed under sail, are again indicative of the shipbuilder's awareness of such a configuration.

This same skill of translating their awareness into real sea craft was evident earlier still among the boatbuilders of Scandinavia from the eighth century. These old Norse builders from the fjords of the North Sea to the Baltic were providing swift, single-squaresail galleys for the first Viking raiders and their subsequent expansion and northern migration. Their boats, built lightly and strongly with minimum internal structure but skillfully planked with overlapping strakes, set a style that was to prevail for nearly 500 years and introduced building techniques still alive today. Aside from their lightness and structure, these longships and traveling ships resembled the Mediterranean galleys and pirate xebecs in underwater hull geometry.

The great galleys of Venice and Genoa gradually gave way, together with the political fortunes of their city-states, and were replaced by even greater and faster sailing galleys of southern France. These warship galleys became popular as far north as Denmark and Sweden because of their speed and maneuverability, but it was the French galleys that established the type and advanced it to its highest development (Figure 1-11). It is said, however, that when a French galley

Figure 1-9. Demi Galleys. A pair of fast Mediterranean boats, lateen rigged. They could sail to windward or, in a calm, move out under oars. These types were semi-workboats or frequently engaged in pirate activity. They were plainly related to the great royal galleys, note the round tuck sterns. From a sketch by Antoine Roux, 1816.

was under sail, its leeward deck rail was so far immersed in foaming water that the galley slaves were up to their waists.

In the fishing industry, the boat owner's moving interest was in sailing speed, which requires the same hydrodynamic configurations as already described. For fishermen, the requirement for speed arises simply from the competition to return a fresh catch to market to command the best price.

In the turbulent channel between Britain and France there were, in the 18th and 19th centuries, tall-rigged fishing boats called *luggers*. They carried a form of fore-and-aft rig, generally on three masts, and an equal number of lugsails and topsails that were not held against the mast with gaff jaws; rather, the upper portions of the sails were controlled to pass around the masts when tacking, while being held close by bridles. These luggers, too, were of the fast hull shape, with easy waterlines and rising sections aft. They were often 60 to 70 feet

Figure 1-10. Mediterranean xebec (chebec) at anchor. From contemporary on-site wash drawing by Antoine Roux dated 1796. There is considerable similarity in hull form here to Chesapeake sharp-built craft.

long, having little overhang, but with long bowsprits and stern outriggers or boomkins. In the winds of the English Channel, with ballasts of wet fish in the hold, these luggers sailed home at nearly ten knots. They not only worked in the fisheries, but were also pilot vessels and were even occasionally adopted by English pirates who sailed out of Penzance and other harbors on the western Cornish coast. These Channel luggers are another example of an indigenous boat developed to the requirements of the environment and economics: a boat with a deep, efficient hull and a driving sail plan. Figure 1-12 shows a noteworthy French 19th-century lugger called a *Chasse Maree*.

Figure 1-11. French reale galley. Bow view of early sharp-built hull for speed.

Chesapeake forerunners

This digression from maritime America, to suggest that other fast types of sailing watercraft originated elsewhere in a similar manner, is not without purpose. Some historians look no further than 18th century Western Hemisphere waters to attempt to identify the forerunners of fast Chesapeake Bay schooners. The builders of fishing vessels of the Channel ports, the Mediterranean xebecs of the Moorish countries, and the 10th century Vikings and their longships—all of different ages and ship demographics—offer no direct evidence of inherited or adoptive shipbuilding knowledge. Yet there is a great amount of visible evidence and recognition of the same characteris-

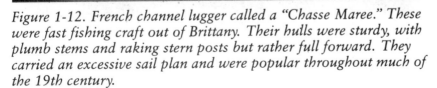

Figure 1-12. French channel lugger called a "Chasse Maree." These were fast fishing craft out of Brittany. Their hulls were sturdy, with plumb stems and raking stern posts but rather full forward. They carried an excessive sail plan and were popular throughout much of the 19th century.

tics of fast hull forms in every maritime community. Among the sailors, the builders, the originators of small sea craft nearer the sea, will more likely be found the thread of awareness and recognition of fast vessels.

It is reasonable to believe that the fast Chesapeake schooners were without immediate influential ancestors; it is best to see them as a natural growth from Chesapeake sloops, which were simply found to be too small. The Chesapeake schooners were built most likely by shipwrights with an intuitive awareness of hull shape, who were not tied closely or at all to the dusty European shipping rules, customs regulations, measurement rules, and all of the other binding restrictions of their craft. However, in the late 18th century many shipbuilding locations in the young and growing country still depended on their European ties. This financial dependency was perhaps understandable for some of the recently liberated colonials, such as tobacco planters and New England merchants, but it apparently was not much of an impediment in the upper Chesapeake Bay region.

A period of refinement

The foreign roots that we have thus far observed were not so much in the minds of the Chesapeake builders as they were subconscious, as in the instinctive bending of a plank in copying the shape of a model. The growth of Chesapeake Bay craft was also nurtured by the magnificently endowed and expansive waterway where the early European settlers found their place and environment to work. The Bay was, in the 17th and 18th century, a place of incubation for shipbuilding ideas. The watercraft grew in size and range, and some, by the time of the War of Independence, were large enough to mount cannons and go to sea. Their development impetus—and practice field—was their employment as pilot boats, blockade runners, smugglers, and privateers.

Revolutionary-era craft of this sort from the Chesapeake were not up to challenging the regular British warships, of course, nor did they pretend to. However, some had been built to British requirements before the war and were delivered with holds full of tobacco, to be converted promptly to ships of the Royal Navy.

After the surrender of Cornwallis at Yorktown, the state of the American shipbuilding industry was tenuous at best. The newfound independence, with its unsettled political disputes and the rocky beginnings of governing the country, left little time or notice to attend the growth of the maritime industry and world commerce. America actually decommissioned or sold most of the few naval vessels, only to begin building again in a few years to arm against foreign threat in the false conflict with France and later the Barbary pirates who were eroding our commerce in the Mediterranean.

It was in such a vacuum that the Chesapeake schooners underwent their period of refinement. In the upper part of the Bay, on the Eastern Shore, in and near St. Michaels, was a cluster of successful shipyards that grew in reputation and experience. Here, at this focal point on the Chesapeake, began the march toward a fully developed type that became known as the *Baltimore Flyer* and, shortly after the turn of the century, the *Baltimore Clipper*—privateers, blockade runners, naval brigs, and vessels that were used internationally wherever fast transportation on the sea was required.

A valuable source

While there is precious little in the way of late-18th-century original or contemporary plans or drawings of Chesapeake schooners that can be cited as immediate forerunners of the Baltimore Clippers, that is not to say there are none. One remarkable source stands out clearly: David Steel's *Naval Architecture*, published in London in 1805, is a most unusual early tome, and while it has outlived its usefulness as a source of scientific knowledge for the profession, it exists as a most valuable study of ship construction at the end of the 18th century. Two examples of sharp-built schooners must be noted, both for their obvious close identity and state of development in the generation of the complete Baltimore Clipper type of 1812.

The first example is a design draft of Steel's in the folio of plates, Number XXIII, labeled, "A Virginia Built Boat, Fitted For A Privateer." This plate shows a handsome lines drawing with body plan, sheer profile, and waterline plan (Figure 1-13). There is little question of the identity: a sharp-built Chesapeake schooner. The author supplied little information of origin or date. It is a schooner, although no sail plan is provided; it could be a topsail schooner, likely a double-topsail schooner, but not a brig or brigantine. This conclusion is indicated from the number and location of shrouds. Although the foremast

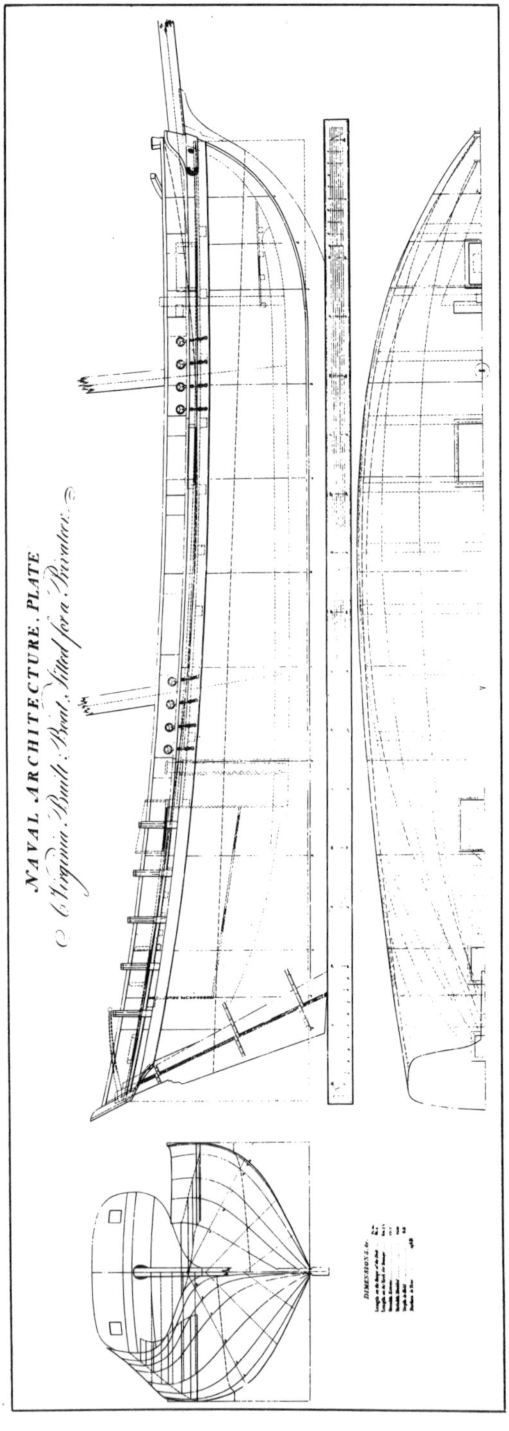

Pride of Baltimore

NAVAL ARCHITECTURE. PLATE

A Virginia Built Boat, fitted for a Privateer.

Figure 1-13. This is an early sharp-built Chesapeake schooner published in Steel's Naval Architecture *in 1805, but is of an early model indicated by its style, circa 1790. Note quarterdeck and square tuck stern.*

shroud chainplates are a bit too far forward (a possible engraver error), the fact that there are four for each mast indicates that it is similarly rigged on both masts, with both fore and main topsails requiring that number. The hull itself is of handsome form; without exaggerated deadrise in the bottom, the feature is certainly distinguished. The schooner does not have a completely flush main deck, but a break for a quarterdeck that rises aft about 12 inches where there is a companionway to the after quarters below. The stern shows a square-tuck transom with a high rise. The upsweep of her counter and sheer as well as the quarterdeck are all 18th-century features. As well, her armament is typical of Revolutionary style. She has five swivel stocks on each side of her quarterdeck, while she is pierced for fourteen guns. The number of broadside guns is not unusual for a Chesapeake privateer, but so many swivel guns on the quarterdeck indicate a different type of hostility than was customary in the War of 1812. This schooner is not large, compared to those privateers of 1812. She is 81 feet 4 inches on deck, with a bit over 22 feet extreme beam, and a draft at her sternpost of 9 feet 9 inches. Her displacement at the waterline, which was apparently recorded when her English stewardship began at the dockyard, was 156 tons.

A second example in Steel's collection is another handsome schooner called "A Fast Sailing Schooner" (Figure 1-14). This hull is a very graceful but shallow form, again with a strong sheerline, high stern, square tuck, and quarterdeck. The sections are fuller with less deadrise; a very pretty body plan. She is but 77 feet on deck, 20 feet beam, 9 feet 3 inches draft. The whole design is less typical of later Chesapeake types, but very rakish, still. She shows at the same time a Mediterranean influence, even though she is obviously of American build; she is also characteristic of privateer use. There is no draft of this vessel in Steel's folio, but rather sectional offsets, specifications, and dimensions from which the reconstruction was made by Howard Chapelle.

Both of these vessels stand out very clearly as examples in the generations' development toward the Baltimore Clippers. Both schooners are undated, but they are American built and were either sold or captured in coming into British hands for their documentation. Their style and fittings retaining Revolutionary or post-Revolutionary character place them as being built no later than 1790.

Pride of Baltimore

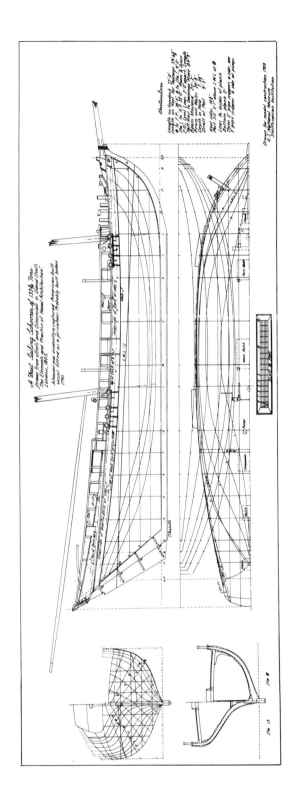

Figure 1-14. This recorded hull is also from Steel's Naval Architecture, *shown as drawn by Howard Chapelle from Steel's offsets. She is a most graceful hull, shallow in midsection with a high rising sheer aft, square tuck stern, and the pre-1800 quarterdeck-break. A lovely model for a fast Chesapeake hull.*

In this and in following chapters, I imply that there was a French influence or connection in the history of the Baltimore Clippers; certainly the French support and near adaption of the clippers during the latter part of the 18th century and early 19th century was most apparent. In this connection, it is appropriate to have the thinking of the well-known authority on the Baltimore Clippers, now gone, but whose works and words still are much with us. Howard I. Chapelle, in a lecture before the Historical Society of Talbot County, Maryland, in November 1960, was heard to say:

> "First we have the partial record of some of the Bay customhouse districts beginning in 1793-1794 under the newly formed Federal Government. Abroad, we find numerous plans of American-built schooners and other vessels, many resulting from French purchases of suitable schooners for privateering and the capture of these by the British Navy.
>
> "So active were the French in purchasing large, fast, and often specially built schooners on the Eastern Shore . . . that the British government was moved to protest to the American Minister."

American owners ignored the complaint and delivered fast schooners with cargoes assigned to French West Indian ports, and those, when successful in running the British blockades, were sold "ship and cargo" to French privateer owners. These were schooners of less than one step away from the extreme examples of ultimate Baltimore Clippers of only a decade to come.

According to Chapelle, the Eastern Shore shipbuilders were by 1811 numerous and prosperous. Talbot and Dorchester counties were then the leading shipbuilding areas. Baltimore had numerous yards and was building large, fast ships, brigs, and schooners, but suffered a chronic shortage of labor. This latter note, it is believed, was not entirely true. It is true, however, that wages paid in Baltimore during this time were higher than those on the rural Eastern Shore, which accounted for a small migration of labor to Baltimore, by this time a significantly large industrial center. Baltimore was attracting skilled shipbuilders at least as early as the beginning of the 19th century. As a notable example, Thomas Kemp, the famous builder of the notorious *Chasseur, Comet,* and others, left St. Michaels, Talbot County, in 1804 to set up a yard in Baltimore's Fells Point. Many privateers were built on the Eastern Shore, but in numbers they could not compete with Fells Point. However, the documentation shows twenty-four privateers built during the three years of the War of 1812 in Talbot County alone.

An industry grows

Early in the 18th century on the upper reaches of the Patapsco River estuary, there was a small community named Baltimore Town. Laid out and chartered in 1730 by the General Assembly of Maryland, it had a population of about 1,000 and was said to be growing. Twenty-two years later, the population was down to 200 inhabitants, and at best estimate one could count only something less than 30 homes, and poor ones at that—nothing to compare with the mansions and plantations of the century-old capital, Annapolis, 30 miles to the south. In the year 1730 in an area to the east of Baltimore Town called Copus Harbor, a William Fell purchased a tract of 100 acres. He had recently arrived from England and married a young lady named Sarah Bond. For the next ten years, Fell continued to buy property in the area, and by 1734 he owned 1,100 acres in a place he then called Fells Point. In 1758, the only son of William Fell, named Edward, had inherited not only his father's land, but that of his father's brother, who had also been involved in the local real estate business. In 1763, the area blossomed into a town named Fells Point.

The location of this town, along the deep-water-protected portion of the Patapsco estuary, near extensive growth of timber, was ideal for shipbuilding and commerce. Streets and lots had been laid out earlier with such nostalgic (and promotional) names as Thames Street, Shakespeare Street, Strawberry Alley, and Petticoat Lane. The lots next to the water at the Point were soon purchased by a Benjamin Griffith and a Benjamin Nelson, followed by Ridgely, Patton, and Hollingsworth—all to become historical establishments such as shipyards and warehouse wharfs known far into the 20th century. In this early group, Mark Alexander of Thames Street and George Wells of Bond Street, together with Benjamin Nelson, soon began shipyards, building the early type of schooners whose destiny became history.

Over the years between 1760 and 1780, developers nibbled away at the town of Fells Point, assisted by political opportunists who recognized the industrial prosperity of the location and its support for the poorer Baltimore Town. In November 1781, the last portion of Fells

Point was annexed into Baltimore, from Fleet Street to Hampstead Street, by order of the General Assembly. The Fells Point community fought the idea of becoming part of the city charter of "greater" Baltimore for another 15 years; this, however, became a fact in 1796.

In another location on the upper Chesapeake Bay, a growing settlement existed about 40 miles southeast of Baltimore and on its Eastern Shore. As early as the 1630s, the first settlers of the upper Bay at Kent Island established a trading post in a little harbor named Shipping Creek. By 1680, a church parish in this location was named St. Michaels, which soon became the name for the surrounding village and the river. The name for the river was gradually slurred to its present name, the Miles.

By the late 17th century (from 1680 on), this community had become a shipbuilding center, and for the first half of the 18th century a most significant shipbuilding community in the colonies. The Eastern Shore was unsuited to raising the same quality of tobacco as Virginia and the Western Shore of Maryland, and with St. Michaels being surrounded by water and forests of building timber, shipbuilding was a natural development. The waterways of the Chesapeake and the overseas demand for tobacco as well as new ships enriched this entire locality, with St. Michaels as its center. Because of its geographic setting, it had all the security of a feudal village.

A Quaker family arrived in 1678 from Yorkshire, England, and, related to the same immigrants who later settled at Fells Point, established themselves on a farm outside St. Michaels called Bay Hundred. Following this, the immigrants, Robert and Elizabeth Kemp, established a dynasty of three generations of Kemps in almost exactly 100 years. Born in 1779, Thomas Kemp had learned his trade as a shipwright by February 1803, and in order to follow his own identity as a shipbuilder without the involvement of local competition, he departed for Baltimore and Fells Point to seek his fortune. He purchased a house in Fells Point on the corner of Market and Lancaster streets. He had married in August — a young lady from Anne Arundel County named Sophia Horstman — and it was from her father, John Horstman, that Thomas purchased the house.

This young man became the builder of several of the most remarkably successful as well as notorious Baltimore Clippers. Rather incomplete records exist concerning his early career in Baltimore, but most probably he first worked for about a year in the shipyard of Joseph Sterett. By July 1805, Kemp had purchased property that became his own shipyard. It was from this date on that he began to turn out fast schooners of the pilot-boat type large enough to be blockade runners and privateers. This was before the conflict with England began in 1812, but many privateer types were being built in America primarily for running from threatening situations. Letters-of-marque were being issued, and there was much promise and encouragement in building fast vessels. Among some of the well-known vessels built in this pre-war time were: *Comet*, built in 1810 by Thomas Kemp; *Kite*, 1807, by Joseph Kemp of St. Michaels; *Lynx*, 1806, by Thomas Kemp, and another *Lynx* certificated by James Cordery in 1811; *Matchless*, 1807, by Richard Spencer, Talbot County; *Nonpareil*, 1807, by William Price; *Model*, 1807, by James Cordery; *Rossie*, 1807, by Thomas Kemp; *Superior*, 1807, by Thomas Kemp; *Robust*, 1808, by Bernard Salenave; *Swift*, 1808, by Hugh Auld, Talbot County; *Telegraphe*, 1807, by Bernard Salenave; and others.

There is some confusion concerning the builder of the *Lynx*. Florence Bourne, in a monograph written for a Maryland historical magazine, claims Thomas Kemp's ledger of 1805-1807 indicates that he built several ships "attributed to others . . . one was the schooner *Lynx*," measuring 99 tons and built in 1806. At that time, according to the same source, Thomas Kemp had some of his work done by others, perhaps subcontractors. One of these shipwrights was James Cordery, who did Kemp's spar work. At any rate, it is a fact that under the name *Lynx* there is but one carpenter's certificate filed and currently existing in the National Archives, and this names James Cordery as its builder. It is possible that this vessel may have been certificated late after being sparred and rigged by Cordery. In the credits of history, it will have to be unconfirmed and any glory jointly shared by Kemp and Cordery. The *Lynx* was not a lucky vessel, in any case.

The *Lynx*, after her untimely capture while anchored overnight in the Rappahannock River with three other Baltimore Clippers (*Arab, Racer,* and *Dolphin*), was taken into the Royal Navy and renamed *Musquidobit* after a town in Nova Scotia. She was a letter-of-marque schooner rather than an out-and-out privateer. Such vessels depended upon their extraordinary speed and windward ability to outmaneuver British warships, and became notable for their ability to run blockades almost at will. As a matter of fact, America's most important commerce with France and other European ports (except Britain) before and during the War of 1812 was carried out by letter-of-marque vessels—most of them fast Baltimore schooners. Merchants in both France and America actually specified that their merchandise be shipped in "sharp-built" Baltimore vessels. The myth that Baltimore Clippers could not be profitably used as merchant vessels loses credibility in light of this hard evidence. It was and is a truth that foreign trade will find a way to move merchandise in war and in peace; in wartime, the transportation is more expensive.

To look more closely at the *Lynx* (Figure 1-15), she was a refined Chesapeake schooner of the newest type, lightly armed (only six guns, 12-pounders), 94 feet 7 inches length on deck, 24 feet beam, 10 feet 3 inches depth of hold, and 223 tons burthen. This vessel, built in 1807 as one of the newly refined Baltimore schooners, may well have been the first of the extreme Baltimore Flyers. Her sail plan was, without any dispute, extreme, and the sail profile, with all light and heavy sails, is an exceptionally beautiful one in proportion. Carrying a fore course with stun'sails as well as topgallant stun'sails and a very large ringtail and main jackyard topsail, she must have been a beautiful sight standing up the Bay before a mild southwesterly breeze. Her rigged scale model in the Smithsonian Institution reflects a little of this.

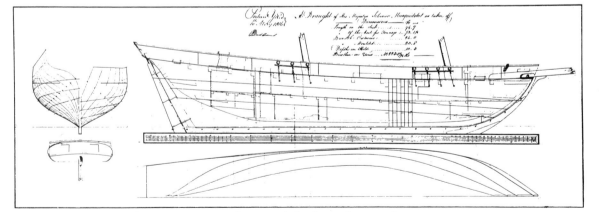

Figure 1-15. The schooner Lynx, *a fine model of a Baltimore letter-of-marque schooner captured early in her career and renamed HMS* Musquidobit.

Of course, Thomas Kemp was not the only skilled shipbuilder in Fells Point, but he built and led the way with great creative freedom and without restraint from European tradition. In addition, he was young. His apprenticeship and training started in the St. Michaels shipyards (namely one "Impey" Dawson's) with a year at Fells Point at Sterett's; he was on his own at 27 years of age. Some two dozen employees worked in Kemp's shipyard, including specialists such as caulkers, blacksmiths, riggers, and expert shipwrights. The cost of these ships in 1806-1811, usually stated in the contracts, varied between $21 and $24 per ton. The *Lynx*, for example, was near 226 tons carpenter's measure, making her basic cost approximately $5,400. In this sort of contract, the owner is obliged to provide the spars and rig, and the total ship cost, ready for sea, could be between $9,000 and $10,000.

Thomas Kemp's largest and most famous ship was one topsail-schooner-rigged, sharp-built vessel named *Chasseur*—and she was a true "hunter" in her career. But when she was conceived and built, *Chasseur*'s owner preferred a commercial fast carrier, and she was documented with a letter-of-marque, not for privateer service. We know that in her first year, 1813, she was not successful. With her first captain, she cleared Baltimore for a voyage to France—a purely trading expedition. She did not, however, get beyond Annapolis. She lay in the Severn River for weeks awaiting a break in the British blockade, and finally returned to Baltimore. Later in the year she tried again, with equal lack of aggressiveness. It was no doubt a question of a too-cautious captain. After the second time, the crew mutinied and the ill-fated *Chasseur* limped home with only a captain and two or three remaining hands.

Within a year the ship was sold, and ultimately she came into New York ownership under the command of a Baltimore resident, Thomas Boyle, the notoriously successful former commander of Thomas Kemp's *Comet*. Her official carpenter's certificate shows that she was 85 feet 8 inches length of keel (probably 115 feet on deck), 26 feet beam, 12 feet 7^1/$_2$ inches depth of hold, and 296 tons burthen, built as a schooner, round tuck and no head, for William Hollins in 1812.

When *Chasseur* sailed from New York, she sailed as a privateer, and Boyle's first destination was the British Isles. When he arrived there in Channel waters, Boyle wasted no time in having his famous pronouncement attached to the door of Lloyd's of London proclaiming that all of Britain was thenceforth under a total blockade. It is not entirely clear as to the exact means used by Boyle to affix his message to Lloyd's door; however, there is no question as to the wording. A copy survives (Figure 1-16), and there is little doubt that the intent of the message got through. It was not long before the insurance rates for commercial ships sailing in British waters, already elevated because of privateer effectiveness, became virtually prohibitive. *Chasseur* came into British waters with a crew of 155 sailors, all but perhaps five or six of whom were taken from America to become crews aboard prize (captured) vessels. It was not until these crews had been transferred to 45 British merchant ship prizes during some five-

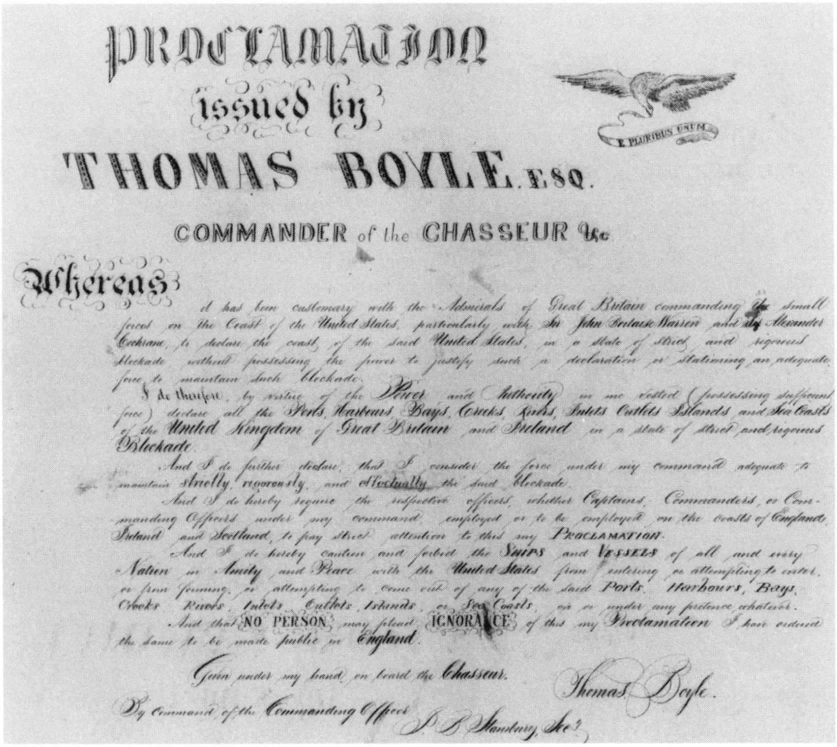
PROCLAMATION

issued by

THOMAS BOYLE, ESQ.

COMMANDER of the CHASSEUR &c

Whereas

it has been customary with the Admirals of Great Britain commanding the small forces on the Coast of the United States, particularly with Sir John Borlase Warren and Sir Alexander Cochrane, to declare the coast of the said United States, in a State of strict and rigorous blockade without possessing the power to justify such a declaration or stationing an adequate force to maintain such blockade.

I do therefore, by virtue of the Power and Authority in me vested (possessing sufficient force) declare all the Ports, Harbours, Bays, Creeks, Rivers, Inlets, Outlets, Islands and Sea Coasts of the United Kingdom of Great Britain and Ireland in a state of strict and rigorous Blockade.

And I do further declare, that I consider the force under my command adequate to maintain strictly, rigorously, and effectually the said blockade.

And I do hereby require the respective officers, whether Captains, Commanders, or Commanding Officers under my command, employed or to be employed on the coasts of England, Ireland and Scotland, to pay strict attention to this my PROCLAMATION.

And I do hereby caution and forbid the SHIPS and VESSELS of all and every Nation in Amity and Peace with the United States from entering or attempting to enter, or from coming, or attempting to come out of any of the said Ports, Harbours, Bays, Creeks, Rivers, Inlets, Outlets, Islands, or Sea Coasts, on or under any pretence whatever.

And that NO PERSON may plead IGNORANCE of this my Proclamation I have ordered the same to be made public in England.

Given under my hand on board the Chasseur.

Thomas Boyle.

By Command of the Commanding Officer

J. P. Stanbury, Sec'y

Figure 1-16. Captain Boyle's famous proclamation, which he had attached to the door of the famous marine insurance house, Lloyd's of London.

and-one-half subsequent months that Captain Boyle felt it was time to return to Baltimore. His return to greetings of the local citizens crowding Federal Hill and the newly acquired nickname "Pride of Baltimore" is now well-known history.

The others

Much has been said here and elsewhere about the great privateer *Chasseur* and her Captain Boyle, and too little about the many others, mostly, perhaps, because of the singular activity of Boyle and his audacity and celebrated homecoming. Added to this, the nature of privateering required fairly covert operation, and there was little publicity or public awareness other than the fairly continuous arrivals of captured prizes in American ports. However, in spite of all this, there is limited documentation of individual privateer success that should and will be mentioned.

The privateer *Lawrence* (Figure 1-17), a Baltimore Clipper built by James Stokes in 1813 in St. Michaels, was an exceptionally fast and responsive schooner, as said by her captain in 1814, the year of British intensification. The records of this private armed vessel's activity are attributed to her captain, who was given to extraordinary correspondence; we are grateful for his reporting because it provides not only a little spotlight on his ship and employment but additional historical confirmation as well. Captain Edward Veazey reported back to the *Lawrence*'s owner on every occasion, even by way of hailing American-bound ships at sea. He was also loquacious in the vessel's logbook. Her log for one week in April (the *Lawrence*'s first voyage), which appeared in the Maryland Historical Magazine in 1908, follows as an example:

April 19th. Latt. 31 degrees 20′ N longitude 11 degrees 15′ W. Captured English ship *Ontario*. Potter, master. Cargo: wine, brandy, salt and corkwood from Alicante to Greenock. Manned her for U.S."

April 21st. Latt. 50 degrees 45′ N longitude 11 degrees 30′ W. Boarded Portugese ship *Rosario* bound to Liverpool. With the captain's consent, put aboard of her 19 prisoners with a sufficiency of provisions and let her proceed. Same day captured English brig *Peli-*

Figure 1-17. The privateer Lawrence, *one of two named after the famous naval hero, is the apotheosis of Baltimore Clippers—a fast, maneuverable topsail schooner with a daring, skillful captain.*

can. Smith, master. From Bermuda to Liverpool. Cargo: sugar, cotton and logwood. Manned her for France.

April 22nd. Latt. 50 degrees 42′ N longitude 12 degrees 50′ W. Was chased by a ship-of-the line from half past 4 a.m. ′till 10 when we had her hull down. Several shots fired but did no injury.

April 26th. Latt. 51 degrees 25′ N longitude 13 degrees 03′ W. Captured the English brig *Ceres.* Follock, master . . . of 8 guns, 20 men from Buenos Ayres for Liverpool. Cargo: hides and horns. Manned her for the U.S.

April 28th. Latt. 51 degrees 7′ N longitude 12 degrees 29′ W. Captured brig *Edward.* Phillips, master. From Cork to Limerick. Cargo: flax seed, steel, etc. Hove the flax seed overboard, took out other articles and gave vessel up as cartel to the prisoners on board, 28 in number.

This was a busy but relatively routine week aboard a Baltimore Clipper. The following week's log has the *Lawrence* continuing in the same general vicinity, in the shipping lanes west of the entrance to the British Isles and the Channel, still encountering Royal Navy patrolling ships. On May 1 she sailed away from a man-of-war brig that came near enough in a calm to engage her in gunfire. This was at about 10 a.m., and by noon the *Lawrence* had her hull down over the horizon. The same night she found herself "alongside of a frigate . . . immediately hauled on a wind and in a very short time lost sight of her." Next day she proceeded up the Channel to Nymph's Bank. The following day "spoke the *Surprise* and *Cathera* out of Baltimore. Had taken two prizes." And the log continued, reporting captures about every other day until arrival in the Madeiras. All privateers were not as successful or probably not operated as aggressively as Captain Veazey's. He reported, for example, in the time noted above, that he had met the American privateer *Yankee* of Bristol out 49 days; ". . . had taken nothing."

The privateer schooner *Lawrence* was unquestionably a most able and swift clipper among all those that were able and swift. In addition, she was commanded by an able and committed captain: a man who understood his mission and in addition knew his vessel, and with great respect. He wrote his owner on stopping in Norfolk on his first outward voyage as well as his vessel's: "The schooner sails beyond my most sanguine expectations. She is in good order for sea."

Captain Veazey further boasts in additional letters to the owner that, upon falling in with the privateer *Yankee* of Bristol, ". . . we tried our sailing with her and beat her in every way. We have been chased by four British men-of-war and escaped easily from the whole of them."

Her partial record for the operational year of 1814, between April and September, states that she captured some 13 enemy vessels. At one time she fought off a brig-of-war with a convoy. She separated and captured eight vessels from this flotilla, one formerly the *Shadow*, a privateer out of Philadelphia. Of this captured assembly, Veazey destroyed four and manned the rest as prizes.

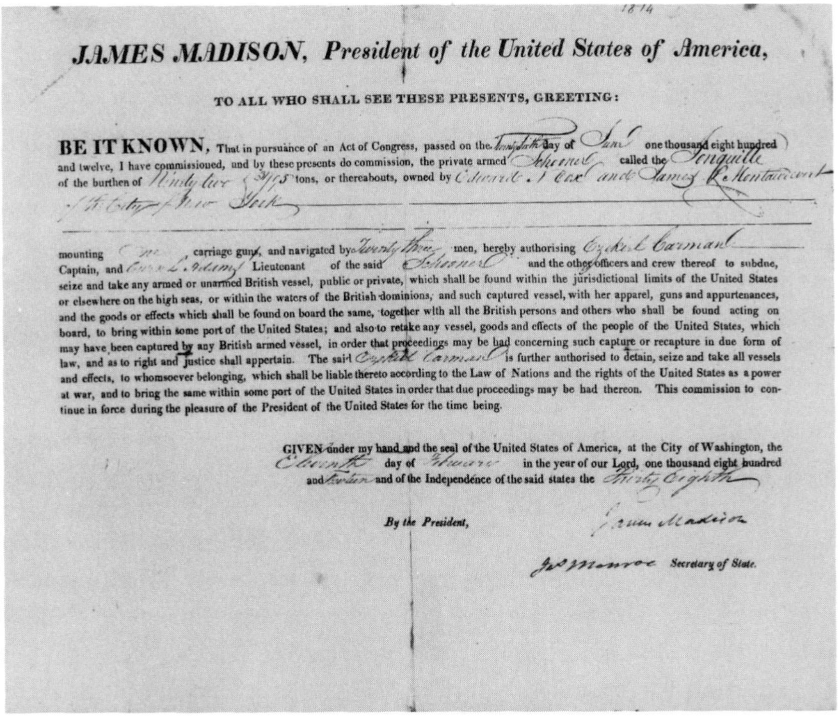

Figure 1-18. A letter of marque—a commission to engage enemy vessels and take prizes, dated February 11, 1814, authorized by President James Madison, and signed also by Secretary of State James Monroe.

The *Lawrence*, according to the carpenter's certificate dated 1813 by James Stokes of Easton Point, Talbot County, was built for J. A. Bosley. She was later apparently sold to Richard H. Douglass of Baltimore. She was 76 feet length of keel for tonnage, 24 feet 3 inches beam, and 11 feet 4 inches depth of hold. Her tonnage by carpenter's measure was 219^{82}/$_{95}$. The registered measurement shows her to be a fairly large schooner of 102 feet length of hull, 25 feet beam, and registered tons of 259.

Maneuvers under sail

Something must be said before going further about the sailing tactics of the privateers. It has been fairly well established as fact that the Baltimore schooners were fast vessels that responded quickly and moved away with considerable acceleration. Further, they could sail to windward better than any other type of vessel that was contemporary. All of these features combined were critical to the remarkable success of these vessels; however, without the proper captain, they were dead in the water, almost literally. We have an example, no doubt typical, of the schooner *Lawrence* under Captain Veazey capturing several vessels out of a flotilla. This sort of exercise was not uncommon, and its success was due to a well-executed tactical maneuver central to which was the ability to sail upwind in an exceedingly better degree than one's enemy or pursuer.

The tactic here (Figure 1-19) consisted of the privateer approaching a convoy of British merchant vessels, convoyed most likely by either a small frigate or a pair of such navy vessels. The British Admiralty followed the time-honored and heretofore reliable strategy of employing heavily-gunned vessels for both offense and defense (frequently a good, conservative system). The vessels used for convoy protection were heavily gunned, even down to the smaller fourth-rates and frigates, most of them three-masted or sometimes two-masted, square-rigged men-of-war. In any case, the convoy vessels were square rigged, built for seakeeping and long passages and well able to fight off similar enemy vessels that might attack; however, they were not prepared for the tactics of Baltimore Clippers when approached precariously closely and arrogantly teased.

The privateers would nip at the heels of the slower merchant ves-

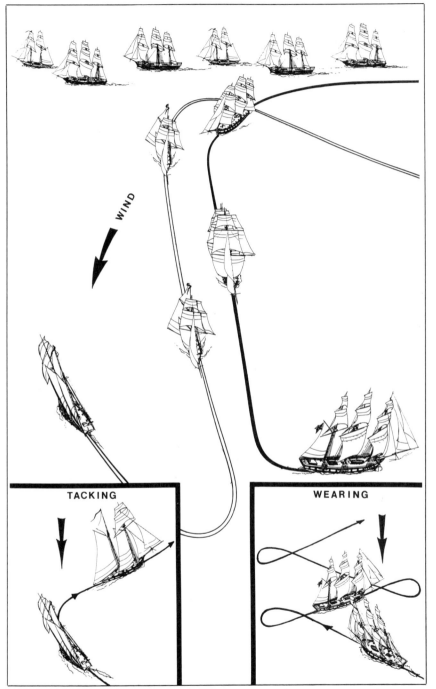

Figure 1-19. Typical chase tactics encountered in convoy raiding.

sels, laying down a relatively harmless or slightly damaging pattern of gunfire. This would generally draw the convoying warship out of the line, bearing down on the nimble privateer schooner, which must be assured that she had aroused the enemy into pursuit. The privateer would then bear off, always downwind, which would please the pursuer because with that vessel's great mass of squaresails, she could go charging along on her most effective point of sailing. This pursuit, a most exciting-appearing affair, could go on perhaps for five or six miles or more, with the privateer as well as her angry chaser cracking on all available canvas. Figure 1-20, showing HMS *Andromache* pressing toward an American schooner, illustrates the chase. The British ship was baited by the faster privateer to get almost within capturing distance; then, with a wide and circling turn into the wind, the fast schooner took full advantage of her superior upwind rig. With her great fore triangular sails and her tall gaff fore- and mainsails hauled sharply in, she headed back to the unprotected convoy, making it a predetermined long, single windward leg. The enemy pursuers were left helplessly in the wake trying to wear about against an unhelpful wind in an unhelpful rig. It would take them at least two or three times as long to work back to windward under square rig, all squaresails set on every mast. The square-riggers were not meant to tack, only to wear around — an ungainly maneuver in coming about. Even when they were trimmed down on the new weatherly course, they could not sail but could at best make about 70 degrees to the wind. In the meantime, in a well-rehearsed routine, the privateer had time to cut out about two or three helpless merchant vessels, capture the crews, either destroy or put prize crews aboard, and depart. This tactic was practiced to create an organized confusion, often routinely predictable, among the enemy vessels.

The better Baltimore privateers were generally trained and practiced, and, taking advantage of their vessels' sailing ability, could carry off these tactics with repeated success. They could also improve their speed by carrying their extensive sail plan in heavier winds than would be prudently possible under normal circumstances and on lesser vessels. One notable example was the use of the unusually large crews carried for manning prize ships. Often these exceeded 130 to 140 men, or in some cases, on outward passages, up to 150. Sailing to windward, the crew would man the windward rail in a heavy windward thrash—a common tactic of racing sailboats known as live ballast. Thus, 140 men on a Baltimore Clipper would amount to at least 10 tons, producing a counter-heeling moment of about 130 foot-tons—a considerable advantage in the power to carry sail.

Proceeds

In the realm of monetary statistics and comparative proceeds from privateer activity, the following figures may give some impression of

Figure 1-20. This rather primitive but contemporary (1813) painting by the English artist G. Tobis shows most graphically a chase by the British king's ship Andromache *of a Baltimore Clipper privateer. Note the extensive press of all light sails including stun'sails on the topgallant and on the running forecourse with a glimpse of the ringtail and a watersail below the main boom.*

return. It should be remembered that the U.S. dollar of 1812 had five or six times the value in purchasing power of today's dollar.

During the 1812-1815 period, typical successful privateers out of Baltimore (Figures 1-21 and 1-22) returned prizes and seized cargoes in estimated values as follows (from the *Republic's Private Navy*, by J. R. Garitee):

Vessel	Prizes	Owner's Proceeds
Nonsuch	7 prizes & cargoes	$94,500
Dolphin	5 prizes & cargoes	54,000
Comet	9 prizes, ransomed, & cargoes	220,000
Highflyer	11 prizes & cargoes	186,000
Rolla	7 prizes in port with cargoes	118,000
Ultor	6 prizes in port, cargoes & ransom	70,000
Midas	7 prizes in port with cargoes	108,000
Chasseur	15 prizes, 2 additional in hold	221,000
Patapsco	3 prizes & cargoes	54,000
Lawrence	9 prizes in port & cargoes	141,000
Surprise	9 prizes & cargoes	178,000
Rossie	5 prizes	68,170

The preceding is a partial list and includes only some of the better-known names. The dollar worth is estimated from incomplete records, but is an interesting comparison. It should be kept in mind that some of these ships were built and operated late in the War of 1812, having sailed less than six months before the war's end. Also, some ships were lost, and most had captured many more vessels but not returned them as prizes; of those returned, many came to U.S. ports other than Baltimore or to French or other friendly harbors.

Other captains, builders

As mentioned earlier, there were other captains besides Boyle and Veazey, and other builders than Thomas Kemp. It is not my purpose or intention to render biographical studies of them even briefly, nor would it be possible. There is extremely negligible surviving documentation, other than fragments, some of which suggest background and confirmation. The builders were apparently dedicated to the privateers, their remunerative specialty, both because of the spectacular

performance of their products and the associated creativity in their purpose. There were the French builders and their employed countrymen—Despaux, Descande, Salenave. There were two brothers, individual builders, named Price, and the builders of the schooners that distinguished themselves—too many and too difficult to cite.

I will, however, mention one of these, a dedicated and skilled builder who, unfortunately, it is believed, could not cope with sudden inactivity when the privateers had no further urgency after the war. This was James Cordery, builder of the *Bordeaux Packet*, the *Courier*, the *Lynx*, and many others. When orders to build were gone and the financial recession grew to panic in 1819, Cordery fell into great depression, which led him finally to a mental institution. He was forced to abandon his extensive shipbuilding property, valuable home, and relative wealth in Fells Point to judgment by the courts. While Thomas Kemp returned to his ancestral home in St. Michaels and a rural livelihood, James Cordery was committed to the terrors of

BATTLE between the SCHOONER ROSSIE, and the SHIP PRINCESS AMELIA, on the 16th of Sept. 1812.

Figure 1-21. The fore topsail schooner Rossie, *built by Thomas Kemp for Isaac McKim in 1807, was a very active and successful privateer. The colorful captain Joshua Barney as her commander was rewarded personally with $32,000 for a three-month cruise on her.*

lunacy in a Baltimore hospital. He died there in April 1820, and his property was put in the hands of his wife and heirs.

Of special interest here is that Mr. Cordery left us a bit of the history of shipbuilding. His papers — one might say his final papers — included a most detailed inventory of his shipyard, building materials, and shipwright's tools, down to the last nail and scraper. The official orphan's court property inventory, included in Appendix 3, is well worth looking at and browsing through. It includes shipwrights' tools common today whose 20th-century counterparts were used in building the present-day Prides; it also names tools long forgotten and unidentifiable, along with several well-known items having nothing to do with shipbuilding. For one who knows sailing vessels and the construction, it is a mild jerk of the emotions to read through this inventory. May James Cordery, builder of Baltimore Clippers, rest in peace.

Growing of independence

From the last years of colonialism through the American Revolution and the period of European wars and instability and finally the naval

BATTLE between the SCHOONER DOLPHIN, the British SHIP HEBE and a BRIG off Cape St. Vincent on the 25th of Jan. 1813.

Figure 1-22. Another successful privateer, the Dolphin, *is illustrated here between two British ships. The* Dolphin *prevailed in this contest and took the ship* Hebe *(left) as prize.*

War of 1812, there was a highly independent shipping continuum in the upper Chesapeake. First the British navigation and colonial tax acts encouraged the colonists to defy the law and engage almost openly in smuggling. The Revolution continued the smuggling and added to an American privateer fleet.

After the British exit in 1783 and the beginning of a new national existence, awareness of the necessity of growth in American foreign trade and commerce became acute. Much of the merchant sector was still aware of the continued need for high-performance ships. The new nation depended primarily on trade, even with unfriendly nations. (American merchants with their ships were contracting with the British Army to supply American flour and other supplies to the Iberian Peninsula, even after the declaration of war in 1812.) Yet fledgling United States commerce was continually bullied by European powers, by their navies and their privateers as well as by pirates in the Caribbean, and foremost by British Navy impressment. Barbary pirates in the Mediterranean preyed on everyone's commerce. French and Spanish letter-of-marque privateers had taken too many American merchant vessels among the Caribbean islands. One American demand for settlement of a merchant's claim for such loss of ship and cargo was not settled until 1915. Such a ridiculously long-ignored settlement as this was not typical, but it does point up the fact that there was prevailing harassment of this young country.

The United States was militarily weak and nearly defenseless against the warring European powers during the quarter-century following the War of Independence. The actions of American leaders, politicians, and merchants were necessarily pragmatic; this was not only effective, but allowed us to retain our national dignity and self-respect. We were, we should be proud to say, the only country that finally balked at paying ransom and tribute to the Barbary states and their pirates in the Mediterranean, and we ultimately sent a naval squadron to deliver the message in 1803. But the success of foreign trade was early understood in the simple terms of reliable delivery of cargo. As long as the unsettled conditions and the treachery on the high seas prevailed, and without a superior national naval establishment (which we totally lacked), the only solution was the export of American goods in fast, maneuverable ships.

In that many merchants on both sides of the Atlantic openly preferred and even stipulated that their cargoes be shipped in Baltimore-built vessels, Baltimore experienced a revival of growth in maritime importance. During the latter years of the 18th century (from the 1790s), the number of shipyards in Fells Point grew to more than 12. Under construction was one of the first Congress-authorized frigates, the USS *Constellation*, the first of those to sail in 1797. The Point handled 60,000 tons of shipping in 1797, and export cargoes the following year amounted to over $1.21 million. There was also a rabble-rousing segment of the population with 47 saloons, and the harbor became a focal point, each enterprise and labor pool feeding on one another.

One highly significant factor toward the end of the 18th century that sparked the prosperity of Baltimore and Fells Point shipping was the turn away from shipping tobacco to the major shipment of flour. The farmers of western Maryland expanded their farmlands to grow wheat, a crop with universal potential. Since Baltimore was closer than any of the other Chesapeake ports to nearby mills, flour soon became the largest export commodity and the most profitable.

A bulk cargo such as flour was not the sort of merchandise normally associated with the construction of fast sailing ships, but as a successful export commodity it attracted shipping agents and ships. And Fells Point–Baltimore became one of the three largest shipbuilding and shipping centers of the new country. The majority of launchings continued to be of the "sharp-built" schooners.

A need for a navy

In this seemingly precarious maritime world where fast ships — but with small cargo holds — were necessary, questions generate themselves. Why, with bulk cargoes such as flour, would merchants look to sharp, fast ships? Most cargo could be carried with greater profit in the large-bellied, full-bowed merchant ships, with thousands more tons on a ship. The voyage would be longer, but with bulk cargo there is no insistence on quickness. But such ships are very vulnerable and attractive to privateers and bullying foreign navies. Where was our naval protection, our convoys? It is difficult today to look back 200 years and believe that in 1789 there was no American navy.

Let us review the statistics briefly, for they reinforce the necessity for a private navy.

After the Revolution and peace, only three naval ships existed as survivors: the *Deane*, the *America*, and the *Alliance*. The *Deane* and the *Alliance* were first-rate, 32-gun frigates; the *America* was a ship-of-the-line launched and completed shortly after the conclusion of war. Almost immediately thereafter, the *America* was presented to France as a token of gratitude for its help in concluding the Revolution. The other two frigates, disposed of by public sale soon thereafter in 1785, left the consequence that the United States had not a single armed vessel.[1] What we had was an empty treasury, an enormous public debt, and no desire for further conflict.

However, peace does not always work to one's desires. A growing situation this same year, after a treaty between Spain and Algiers, created an open door of opportunity in the Atlantic for roving pirates from Moslem states. The first evidence of the new menace and harassment to United States commerce showed up in the capture of an American merchant vessel named *Maria* in July 1785, and five days later the *Dauphin* of Philadelphia. Both ships were seized by Barbary pirates (Figure 1-23) and their crews taken as slaves to Algiers.

At this time, the United States Department of State negotiated with Morocco for a treaty of immunity from piracy by paying a large cash sum. This was the sort of foreign relations the United States felt was more economical than investing in a new cluster of warships. After much discouragement and costly negotiations with all of the Barbary states—Algiers, Morocco, Tunis, Tripoli—the best we could do with Algiers, over nearly ten years of wrangling, was an annual tribute of $22,000 and a ransom for the captured Americans of $1 million. This was our first experience with Mediterranean terrorists, in 1785. By March 1794, with such terrorism continuing, Congress finally and reluctantly passed an act creating a new naval establishment and authorizing six large frigates: *Constitution*, 44 guns, 1,576 tons, built at Boston; *President*, 44 guns, 1,576 tons, built at New York; United States, 44 guns, 1,576 tons, built at Philadelphia; *Chesapeake*, 36 guns, 1,244 tons, built at Norfolk; *Congress*, 36 guns, 1,268 tons, built at Portsmouth; and *Constellation*, 36 guns, 1,265 tons, built at Baltimore. Captains and officers were appointed and commissioned in June of that same year, most of them becoming famous or notorious names in our naval history.

The interim treaty with the Algerian terrorists signed in 1795 stated that the building of our frigates was to be suspended when a peace treaty had been arranged—a clear example of our timidity and political stumbling. Within a year after the treaty, only one of the frigates was ready to sail, two others nearly ready to launch, and the rest only in frame. Congress authorized the completion of two and commissioned the completed one, but suspended work on the others. In September 1797, the United States frigate *Constellation* was the first to be completed and get to sea. She sailed under the command of Captain Thomas Truxton and had been built and commissioned at Fells Point, Baltimore.

Figure 1-23. A rather active Mediterranean pirate felucca by Antoine Roux in 1816. She is armed with two heavy bow long guns, indicating she has capability under oars.

Before any of these first frigates were completed, much trouble persisted on the high seas in addition to the Barbary pirates. The French, English, and Spanish conflicts led to increased bullying of American merchant ships. In 1797, the U.S. Department of State reported the capture of 32 ships, brigs, and schooners by French privateers; the newspapers had reported the loss of some 300 more. Congress was moved by this alarming situation to "purchase or hire a number of vessels not exceeding 12 . . . to be armed, fitted, and manned." The frigate construction that had been suspended in 1796 was re-started; a Department of Navy secretary with cabinet rank was created, a Marine Corps established, and further ship acquisition by the Navy authorized.

So, in the spring of 1798, our naval establishment consisted of a floating force of 12 frigates of 32 to 44 guns each, 12 ships of no less than 20 guns each, and 6 not exceeding 18 guns — along with an unspecified number of galleys, small gunboats, and revenue cutters. United States naval force was now moving, however poorly organized.

This number of ships authorized for building and purchase might seem an impressive naval establishment for the small and struggling United States. England did not consider it a naval threat, if they thought about it at all. But these were critical years, and few ships from the European naval forces were spread as far as the Western Hemisphere, aside from the West Indies station. The American naval force was essentially defensive, created out of necessity to protect our growing and active maritime trade. On a continent far from the profitable markets of Europe, the United States had a great need to protect merchant trade routes as national lifelines, which went essentially toward Europe and particularly into Mediterranean ports as well as those of the West Indies. These were lucrative markets, and much of the American exports were bulk cargoes. The defensive forces were not to be used as escorts of convoys; the merchants and their vessels were not so organized nor their vessels so numerous nor the navy so strong as to establish such a system. Armed merchantmen, superior sailing performance, or both, was the obvious solution. It was such a critical situation that became a significant part of the crucible creating the sharp-built schooners from the Chesapeake.

The British

It is interesting to describe the British naval establishment at the end of the 18th century. It was not an armed sea force quickly established to counter the sudden threat of a young and startlingly successful military dictator charging around Europe. It was centuries old, highly organized and maintained to the latest state-of-the-art. This was a maritime power to face the combined naval forces of Napoleon, an enemy with the great ships inherited from the former French Royal Navy as well as the navy of Spain. The British Royal Navy was the navy of Nelson, of seasoned veterans of years of victorious encounters.

There can be no direct comparison, ship by ship, of the first American naval force with the British Empire's naval establishment. A brief description of this potent and arrogant navy will serve to better illuminate the historic stage where our tenuous young Western nation was trying to set foot with the least amount of disturbance. The largest of British naval warships, named ships-of-the-line, had multiple gun decks. They rated from a vessel like Nelson's HMS *Victory*, as a *first rate* of 2,200 tons with three gun decks, to a *fourth rate* of over 1,000 tons with two gun decks. The American navy had none of these. The closest the new American ships could compare to the British was a *fifth rate*, comparable to a heavy frigate. American frigates were powerful, effective, and relatively fast, but there were only six authorized by Congress, twelve altogether in 1798. The British fleet faced the combined ships of Napoleon at Trafalgar in 1805 with 88 ships-of-the-line and 125 frigates.

This contrasting picture of two nations' vastly different sea strength is highlighted here to give emphasis to the direction of shipbuilding and the necessity for a private navy in the United States in these first years of development. After Napoleon's fleet was defeated at Trafalgar, the British continued and even stepped up their practice of impressment of American seamen to make up for battle attrition and desertions. Although some British naval vessels were freed from the European theater and thus increased their numbers in American waters, their campaigns and obligations continued to occupy their now unrivaled sea power. The United States had no means to oppose such strength on the sea, to protect or continue our sea trade, other than with faster and more-maneuverable ships. These were the qualities that were so typical of Baltimore- and Chesapeake-built schooners.

It is true that ships with these qualities were also in the minds of New England's and New York's builders, who turned out some schooners remarkably like those of the Chesapeake, particularly the vessels from Salem, Massachusetts, as seen in contemporary paintings of early 19th century. These fast schooners from New England, compared with those of the Chesapeake, had masts raked a little less, bows more embellished with trailboards and figureheads, and hulls that were not as low and rakish. The builders had not quite "gotten the hang of it" up there beyond the Mason and Dixon Line.

As a matter of fact, the Chesapeake builders' products were built not only for Baltimore's owners. The capacity of the Fells Point shipyards was too large for limitation to Baltimore orders, and the demand for privateers was too great for Baltimore's economy and ship-owner syndicates. The building of Chesapeake ships became a national enterprise, and Congress recognized the necessity to be most liberal in the policy of issuing letters of marque and reprisal.

In the years from 1810 to 1815 there were, in Fells Point, 11 shipyards, and during that time their concentration was on "sharp-built" schooners, as they were colloquially known. But it was before this period that the "private service"[2] vessels began to be built with considerable concentration, to account for the harassment of American commerce at sea, which had begun by 1800. During the war years, the Baltimoreans continued to use Eastern Shore shipbuilders, mainly from Talbot County, the home of Thomas Kemp as well as of the Harrisons and Dawsons of St. Michaels. It was also common practice at this time to send unfinished and unrigged hulls from there to Baltimore for completion and outfitting.

For a growing country whose economy was never better than marginal, the first decade was a struggle between pragmatism and pride. On the one hand, President Madison abhorred the thought of warring again with England, but on the other he was harassed by the continued arrogance of the British. They took American seamen at will and blocked American trade in the West Indies, and offered no help in the wars with Tripolitan pirates. The British scoffed at the new form of government and scorned the Constitution as a document espousing a government by some new radicalism. The new country was little better off than it had been before the Revolution. It is not far wrong to refer to the War of 1812 as the second American Revolution. It came finally after all patience was exhausted. However ill-prepared militarily this country was, however ridiculously outnumbered in naval vessels, it was necessary to salvage the nation's self-esteem and a semblance of true national independence. And the most improbable fact of all: In the end, the war was successful.

A very large extent of credit, and credit that past naval historians have not recognized for one reason or another, is due to those fast and active schooners and brigs called Baltimore Clippers originating in the upper Chesapeake Bay. It is fortunate for this nation that their growth and development, for more time than can be documented, had ripened to maturity by 1810. The Baltimore Clippers were ready to move into an unchallenged field with a desperate need. Thanks to Baltimore's industrious teamwork, investment capital, experienced designers and builders, and young and skillful captains and sailors, they did.

Finally, when the British king's armed ships and troops had had enough of their embarrassing frustrations and defeats (including the well-known attempt by a large naval squadron under Vice Admiral Cochrane in 1814 to destroy the shipyards at Baltimore's Fells Point), England decided to let us go. In early 1815, the Treaty of Ghent brought the beginning of the end to the American privateer era and production of these remarkable vessels.

The Baltimore Clippers had rendered a service to a nation that her navy was unable to do and which her government was unable to afford.

CHAPTER TWO

The Baltimore Clipper:
A Unique Identity

We have seen that the Baltimore Clippers did not just spring from the ground like crocuses, or from the sea; the type originated and developed over nearly half a century. I have traced the Baltimore Clipper's ancestry as positively as any other historian, possibly more so, and perhaps with more profile for counter-argument. Be that as it may, we must move on to the more descriptive side of this beautiful nautical creature.

The remarkable character of these vessels is that each was unique, but at the same time all of a species, the species being more identifiable in general terms than in specifics. The boundaries of the term *Baltimore Clipper* must be set and understood, as the references I make to these vessels are limited to these boundaries.

The name itself was not used or applied until the days of the Baltimore Clippers were nearly over. From the first, their speed, audacious sailing performance, and notoriety generated names, the most common at the time being "Baltimore Flyer." This name did not last long after, but it was the one that accompanied their brightest era, the time of their excellence, superiority, and maximum performance, from 1805 to 1815. Those years saw as well their most extreme and unrestricted shape, proportions, and spread of sail, and so it is within this time frame that we will identify them as Baltimore Clippers (before 1805 and after 1815, they were "pre-" and "post-" Baltimore Clippers, respectively). At this named time, the builders, captains, and crews of Baltimore Clippers identified their vessels not by name but by uncommon visual descriptive characteristics.

As today, the builder was required to officially entitle a new boat or ship upon completion by writing out a brief description for the public record called a "carpenter's certificate." This certificate listed the names of the vessel, the builder, and the owner, the location of construction (county, town, or city), and the date of completion (month and year). The required description of the vessel, left to the builder or his representative, was less defined but generally included the dimensions, thus (in feet and inches): length of keel, beam (maximum breadth), hold (depth of), capacity in tons (carpenter's measure). That is:

$$\frac{(\text{Length of keel x beam x beam}/2)}{95} = \text{Tonnage (carpenter's measure)}$$

Finally, the vessel was described very briefly in the builder's own words. It is here that we can find the true terms of identity, in the builder's sparing and abbreviated description of his work. Typical examples, for Maryland and Chesapeake records of the early 1800s, are: first the rig, such as *schooner, brig, sloop,* or *ship* (sometimes further, for clarity, *one deck, two masts*). The hull might have been *pilot boat, sharp built, privateer style, flush deck,* or *full built.* And, finally, any particular features, such as *square tuck, round tuck, man's head, no head,* or *no figurehead,* were explicitly mentioned, with a few variations (allowing for more or less loquacious builders). Thus, the carpenter's certificate is a primary source for definitive, original references to individual vessels; it was the equivalent of a birth certificate, or, in today's terms, the basis for an automobile title or a boat title.

In an example from the records of the National Archives (Figure 2-1), we can see exactly how Thomas Kemp listed and described his famous *Chasseur.* One may read, with a little difficulty, that *Chasseur* was built for William Hollins during "the year of our Lord Eighteen Hundred and twelve [1812]," that she was finished ". . . privateer built, with a round tuck and no head," and the ". . . following Dimensions to say Eighty five [85] feet Eight [8] inches keel twenty Six [26] feet Beam twelve [12] feet seven and a half [7¹/₂] inches hold and that she Measures two hundred Ninety five [295] Tons and

Ninety ninety fifths [⁹⁰/₉₅] of a Ton Carpenters measurement or thereabouts." (Although the dating may seem contradictory, with *Chasseur* having been built in 1812 and the certificate being dated January 1813, Mr. Kemp probably did not get around to certifying the vessel until 1813, quite possibly when she was sold.)

Descriptive terms

The descriptive terms *no head, round tuck, sharp built, pilot boat,* and several others require additional explanation, primarily because they are most frequently used for Baltimore Clippers. (These terms

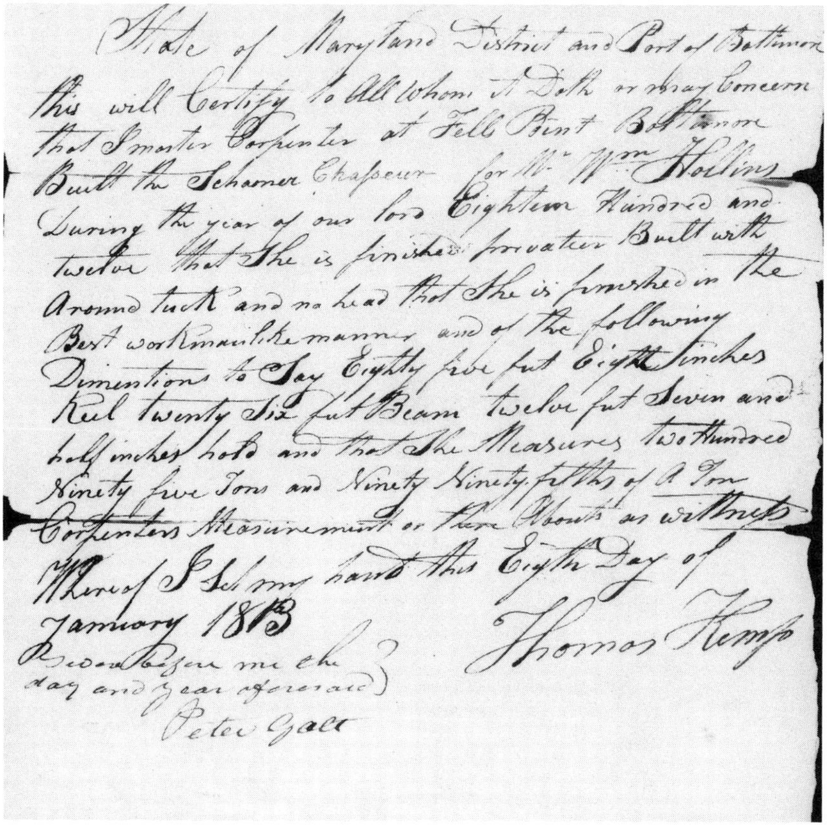

Figure 2-1. A photocopy of the actual carpenter's certificate of the famous Chasseur *signed by her builder, Thomas Kemp, January 1813 (although she was built during 1812).*

are often definitive and distinguishing when related to other types of vessels.)

No head simply means there was no figurehead or scroll head on the end of the stem or gammon knee at the forward extremity of the hull (Figure 2-3). This was invariably the case with the privateer-built schooner.

Round tuck as opposed to *square tuck* is a bit more in the manner of shop talk. It is worth saying that this type of stern was, in the early 1800s, a structural form reinvented for schooners being built larger and faster. The round-tuck stern had its origins in the Mediterranean in the Middle Ages and early Renaissance. Instead of extending the bottom planking aft to a flat transom or wineglass-shaped flat stern, the planking was curved up to a transverse timber called the transom beam resting on top of the sternpost; this was a rounded tuck of the planking ends. The round-tuck stern was clearly of Mediterranean heritage, used nearly exclusively in French, Spanish, and Italian ships. The square-tuck transom was popular through the 18th cen-

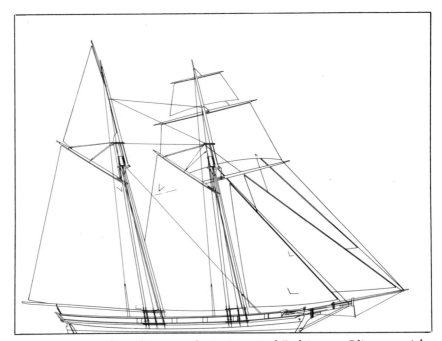

Figure 2-2. Profile of a typical 1812-period Baltimore Clipper, with the standard working rig of a fore topsail schooner.

tury in northern Europe, particularly in the Netherlands and in England.

In describing the new vessel for the certificate, the master carpenter used one of two terms to indicate the hull shape. Either *full built* or *sharp built* was the standard call for, respectively, a merchant-type hull or a fast-sailing hull destined for letter-of-marque or privateer service. Sometimes, as in the case of *Chasseur* and Thomas Kemp, it was very straightforwardly stated *privateer built*. The term *pilot boat*

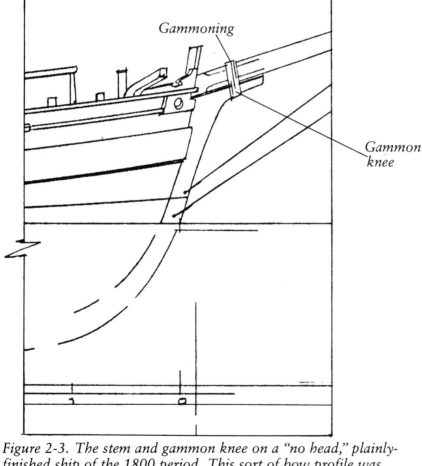

Figure 2-3. The stem and gammon knee on a "no head," plainly-finished ship of the 1800 period. This sort of bow profile was found on many poor working merchant ships in both Europe and America, as well as Baltimore Clippers.

describes essentially the same type of boat as the term sharp built. The expression *flush deck* typifies the low-freeboard style, with a clear stem-to-stern deck and no break in level of the privateer sharp-built vessel, invariably a Baltimore Clipper.

These descriptions, essentially the summary of those found on carpenter's certificates, are a reasonably accurate identification for the style of vessel of interest here. In the critical building years of 1810 through 1815, they constituted the majority of all vessels built in Baltimore and the upper Chesapeake Bay shipyards (see Appendix 2).

Common features

Baltimore Clippers are named for several features in common: their characteristic employment as privateers; their like performance and capabilities; and finally, their very similar physical structure. However, like individuals of the human species, no two Baltimore Clippers were exactly alike; there were never any duplicate copies or sister-ships. Their builders were known for their independent attitudes and philosophies, and like creative artists they grew with their creations, attempting with each of their products to build a better one. After 1810, being produced in quantity because of the great demand, the Baltimore Clippers enjoyed a plateau of great reputation, with small refinements.

It is during this period that we must consider the typical image of the Baltimore Clipper, to be preserved and considered the standard—sometimes called the *extreme* Baltimore Clipper, but that may not be the best adjective; a better word would be *ultimate*. While it is true that no two were exactly alike in size, rig, or detail, there is enough sameness to establish a typical profile. It is interesting, in looking at Figure 2-2, to first establish the rig, shown here as a fore-topsail schooner. This is not an unusual rig, in the context of the early 19th century, but it could be confusing. A fore-topsail schooner has squaresails only on the foremast, particularly the fore topsail. There is also a double-topsail schooner, of which there were many; the old records do not tell how many or indicate the preferences. It is logical to speculate that there were probably many more fore-topsail schooners, as a fore-topsail schooner is easier to handle, requires less crew, is more economical, has less weight aloft, and will sail and maneuver with equal or better agility; the total downwind or reaching sailing speed potential is almost the same.

Looking then at this typical rig, we see specifics found only in Baltimore Clippers. First, the headsail rig, or foretriangle between the foremast and the bowsprit-jibboom assembly, is much greater than that of the contemporary merchant vessel, whatever its rig. The bowsprit assembly is longer, the mast is proportionately farther aft, and the foremast is proportionately taller. In this triangular space, a Baltimore Clipper notably took every advantage. The clippers' builders and captains and their forerunners learned that these triangular sails were essential windward drivers; they learned also not to cut up this area with many smaller sails. The forestay does not terminate, as in the customary contemporary merchantman, on the stemhead or thereabouts; rather, it leads from the schooner's foremasthead to the bowsprit end. The jibstay terminates at the end of the jibboom and the foretopmast stay also, sometimes beyond on an extension pole. On these three stays, there are only three very large triangular sails; in "working" weather, perhaps but two. Together with the square fore topsail, the foresail on a gaff, and the large gaff mainsail, there exists 75 to 80 percent of the entire driving power. This is a more efficient sailing rig than had ever been devised before.

The masts of this schooner rig are proportionately taller than those of most previous schooners, which allows the shrouds to rise from the channels at a lesser angle to the vertical. As they meet the crosstrees, they will allow the squareyard to trim around through a greater and very advantageous arc for hard-on-the-wind sailing. Also, there are on this single topsail rig but three lower shrouds and two topmast shrouds, as opposed to the usual four or five or more on a fully square-rigged mast. All of this contributes to less windage and to sharper windward trim in the matter of the topsail and the light upper sails on the foremast.

There was sometimes an intermediate sail between the masts, known today as a fisherman staysail. It is not clear what this sail was called in 1810 — perhaps the main topmast staysail, but, more likely, something in a seamanly, rough vernacular. It is known that this sail is not easy to set, has interference problems in tacking, and overall is not particularly effective. Downwind and reaching, it blankets the fore topsail, chafes considerably, and is generally not much used.

On the mainmast, the great, gaff mainsail is the largest single sail. The sailmaker is put to testing his skills to create this piece for maximum performance. It usually has three reef bands and, together with the foresail and forestaysail, is made of the heaviest weight of cotton sailcloth—so heavy that when wet, it is stiff as shoe leather. Together with the fore topsail, the four lower sails—main, fore, forestaysail, and jib are considered the working and fair-sailing weather combination. In lighter winds, as light as 15 knots, the main gaff topsail, the fore topgallant, and the flying jib would be added. In winds of lesser force, the captain would likely call for the ringtail and stun'sails (studding sails).

The entire sail arrangement on a topsail schooner such as pictured, together with the various running and standing rigging, produce a system for sailing that truly can be likened to an efficient machine. An easy capacity to speed up or slow down, to accept greater or lesser wind force, to sail closer to the wind or bear off, to come about or fall off and even bring the vessel to a quick stop—these were all the capabilities of an ultimate Baltimore Clipper.

The outboard hull profile reveals other characteristics in the clipper's lines that are also unique: the low, flat sheerline and minimum freeboard, with no change in deck continuity from forecastle deck, waist, or quarterdeck. There was always a single, broad wale strake extending the full length of the hull from before the hawse to the lower transom fashion piece. The simple and plain head appearance shows no headboards, stem knees, or trailboards, common in the 18th century and still common contemporaneously. Especially, there was no figurehead—the essential meaning of the builder's term *no head*. There was customarily a short stem projection called a *gammon knee* to form the carrier piece of the gammoning below the bowsprit (Figure 2-3). (Gammoning is the rope winding or lashing of the bowsprit to this stemhead projection and thus its fastening to hold it in place against vertical movement.) This was important, for the bowsprit carried the sailing thrust and lifting tension of the sails of the powerful foretriangle. The gammon knee was probably Chesapeake functional creativity, although there are similar stem profiles from the Mediterranean. It relates to the term *clipper bow*, which is universally recognized.

There was still some individuality and experimentation during these years. One 154-ton sharp-built hull, built in Baltimore in 1813, was rigged as a "chebec" (Figure 2-4). Where during this period over 90 percent of all Baltimore's fleet of private vessels consisted of the typical two-masted topsail schooner type (half of New England's and two-thirds of New York's vessels were schooners), this xebec was obviously built for deception when sailing as a privateer. Named *Ultor*, this Baltimore Clipper with a Mediterranean rig was owned by a syndicate of four investors, a common form of ownership. Her rig definitely supports the contention explored in Chapter One that Chesapeake builders were quite aware of these Mediterranean types noted for their speed and maneuverability. The *Ultor* proved to be a

Chebec espagnol a voiles latines, courant vent largue.

Figure 2-4. A contemporary print by the famous 18th-19th century marine artist Beaugean shows a finely-detailed Mediterranean chebec of the 1800 period. She is armed with ten heavy broadside guns plus two substantial swivel guns aft. She flies the flag of Spain and could be a naval vessel. Her officers on deck seem to be in uniform, and she is fitted with hammock nettings for the crew as well as splinter protection.

most successful privateer. Still cruising in early 1815 and unaware of the recently signed treaty of peace, she took a large (411-ton), 13-gun British vessel in the Caribbean. She profited her owners some $70,000 during her two years at sea.

It is my belief that the identity of a Baltimore Clipper was not so much in its rig as in its hull. The hull was not like that of a xebec of the Mediterranean or any other European craft, although there is some likeness that may have ancestral roots. Over the centuries of maritime experience, the characteristics of fast sailing vessels are no great mystery. But beyond such features as the sharp entrance at the bow and the long, fine quarters aft, there was more to the uniqueness of a Baltimore Clipper.

To begin with, these Chesapeake-built schooners were clustered typically in the same size range. They were not built to carry bulk cargo; they were particularly unprofitable as merchant ships except when delivering valuable wares through enemy or hostile blockades. Their size range, expressed in a ratio known to shipbuilders as displacement/length ratio, classified them in their time and even today as lightweight vessels. This does not mean that they were built of lightweight material or, particularly, of light frames and planking; these materials, with the dimensions used in 1810, would now be considered almost massive.

Their specific displacement/length ratios were between 250 and 180, with few exceptions. These numbers are dimensionless and can be used to compare the relative weights of any ships, regardless of size. Vessels over 500 displacement/length are considered exceptionally heavy and burdensome; those below 200 are applicable to light-weight racing yachts. These figures are used for ships in conditions of no cargo.

Other factors

There is little doubt that a Baltimore Clipper's speed and agility was a combination of a number of factors: the captain's experience, special skill, and spirit; a well-trained crew; the sail plan's power, and the shape of the hull. There is no technical or objective analysis for the human factors, although we are aware that diligent captains trained their crews in sail drills, gunnery drills, and leadership structure—organization for the drive and response in the ship. The hydrodynamics of the hull and the aerodynamics of the sail plan deserve a bit more explanation to help in understanding the remarkable mobility of the fast schooners from the Chesapeake.

Most people have experienced these dynamics literally or figuratively in "moving against the tide." Moving a car or a wheeled vehicle through a road of axle-deep soft mud, wet snow, or other thick fluid requires power. An aircraft pushed through atmospheric air requires power. Power is force through a distance in a unit of time. It is the same for a sailing vessel as for an aircraft or truck or any physical mechanism doing work. The sailing vessel is unique in that it is moving through two fluid media at once. One, air, happens to provide the force by sail to move the hull through the other, a heavier fluid—a rather roundabout transference of energy. Nevertheless, the sails, the masts, the rigging, the entire apparatus for sailing, is a large part of the resistance in moving through the atmosphere. As one astute observer, an engineer, once said while looking at a graphic illustration of a Baltimore Clipper racing along with her whole sail plan evident and the hull leaving a white foamy wake: "My God, think of the power to just move that mass of canvas and rig through the air!" He was very correct; he was speaking of the wind as it dragged through whole complexes of masts and spars and rope—the entire rigging fabric, including the sails.

The sails provide the driving force in directing wind to them as airfoils and in making a diverted force component pull in the intended direction—but not for free. A large toll is exacted: perhaps 50 percent or more of the total wind energy is bled off in drag or resistance in moving the whole superstructure of sail and rig through the air; the rest is the hull drag or resistance of the water, a fluid 800 times as heavy as air. Nevertheless, there is still enough energy left over to pull the hull along through the heavier medium. In the Baltimore Clipper's case, we know now that the energy absorption and transference was adequate in certain points of sailing and sea state to move those hulls to 12 and occasionally 14 knots.

To fulfill these maximum expectations, the hull was rightly shaped. Its configuration has been discussed; the "sharp-built" hull was understood. But the rig also was appreciated and its resistance recognized by the late-18th-century and early-19th-century builders—while nowadays, with our remarkable hindsight and 20th-century technology, we marvel at the complexity of the old rig. However, compare it to any of the contemporary slow-speed, full-built merchant hulls, whose square rigs with three masts, all in three parts, the whole of the assembled standing and running rigging, needed or not, was like a thick web compared to the slickly reduced topsail schooner. With their bluff bows on fat-bellied hulls, built for maximum cargo stowage, the merchantmen were simply obese floating transports. It is a comparison of fluid drag and energy resourcefulness and a tradeoff between cargo volume, delivery time, and, in 1812, being an effective privateer.

Baltimore Clippers were built in both rural and urban surroundings in the late 18th and early 19th centuries. It is better, of course, that a clipper or any ship is built in a community where shipyards, building supplies, ship's chandleries, and a labor pool exist. On the other hand, for wooden ships, it can be argued that it is more desirable to build where the basic material source (timber forest) exists. Timber in the form of felled trees and logs is difficult to transport, which, when it must be done, adds to the ship's cost. Ultimately, the urban shipyards of Baltimore at Fells Point produced the greater number of schooners. It meant transporting timber from the sources, both Eastern Shore and western Maryland, to Baltimore—from the east by water on lumber schooners, and from the west by timber wagons hauled by oxen.

In either case, the choice of wood was limited to Maryland and Virginia trees, which were not greatly restricted. Depending upon the cost and the owner's agreement with the builder, the superior wood for the hull and frame was white oak. The oak trees grew both in the open and in forests. The forest oak grew tall and clear of blemish, and the wood was more useful in longer lengths both for keel and planking. The pasture oaks, with their low, spreading branches, were excellent for the natural crooks required for hanging knees, lodging knees, breasthooks, and other pieces for corners needing continuity and reinforcement. While oak frames and planking made an excellent and elegant vessel of superior strength, oak was also, like other things of high quality, more expensive. Worked with hand tools (see Appendix 3), it meant slower sawing of long lengths or short, bulky, difficult shapes. As described today, the work was most labor-intensive.

So, for less-expensive ships, softer, more easily worked wood was used—basically the pine species, generally the preferred longleaf or Southern pine, sometimes referred to as pitch pine. This was an excellent planking wood, and when freshly cut was worked easily, seasoned quickly, and, after being fastened in place on the ship's frame, took on a permanent shape and hardness with the crystallizing of the resin it contains. A typical, well-made ship would have been framed in white oak—keel, backbone, and transverse frames—and planked in longleaf yellow pine. A ship's planking constitutes the greatest amount of wood in any single structural application, and in a well-built ship it must be carefully selected in the longest lengths possible.

One typical contract in Fells Point (between builder Thomas Bond and Tyler & Foster, dated April 29, 1793) for the construction of a schooner of 70 feet keel length and 26 feet beam and other standard dimensions, called for the best white oak timber (frames) and planking below the "wail" (wale) to be 3 inches thick, the whole to be secured with locust and white oak "trunnels" (tree nails or wooden pins) and a sufficient quantity of iron. The timbers above the wale were to be of red cedar, locust or white oak, and the planking above the wale to be of pine or white oak, at the option of the builder. This vessel, while not a sharp-built schooner, was typical in the choice of woods for a well-built ship in Baltimore at the turn of the 18th-19th centuries.

The wale referred to is a heavy strake (line of planking) or several adjacent strakes of greater thickness, generally located above the waterline just below the deck line and intended as one of the longitudinal strength members. The planking thickness specified in this contract indicates that the vessel must have been a conventional full-hulled merchant ship for heavy service. The thicknesses are much greater than for a typical Baltimore Clipper, which would have been $2^1/_2$ to $2^3/_8$ inches outside below the main wale, and 2 inches inside. The contract also describes the structure of the quarterdeck, indicating again a configuration not typical in Baltimore Clippers, which invariably had a continuous weather deck, called a *flush deck*.

It is interesting that this contract verifies the formula in common use for measured tonnage as the length of hull (between perpendiculars forward and aft at the posts) multiplied by the breadth and again by the half-breadth of beam and divided by 95; carpenter's measure-

◀ 61

The Baltimore Clipper:
A Unique Identity

ment used length of keel instead of hull. (Tonnage must not be confused with displacement; see Chapters 4 and 5.)

The building procedures and timber sequence had stabilized by the end of the 18th century. There seemed to be an abandonment of the inherited and disuniform methods of framing used in northern Europe, and a more regular frame that became a standard. This method appears even in an example of a French privateer set up in frame in 1790 on keel blocks (Figure 2-5). This handsome watercolor sketch by Antoine Roux, the celebrated French marine artist of that period, clearly illustrates double sawn frames fastened or sistered together and set at uniform spacing along the keel. The vessel is ready for planking, and it appears, through a bottom opening in the framing for interior access, to have a bilge stringer begun on the starboard side. The builder clearly intends to let the single part of each doubled frame extend above the deck as a bulwark stanchion. A scaffolding

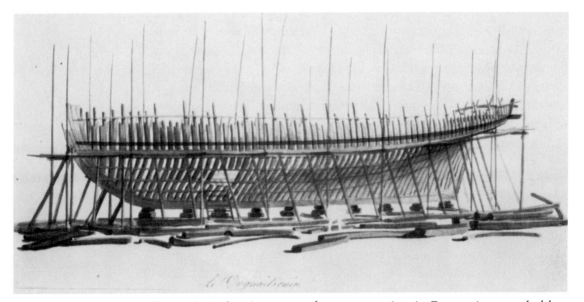

Figure 2-5. A privateer under construction in France is remarkably similar to a Chesapeake schooner in the same phase of building. This is not surprising in that French builders were very impressed by sharp-built Chesapeake vessels and studied their construction. This vessel has more closely spaced frames than was customary in Chesapeake construction and would result in a heavier vessel. Her identity, according to the artist, Antoine Roux, is Dugnaitrouin.

platform is erected at the level of the main wale, which is at least partially in place. There appears to be a temporary batten above the wale to indicate the beginning line for the sheerstrake. These integral parts, shown so explicitly in this painting of 200 years ago, are easily identifiable and indicate the same sequence of building that was used in late-18th-century America and has been used continually since in the construction of wooden schooners of this size. Such a method was not evident in vessels built in either America or northern Europe 30 to 40 years prior to this artist's work.

The deck structure of a Baltimore Clipper is also shown in a contemporary plan of deck framing of the Baltimore Clipper *Flying Fish* (named HMS *Flying Fish* for Royal Navy service), built in Baltimore in 1805. This drawing (Figure 2-6) was made from dockyard plans in Portsmouth, England, in 1806. The deck beams are rather generously spaced, with lighter carlins in between; this system is no longer used because of its inflexibility to placement of hatches, ladders, companionways, and other deck openings. The deck framing also shows a uniform distribution of lodging knees along the sides and in the way of the masts—clearly man-of-war style. The schooner was also three-masted and not typical in rig (Figure 2-7). Although built in Baltimore, apparently for a British account before the 1812 conflict, it is most interesting as a sharp-built schooner. The hull is basically the same form as of the best of the later privateers. She measures 59 feet 6 inches keel length, 21 feet 3 inches beam, 8 feet depth of hold, and a tonnage of 106 $^{45}/_{95}$ carpenter's measure. Her body plan (Figure 2-8)) shows an elegant shape with very graceful rounded sections of ample but not extreme deadrise.

The lines and profile plans of this unusual Baltimore schooner show also an apparently alternative stern, or an altered one. The stern profile on the sail plan (Figure 2-7) shows the short transom with an outboard-mounted rudder and exterior sternpost. It may be a square-tuck stern, but the body plan (Figure 2-8) showing the after sections is not explicit on this. Dotted lines on the plan appear to show a change in the position of the transom. My best guess is that the deck length was increased with the rebuilt overhang of the transom and the inboard rudder.

There is no doubting her unusual rig. She is a three-masted, double-topsail schooner. Being a pre-1810 example, she shows evidence

Pride of Baltimore

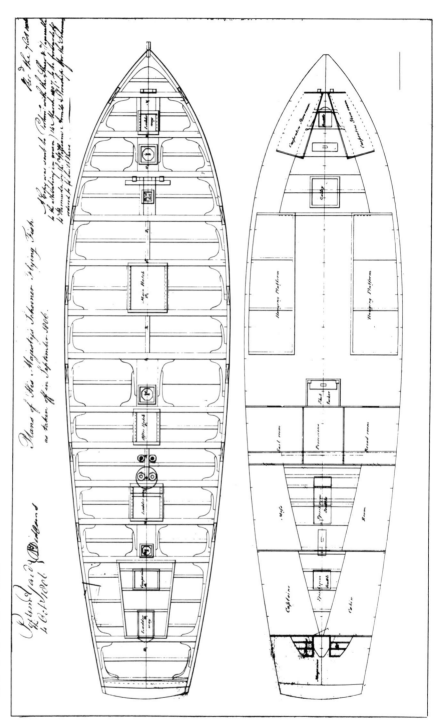

Figure 2-6. The deck plan of HMS Flying Fish, a three-masted or tern schooner which qualifies as a Baltimore Clipper by the shape of her hull and locale of building.

of experimentation and transitory detail: that is, a spritsail yard beneath the bowsprit. Altogether, she is a small schooner for three masts and two large boomless gaff sails. She may well have been a fast boat but a busy one.

The collection of work by Roux includes, interestingly, a painting of a deteriorating hulk on the beach (Figure 2-9). Enough of her skeleton remains that one may speculate confidently that she was a vessel of a little larger size and probably at least 50 years older than the French privateer described earlier (Figure 2-5). A few frames still rising from her bottom show a distinct full body with the rise and inward curvature of tumblehome, a characteristic of the ships of the Renaissance that continued through several centuries to the full-bodied 18th-century ships. The framing procedure of ships of the 18th

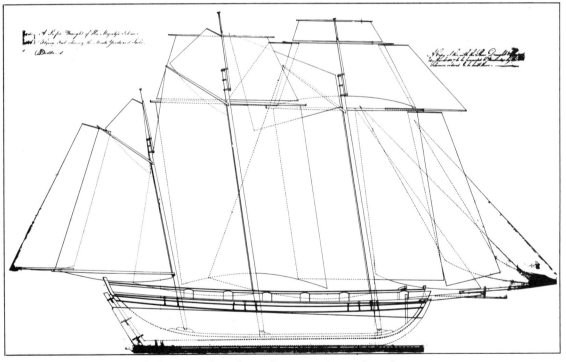

Figure 2-7. Sail plan of Flying Fish. *These drawings are taken directly from the original British dockyard drawings over 180 years old, and the poor quality of reproduction reflects the poor condition of the originals.*

century and earlier still demonstrated a tendency (and necessity) for the planking to proceed simultaneously with the frame—a methodology inherited from the medieval era and before, when most vessels were built "shell first" and their planking edge-fastened as the hull took shape without a frame. Perhaps without realizing it, Antoine Roux has illustrated in these two paintings the end and the beginning of two different, historical theories of ship construction: an old ship slowly disintegrating on the edge of the sea, and a new ship rising in frame, representative of a new and enlightened approach that held the promise of the future.

While there were apparently no artists illustrating the construction of Baltimore-built ships at Fells Point or the yards on Maryland's Eastern Shore, these Chesapeake ships were probably built very much like this one near Marseilles, depicted by Roux (Figure 2-5), in their time. As a matter of fact, this watercolor sketch quite likely may have reflected the American maritime influence and significance in France. There was at that time, and before, a strong Franco-American relationship.

In the first years of the 18th century, for instance, a shipbuilding interest in France transported a Maryland-based group of shipbuilders to be set up in France. Baltimore's port records and customs entries show a significant trade entering from France, particularly in Baltimore-built letter-of-marque schooners during the War of 1812

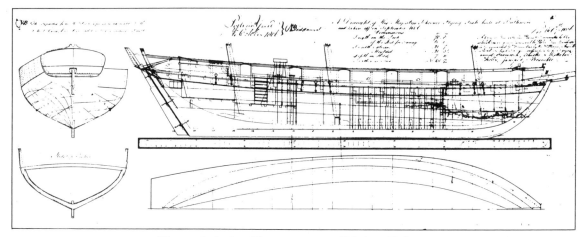

Figure 2-8. Profile structure of Flying Fish.

through the British blockade. Not that the Baltimoreans or Maryland citizens were fluent in the French language, but it was certainly not uncommon to them. The fact that many of the privateers carried French names indicates some friendly association—consider the largest privateer of Thomas Kemp, with her proud French name, *Chasseur*. There were *Vidette, Garrone, Bordeaux Packet*, and others advertising the French connection. Another example is the *Ultor*, built in Fells Point in 1814 and rigged as a French Mediterranean xebec. (This unusual Baltimore Clipper was built by French-American shipwright Andre Descande for French owner Pierre Gustier.)

There also, with this evidence of mutual admiration, must have

Figure 2-9. A ship's hulk near the beach painted in 1799 indicates an old vessel of the 18th century at the end of its life, a contrast to the vessel of the previous painting which is just beginning.

been some give and take in building methods. The American builders were not of a long heritage of shipbuilding tradition and should have been open to learning, but philosophically it would have been indirect. They were much aware that the successful vessels they were turning out were their own in style and design.

With this seemingly cosmopolitan involvement, it is interesting that there was so little in documentation of these Baltimore schooners.[1] Particularly, there are neither drawings nor even good graphic representations. We must conclude that apparently the builders did not use drawings or prepare anything called a design for their guidance—but this is questionable. We know that at least one builder, Thomas Kemp, had a drawing room in his house at Fells Point where he is said to have done his design work. If he did, there must have been others; yet no such materials have come to light. There are building contracts preserved in good condition, along with the official shipping records and carpenter's certificates (Appendix 2). Because builders, like all skilled craftsmen, must protect their special knowledge, it is not strange that, in terms of design drawings, not one scrap of paper (if any existed) has survived.

Some skilled builders, particularly in the isolation of the Chesapeake's Eastern Shore, may not have been sophisticated enough to work from drawings. Perhaps only a few such capabilities existed in Baltimore. It certainly was before the technology of blueprint duplication but not before the availability of some methods in naval architecture procedures. Reluctantly, I must conclude that these were very slow in reaching the Chesapeake builders. Yet, while such new procedures would have been helpful, they were circumvented by native intuition, traditional knowledge, and inspired creativity.

With these assumptions it would be interesting to reconstruct, together with knowing what *has to be* done, what *must have been* done—and to visualize it, more or less, step by step.

The importance of design

In the building of a ship or a boat, one cannot ignore design, whether for a 1,000-passenger cruise ship or a small rowing skiff; whether it is a formal, many-blueprint "high-tech" design or simply in the mind of the builder. It can be a good design or a bad one. A design most fun-

damentally is a concept that grows with refinement. One needs more
than just a concept to turn ideas into reality, and that is the purpose
of design. At any rate, there are several ways to approach ship design
with hope of achievement. Experience tells a good designer that he
must sort out the various goals and requirements and that priority is
on the side of creating a vessel that will cope successfully with the
natural elements. However, it is not enough to design a ship merely to
survive—although, when one is faced with the very worst, survival
becomes most basic. Performance has become a requirement ever
more evident and more urgent; it has always been important in the
maritime world. It was this priority and awareness that pushed marine design along from the first primitive log canoes. Performance
was a most urgent requirement for the builders in Fells Point as the
19th-century shipbuilding scene there first unfolded.

Whatever the motivations in the design of a ship, the first consideration must be its mobility in the sea—how it will respond, how safe it
will be, how quick, and perhaps how comfortable, how sustainable,
and all the rest—in order of importance, to satisfy the mission. In this
pressured first decade and a half of the 1800s in the upper Chesapeake maritime circles, the prime mission of the sharp-built schooners was speed and maneuverability under sail. Here, the first direction
is toward the elementary sea, and for this reason, if for no other, a
ship or boat must be designed from the *outside in*, not from the inside
out. It is the latter tendency that produces some very ugly, very poor-
performing, and most often marginally unsafe vessels.

An honest and experienced designer will rightly question a prospective owner who will give the carrying capacity, extensive living
accommodations, and other non-critical characteristics first importance in a proposed seagoing vessel. The designer will take his direction from those who put the ship's future and safe and successful
operation in his hands. The concept then becomes clear, and he can
proceed to delineate the hull's configuration.

In 18th- and 19th-century America, particularly in the Chesapeake, original and creative ship conceptions were commonplace.
Post-colonial builders most often began by modeling a hull shape in
wood. This was done as a half hull, or *half model:* one side of the
vessel, from its longitudinal center plane. This is the old and traditional *half-hull method*. The model was carved and faired to suit the

trained eye of the builder. He sized the model to a convenient scale proportional to the ship he intended, and when the shape suited him, he proceeded to *lift* the hull form and convert it to expanded patterns from which he reproduced full-size ship's parts. This process was and is called *lofting*. In the mid-19th and 20th-century world, the traditional method of lofting is based on a master draft or print called the *lines drawing*, which takes the place of a half model but is still the designer's expression of form concept. The lines drawing is prepared with three related views according to a geometric procedure in orthographic projection. In today's technology for multiple ship configurations and some yacht forms, this process takes place by computerization.

The builder's objective, whether from the half model configuration or the designer's lines draft, is to expand the shape to the full size of the vessel. The ratio between the model or draft size and the full-size vessel is the scale relationship, which may be expressed in inches per foot or in the (now more common) direct mathematical ratio such as 50 to 1 or 100 to 1. In either case, it is a tedious process to enlarge and redraw at full size. The traditional method of lofting was formerly, and still is perhaps, done in small shipyards to delineate the full-size lines drawing on the mold loft, a large wooden floor of extensive area. There are two purposes here: first, to *fair* the lines (that is, to eliminate any small errors or surface discontinuities that do not show up on the small-scale drawing or model); and, second, to locate in this large, lofted form the shapes of structural members such as the transverse frames, which are drawn into the lofted lines that generally delineate the inside or *molded* surface (the surface inside the planking, or outside the frames).

When the patterns are taken from the lofted form, they are transferred to the ship's structural material, whether it be wood or metal. In the 18th- and 19th-century building yards, the first structural member was the keel, and it generally needed no lofting. The designer directed its shaping and readiness by simply stating its length and its sided and molded dimensions. (The *sided dimension* was its width and the *molded dimension* was its vertical depth.) The keel length in the days of wooden ships was a most important dimension, being one of three key figures that determined the ship's *tonnage* or *burthen* (the basis of the ship's measure), the other two figures in the equation being the ship's maximum breadth and its depth of hold. It was this tonnage measure that fixed the cost of a ship, her taxability, port costs, revenues for passage, and sundry fees; it was also a ship's figure of comparison to other ships. Again, keep in mind that tonnage is unrelated to the ship's real weight or displacement, although it is always expressed in "tons."

Returning to construction, the first procedure was the "laying of the keel." This much-quoted and ceremonial process was the observance of the beginning of the real ship, even though it had begun perhaps months before in the designer's mind and models or in the builder's loft and shop, together with other parts simultaneously begun before the keel. This keel—shaped, sided, and molded and with key scarfs cut in its ends—was set upon the keel blocks upon the building stocks, which may or may not have been inclined to level ground, depending upon the launching intentions. Even in the beginning, the shipbuilder—as does most any prudent workman—looks beyond tomorrow. The method of launching dictates the positioning of the ship upon the ways, together with several other considerations such as the weather, the direction of the compass, etc. Large wooden vessels were built outdoors, with little or no protection from weather, and the anticipated time of construction often exceeded 12 months (although the building time could and would be shortened, depending upon emergencies). In Fells Point in 1810-1814, some sharp-built schooners were launched in less than 90 days from keel laying.

After the keel was officially dedicated (or, perhaps, officially ignored), the building proceeded with the first assembled frames in the middle portion of the hull's length. This frame positioning gave the ship its first three-dimensional aspect, particularly when, as was customary, the ends of the ship—the stempost and sternpost—were in place at the time. Being the rib-like structural members in the ship's anatomy, the frames give the hull transverse strength. When the frames are all in place, with the after frames progressing toward the stern in ever-deepening wineglass profiles, and the forward frames progressing like sharpened V's toward the stem, the true ship's shape has emerged. Framing is perhaps the most exciting, as well as most exacting, part of construction: There must be no relative change in position between the frames. They must be most solidly held in place, and their longitudinal spacing must be exact to minute tolerances, generally monitored by an accurately made master spacing tool; the builder must continually inspect and examine this positioning, to prevent the ship from becoming longer or shorter than specified and to avoid the related development of unfair form. Also, each frame must be plumb and stand parallel to its adjacent frames, for which plumb bobs, declivity boards, and levels are the basic tools. (The traditional practice in the early 19th century was to erect the frames perpendicular to the keel. If the keel was laid on keel blocks and inclined to the designed drag — that is, deeper aft than forward — it was necessary to use a "declivity board" to check the perpendicularity.)

Finally, with frames in place, held with temporary shores and longitudinal battens, the permanent structure proceeds. The bilge stringers — heavy longitudinal timbers running the ship's length on the inside of the frames — are fastened with heavy iron bolts along the bilges at their outer and upward curvature. At the same time or earlier, another key longitudinal timber is placed and fastened directly above the keel but separated by the transverse, intersecting frames. (The frames are assembled from many pieces, sided each to the other in double thickness and in alternately overlapping sections called *futtocks;* the lowest of these, crossing above the keel and symmetrical in port-starboard distance, is the floor.) So, on top of the floors and the sistered futtocks is fastened the keelson — a long, longitudinal timber, slightly smaller than the keel. This total longitudinal assembly, keel and keelson, connecting the ends of the vessel, is the *backbone* — and a strong and stiff girder it is, formed by the many integral wooden trusses of floor, keels, keelsons, floor futtocks, and so on.

The fastenings used in the early 19th century to hold the integral parts together were iron rods (drifts) driven through heavy assemblies, wooden tree nails (trunnels) holding the sistered frames, and iron bolts holding heavier timbers such as stringers to frames. Heavy iron nails were coming into increased use in this era also.

Next in the process comes the planking and installation of the inner ceiling, after placing the deck beams. The latter are heavy transverse timbers with about the same sectional dimensions as the doubled frames; there are not as many deck beams as frames, however, and they are placed with respect to the location of hatches, cabin trunks, and other deck openings. The deck beams are rested at their outboard ends on the upper longitudinal girder or *beam shelf,* which runs continuously along the inside of the frames at their upper ends (this may be a built-up assembly). Beam ends are notched to fit this type of stringer, which is an essential structural part.

As the planking is bent on in place, working from the keel up and the sheer down, the shell gradually closes. At the same time, internal parts go in: breasthooks, stern knees, transom frames. The main wale is fastened on often before the other planking, and this is an external, heavy plank form, generally half again as thick as the planking. It follows the upper main deck or sheerline, perhaps a plank-width or two below it.

At some time in this process, when the hull is partially built, there comes a change. One day, as the ship's carpenters are working with their hammers and mauls, driving down the drift rods, bolts, and heavy nails, the sound of the hammer no longer is a dull "thunk" or "thud." There is a different, harder, higher-frequency sound, nearly a ring to the tools as the ship's structure absorbs the vibration. The growing structure is no longer an assembly of many parts held together by nails and bolts; it has become a single thing. It is not too poetic to realize that a monolith now exists. Perhaps a Baltimore Clipper is born. It will simply have to be finished and fitted for its destiny.

An important resource

I have implied that the Baltimore Clippers were not designed in the conventional sense and understanding of design. No drawings of hull configuration, no patterns have been found, although there must have been some; they apparently did not survive. There were half models, generally of the simplest sort. (One rather deteriorated such model does still exist and was a part of Howard Chapelle's collection.) There was no design precedent, even in the more sophisticated British and other technically advanced shipyards, for sail and rigging plans of ships. Many procedures, such as rules for masting and rigging for this, had been recorded, but none for Baltimore Clippers. We must be grateful to a more common source: the marine artist.

Beyond the written word and recorded documents, a source for research and replication of a true Baltimore Clipper's image is found in the marine paintings of the period. Some of these were done by the most skilled marine artists during a period of artistic realism and representational painting. Many of the paintings were done by lesser artists and would be perhaps best classed as primitives; we must not, however, neglect to examine any of these works.

It is also important to examine other types of ships of the period, preferably those of similar size and purpose. The artists, whether they were skilled or unskilled, were realists and most often painted the ship and her rig in accurate detail. It will be useful to refer to some examples here.

The purpose of showing these illustrations of vessels, some of them different than the Baltimore Clipper, is to exhibit the striking contrast between the ordinary, conventional, small vessels and the fast-sailing schooners. Let us look at such a contrast.

Figure 2-10 is a reproduction of a painting from the Mariners' Museum collection (Newport News, Virginia) by Antoine Roux, perhaps the most famous of the late-18th- and early-19th-century marine artists and the patriarch of a family of marine painters of Marseilles, France. This watercolor painting, dated 1803, is of his characteristic style. It depicts a French merchant brig or, more accurately, a variation of the rig called a *snow*. A snow has a small pole mast close to the mainmast for hoisting the fore-and-aft gaff main; this makes it possible to lower the gaff of this sail independently, which is (was) not possible on a brig.

This vessel is a typical slow-sailing merchant vessel; and, compared with a fast topsail schooner from the Chesapeake, it can only be said, to its credit, that it could carry a more profitable cargo. The detail of its rig shows a vastly more complex arrangement of yards and tophamper, requiring a crew perhaps twice as large as that for a topsail schooner. Both masts are in three sections. Although no topgallant yards are shown, there are topgallant poles (the uppermost mast sections) set. The weather that is evident in the painting indicates the prudence of striking these upper sails. On the bowsprit there is a spritsail yard shown without the sail. (Such sails at this time were little used and were gradually becoming obsolete.)

The ship carries but one gun to starboard and probably another on the opposite side. These are for protection against the ubiquitous Mediterranean pirate presence—although most merchantmen of this period were armed, more so than this poor brig.

The painting scheme on this vessel shows it to be typical of its period: a black hull with a broad ochre stripe on the main wale and the projecting rails, and covering boards painted to match the color of the wale. The rails and covering boards here indicate that the vessel had a quarterdeck, a main deck, and a forecastle deck. She was steered by a tiller, and carried a ship's boat on the main deck and a smaller gig on stern davits. A large anchor stock is shown on the after side of a projecting cathead, and the shank seems to have been brought into the forecastle deck by topping tackle from the foretop.

Figure 2-10. This is an excellent graphic impression of a contemporary early-19th-century merchant vessel. Although she flies the French flag, she is typical of hundreds of small, poor merchantmen sailing in coastwise or ocean trade, or both, in European waters.

The flying jib is furled, and the jib has not yet been brought in by its sheet from the previous starboard tack position. The brig seems to be in the process of shortening sail for a run before the wind.

To contrast this French brig (snow) with a typical topsail schooner out of Baltimore, we can look at another painting, also done in the Mediterranean and only a few years later, of the Baltimore Clipper *Patapsco* out of Baltimore, sailing into the Bay of Naples (Figure 2-11). Our records (carpenter's certificate) show this schooner to have been built by Thomas Kemp for a consortium headed by Henry Fulford in September, 1812. She was 74 feet 3 inches on her keel, 24 feet 2 inches beam, 11 feet 5 inches hold, and 215.6 carpenter's measure. She had the usual "round tuck and no head." The painting, by an unnamed Italian artist, shows the typical Baltimore schooner rig described earlier that sets her apart from foreign schooners and most other American schooners. Her forestay carries a very large staysail out to the bowsprit's junction with the jibboom. Her fore triangle is complete with jib and flying jib on an extended jibboom. A double-topsail schooner, with square topsails on both masts, she is shown flying not only topgallant sails on both masts as well, but also royals—her fore royal is lowered to the topgallant yard. This much working sail is unusual but apparently is an alternative for the more common stun'sails for light weather. The *Patapsco* is shown to have the usual large fore-and-aft fore- and mainsails. The foresail is straddled by the typical double mainstay and, according to standard American practice, is overlapping the main with a boomless foot. The mainsail extends beyond the stern by approximately 30 percent of its foot on a loose-footed boom. The vessel is pierced for 16 guns and showing eight on her port side.

There is some graphic evidence of another interesting Baltimore Clipper, though not in the form of a painting. The description is based on a fine model in the Smithsonian collection in Washington, D.C. (Figure 2-12), made from plans existing in the Swedish Archives. The fore-topsail schooner, said to be built in Baltimore in 1812, was apparently built for a foreign account. There is no known record of a carpenter's certificate, but the schooner was sold to Sweden, and the naval officials of Sweden's king were apparently so impressed with the vessel, named *Experiment*, that they ordered four duplications. The model shows a very graceful combination of hull and rig of a typical fore-topsail schooner. Her squareyards are comparatively short but make up in sail area in height of sails. It is thus a lofty, narrow rig with a double fore topmast and an extended jib-boom. The vessel carries no armament, but her dimensions and form

Figure 2-11. A contemporary portrait of the Baltimore Clipper Patapsco *entering the Bay of Naples. The artist is unknown, but the port of Naples has been known for its prolific artists whose livelihood was painting ships entering their beautiful harbor. (The author owns such an example painted in 1937 of the U.S. warship in which he was embarked.)*

show a relatively small schooner of shallower-than-normal draft, suggesting blockade running and shallower water. The museum records (Sjohistorica Museum, Stockholm) indicate that the vessel was 71½ feet between perpendiculars (molded waterline), 23 feet extreme beam, and 96.5 tons displacement. Altogether she is an excellent example of the extreme Baltimore Clippers at the peak of their curve.

Returning to another vessel painted by Antoine Roux from one of his sketchbooks, dated 1790 and in the collection of the Peabody

Figure 2-12. Baltimore Clipper Experiment, *a handsome model of a typical Chesapeake schooner of her time. This vessel was built in 1812 and purchased by the Swedish Navy in 1813. Her waterline length (less molded posts) was 71 feet 6 inches. Her extreme sail plan is evident in her tall spars. She has an additional fore topmast pole extension and an extremely long main gaff topsail pole as well as an additional outer jib stay.*

Museum of Salem, Massachusetts, Figure 2-13 shows a very rare image of an early Chesapeake-type topsail schooner just prior to the well-known privateers. It is unfortunately an unfinished sketch, but is typical of Roux's literal interpretive eye; it would be similar to a candid camera shot if the artist were a photographer. The nameless schooner is apparently lying under shortened sail, perhaps waiting for a pilot outside the port of Marseilles, which was the artist's habitat and the typical locale for his paintings.

She is a double-topsail schooner with squareyards on both masts. She interestingly carries no guns; obviously she is a fast schooner and is confident that she needs none. She is, characteristically, a very plain and understated vessel. Her foresail is in brails and boomless, as was usual. Her fore course and both square topsails, as well as her

Figure 2-13. An unfinished watercolor sketch of a double topsail schooner obviously of the Chesapeake. She is an early model, 1790, and shows a square tuck stern. She is another example of Antoine Roux's prolific brush at that time.

middle headsail, are loosely filling with a quartering breeze. The main gaff is dropped and the sail is lifted on the mast in the customary temporary habit of standby. The deck rails are rigged with nettings, at least to the quarterdeck break, which is a low step from the main deck. This is an early structural style predating the completely flush main deck (see Figure 1-14, Steel's "Virginia Built" boat, circa. 1790).

There is evidence here that confirms a long, controversial question of how spare spars or spar material was carried to account for the breakage of light-sail spars on Baltimore Clippers. This question is likely answered here by the outside quarters exhibiting lashed poles, quite probably spar material.

The schooner is flying the American ensign, with 13 stars in rectilinear arrangement. Note also that this schooner has a full transom stern with the old square tuck and a very graceful lower line with rising wale. The waist scuppers indicate a rather high main-deck freeboard—a prudent idea for a lofty merchant schooner. The artist left the sketch unfinished, not showing a separate jibboom on the bowsprit or indication of dolphin striker and martingale.

In the next illustration, Figure 2-14, we see a full-blown privateer-type topsail schooner. This painting is from the Mariners' Museum collection, and is by the famous British marine artist Thomas Buttersworth (1797–1827). The painting is undated and the ship unidentified. The 12-gun schooner is sailing hard on a brisk wind and heeling to such a degree that her lee rail could be awash. She is pointing exceptionally high, with the square topsail braced around as far as it will go and fore- and mainsails sheeted in also to the limits. The jib and forestaysail as well are drawing their limit, and the flying jib has been dropped and the topgallant let fly. She is probably making less speed through the water than she would if her sheets were just started a bit. However, it makes a dramatic scene.

The background of the painting indicates that it is near a rather mountainous coast with a harbor nearby. The style of rig on the small vessel to the right and the onshore line strongly suggest a Mediterranean harbor, probably near Marseilles or Toulon, France. This would set the time after the Napoleonic period, perhaps in the second decade of the 19th century.

Speculating a bit further, the rig (single-topsail schooner), the six gunports to the side, the loft of the mast, and the extent of jibboom, establish a true image of an extreme Baltimore Clipper of letter-of-marque style. Flying the British ensign on this foreign shore indicates a Navy vessel on station. She appears very like the Baltimore schooner *Lynx* (Figure 1-15), captured by the British in 1813 in the Chesapeake, having been trapped with three other Baltimore Clippers when they were relatively new vessels. (As mentioned earlier, the *Lynx* was taken into the Royal Navy and remained ignominiously

The Baltimore Clipper:
A Unique Identity

Figure 2-14. A lesser-known painting by the well-known Thomas Buttersworth: a topsail schooner flying a British flag. She quite possibly could be the captured Baltimore Clipper letter-of-marque schooner Lynx.

HMS *Musquidobit*.) There appear to be approximately 16 sailors evident, high on the windward rail — a good place to be, in the schooner's sailing attitude.

The Treaty of Ghent

Had the War of 1812 continued much beyond 1815, the supply of new sharp-built privateers out of Baltimore would have lengthened what may seem to be an endless line of Baltimore Clippers. But the war did not go on. As in most conflicts, rationality eventually prevailed, urged on by frustration, exhausted participants, and funds that were not inexhaustible. The United States, a poor country at the start, could not afford to maintain the small, young navy that fought aboard their pitifully few frigates so valiantly. Toward the end of hostilities in early 1815, there were insufficient funds to put the larger frigates to sea; the majority were harbor-bound by the winter of 1814. As valiant as the several victories by U.S. ships over British ships had been with superior tactics, seamanship, and gunnery, it was not a factor in the war's conclusion. The British naval forces and their combined military strength were insignificantly touched by United States ships. The land battles were small skirmishes, except perhaps the Battle of New Orleans and the victory by General Andrew Jackson; unhappily, a peace treaty had already been concluded before it happened.

Clear evidence exists to tell us that the emissaries of His Britannic Majesty were brought to the peace negotiation table by frustration and economic pressure. The only important military problem facing Great Britain, and the oldest, was the problem with Napoleon and his French Republic. Waterloo was still, at the end of 1814, only a peaceful village in Belgium.

The members of the British Parliament felt the sting of bitter complaints from citizens representing the coastal fishing industry and the ship owners whose vessels had been lost to American "piracy" (they were not going to recognize the legitimacy of privateering or the letters-of-marque). The great number of British ships lost — reliable estimates exceed 600 — was not an inconsiderable item to the powerful marine insurance lords led by Lloyd's of London. The government in the halls along Westminster Embankment was acutely aware of public unhappiness and the Treasury's leaky bottom.

British delegates met with those appointed by the President James Madison of the United States in Ghent, Belgium, in the autumn of 1814. There was considerable wrangling and a tendency to backslide, much blustering and attempts to bully the American impertinence. Reality and practicality finally wrestled down a ten-part agreement; this was due largely to the adroitness and rightful reasoning of the notable American delegation, with its distinguished leaders John Quincy Adams and Henry Clay. The Treaty of Ghent was finally signed on Christmas Eve, 1814, and ratified and proclaimed by President Madison on February 18, 1815.

The Baltimore Clipper:
A Unique Identity

CHAPTER THREE

The Demise and
the Heritage

After the War of 1812 was over, most of the citizens
were relieved and merely glad that the trouble was gone. The celebrations, such as they were, had no great moving spirit. The Treaty of
Ghent was more of a mutual agreement to return to the status quo
before 1812. There were no notable concessions; a few questionable
boundaries were firmed up, and the ownership of some small islands
off the coast of Maine were established to satisfaction. Nothing was
said about impressment of seamen, its illegality being understood.
The most important thing about the settlement and peace with England was the silent recognition of mutual respect: This time, it was a
settlement between two nations.

In Baltimore, there would be a change in the shipbuilding industry.
It was symbolically and in fact the end of an era; it further was an
abrupt end of a shipbuilding boom, and this is reflected statistically
in the registration records from 1815. There was literally no more
market for privateers, and there was a great scramble of selling and
converting and transferring of registrations.

Thomas Kemp moved from Fells Point back to his home on the
Eastern Shore and built a manor house at Wade's Point, outside St.
Michaels. When he died in 1824 at age 45, there still was no demand
for legitimate letter-of-marque or privateer-style vessels.

Of the hundreds of sharp-built privateers and letter-of-marque vessels that sailed out of the Chesapeake before and during the War of

1812, what happened to them all? We know of those that fell into the hands of the enemy—all told, hardly more than a dozen, for the most part taken into the British Navy, and well recorded. Others were lost at sea, and of these there is no reliable record.

Of the some 70 Baltimore privateers surviving after the War of 1812, it is documented that 24 of them were sold to foreign buyers; four others were reported lost at sea after 1815. The remainder were sold into the merchant trade. Their success as merchant ships was poor, however. Their holds were too small, they were too sharp in the ends, and had too quick a rise to their bottoms; and there were too few interested as crew without the incentive of prizes. Also, it has been said that the privateers were built too quickly and too cheaply and could not last more than two or three years before rot and leakage ended them. That judgment is not without a little merit, but it is not a general truth. From the examples of Fells Point builders' contracts, we can plainly see how specific builders agreed to build the vessels, and such quality of structure was typical of Baltimore ships in the years leading up to 1812. As the war pressures increased and the number of ships multiplied exponentially, quality, without doubt, gave way to necessary haste. However, it would be illogical to believe that pine was substituted for oak, for there was plenty of both. More likely, the haste in some construction was responsible for careless caulking, poorly fitted scarfs and plank ends, and the like, which would lead to leaky hulls with consequent shortened life.

On the other hand, there is evidence of many of the privateers and letter-of-marque schooners being sold to the south—not necessarily to Southern states, but to southern countries. The destiny of those ships was to Cuba, the Caribbean islands, and South America. During these years, there was considerable growth in the Southern Hemisphere and shifting political climate, and with this came a demand for fast sailing vessels.

For better-known individual privateers such as these, it is sometimes possible to follow their subsequent use after their privateer service. The foreign buyers were largely from Havana, Cuba, and the privateers included the *Comet, Chasseur, Amelia,* and *Patapsco* (Figure 3-1), among others.

For a few years after the signing of the Treaty of Ghent, Baltimore-owned and -built schooners (many changed to brigs) enjoyed a reasonably rewarding trade to the West Indies. The export cargoes were frequently flour and cotton, returning with coffee and sugar. Major Caribbean ports were Havana and Port au Prince.

At this same time there was considerable unrest and revolution against Spain in South America, and the fast schooners were particularly useful for illegal or borderline trade, running blockades and supplying war munitions. The former, much-admired Baltimore Clippers were involved in what became commonly known as South American raiding, and this rough and more irresponsible use only hastened their demise.

Figure 3-1. Privateer Patapsco, *the two-topsail schooner out of Baltimore engaging in a night encounter with a British warship, September, 1814.*

This service was most attractive to many of the former captains and crews, who had enjoyed the handsome income and freedom accorded them as American privateersmen. With their Baltimore-built schooners, they continued this seemingly endless, fortuitous life. And Baltimore as a supply port could service both the Spanish and rebel forces. As a matter of fact, Baltimore became a strategic part of this South American revolt. Blank commissions were printed and supplied in Baltimore for private armed vessels. The names of the vessels even continued to be typical of those of their predecessors. It is not an especially bright chapter in the history of either the port of Baltimore, its entrepreneurial bankers and investors, or the ships and crews that participated.

The entire enterprise soured by 1820. Many of the more noble and respectable Baltimoreans backed away from favoring anything to do with the South American raiders. In many cases, these privateers, being too hastily and poorly legitimized, became involved in outright piracy. Interpreting the matter literally, Baltimore was engaging in acts of war, not only against Spain but against non-belligerent ships from Europe. There is evidence of these Baltimore vessels returning to unload poorly diguised prize goods and booty not only from Spanish sources, but from Portuguese, Dutch, and French ones as well.

What a sad end for Secretary of State James Monroe and his successor, John Quincy Adams, to be forced to respond to complaints of the foreign embassies. For this was the final episode for many of those great exploiters of speed and sailing performance that had been hailed with such esteem when warring against England. One of the most shameful examples was that of the old *Comet* (see Chapter 1), built by Thomas Kemp in 1812 and so successfully and honorably sailed by Thomas Boyle. The only slightly less famous *Hornet*, under her last South American flag and named *Alerta,* was returned to Baltimore under arrest and with the evidence of her guilt on board. But the darkest and most miserable work was still before some of the surviving vessels after the South American adventures were curbed: the involvement in slave running in the 1820s by splintered remnants of the great Baltimore Clipper fleets of the decade before. It was this use that was responsible for besmudging the reputation of the clippers as a whole.

The slave trade

Before 1801, it was legally possible to employ ships to transport slaves as long as those ships were not built or fitted for the purpose. Consequently, the slave trade was about the same as other profitable merchandising: The use of large ships to hold the maximum quantity of black bodies was the formula for delivering the greatest quantity of merchandise in every arrival. In 1808, the importation of slaves was prohibited by Congress. The law was further strengthened ten years later by increasing the penalties against anyone involved, especially the owners and operators of slave ships; this reflected the consternation of Congress. Responding again in 1820, Congress labeled the slave trade "piracy," and punishment for slavers was death, although the enforcement of the law was indifferent. Even so, as part of the Treaty of Ghent, the British Navy, as well as the United States Navy, was involved in pursuing slave ships, so the occupation of transporting slaves on the high seas required fast ships.

When there is risk of apprehension on the high seas in such trade, the tendency is to utilize faster, more evasive transportation. The avoidance of risk, along with the increasing penalties levied by law and the specialization of vessels and expert captains and crews, results in higher prices; this situation existed in the years approaching 1820. For the owners and captains of fast schooners, many of which had recently been active as South American raiders, the negligence of enforcement added to the attraction of becoming involved in the slave trade.

Having served their country to spectacular success, some of the Baltimore Clippers fell on hard and shameful usage after their original purpose ceased. After the War of 1812, they were still fast and maneuverable vessels, but in the hands of greedy owners, captains, investors, and suppliers with no motivation other than easy money and with no moral principles, the ships were as captive objects. We must not let them slip into oblivion so easily; it is the greedy people who possessed them that we must hold in contempt.

I must make a distinction between the Baltimore Clippers—the earlier veterans of the 1812 conflict, the extreme schooner/privateers and blockade runners that were sold or drifted into the South American revolutions and ultimately the slave trade—and the sharp schooners for the coastal trade during and after the third decade of the 19th century, which were different vessels and cannot technically be identified as Baltimore Clippers. Some of the schooners of the 1830s were built for the fruit trade; those built as slavers were illegally built, or illegally sold to foreign owners. These vessels were poor copies of the fast-sailing, lofty schooners of the earlier 1800s: Their masts were shorter, the hulls fatter, and they frequently, because of the current

Figure 3-2. The notorious Baltimore-built schooner Amistad. *This Spanish-owned vessel out of Cuba, undoubtedly an original Baltimore Clipper, worked the coastwise slave trade. She cannot be traced through records to her original identity. Her days ended when fifty-three black slaves in her hold revolted and took the ship to Long Island, New York.*

nautical styles, carried decorated headboards. If there is any similarity they should be identified as post–Baltimore Clippers to avoid confusion.

These newly built vessels cannot be identified as Baltimore Clippers; they did not have the characteristics of the letter-of-marque and reprisal vessels of the earlier years. It is unfortunate that many students and historians of this era of our maritime history have carelessly and incorrectly referred to the whole lot as Baltimore Clippers, for it is only the deliberately built vessels that deserve their sullied reputation as slavers.

The true Baltimore Clippers were the schooners and brigs that evolved from the Revolutionary period and then erupted out of Baltimore shipyards into the refined sailing machines of the first decade of the 19th century. These were the successful vessels that first attracted the attention of shipping investors at this time, not only in America but in Western Europe.

There was a significant difference in build between the new schooners built in Baltimore and elsewhere for coastal trade, some of which fell into disreputable employment, and the slave vessels. Between 1836 and 1841 some dozen and a half ships were built in Baltimore or the upper Chesapeake and recorded as "slavers." All but three were described as schooners; the others were two brigs and one three-masted vessel. These schooners were smaller than any of the privateers of the early 19th century, their tonnage averaging less than 100, as compared with a typical privateer schooner, for example *Lynx,* built in Baltimore in 1812, which had a registered tonnage of $225^{18}/_{95}$. The difference in tonnage is one characteristic contrast between the two types of schooners.

Lynx's profile and sail plan are most distinctive for her period, with no decoration, a plain head, a long bowsprit, and three large headsails. Her hull has the lines of an oceangoing vessel, with a deadrise to her midsections of approximately 30 degrees, a sharp but not hollow entrance, and a fine run under her quarters with slight hollow above the waterline. She is pierced for 14 guns above a minimum freeboard of 3 feet. Her masts in profile show a substantial rake of between 15 and 16 inches.

Less is known specifically about the so-called "slaver Baltimore Clippers" of the 1830s, but it would appear from one set of lines drawings that the smaller schooners were fuller in section with less deadrise, for greater hold capacity. These were, according to ship styles of that period and according to the customs records and register, decorated with head knees, trailboards, and figureheads or billetheads. Their freeboard was (logically) proportionately greater.

However, despite the great traffic in slave ships, it is not possible to label a slaver as a type, for there was no such thing as a typical slave vessel. Many of the vessels were built larger, of ship rig and corresponding tonnage, with built-in 'tween decks for the terrible human stowage. Many were Spanish-built schooners and brigs; many were older, nondescript vessels.

Lost to time

It still is something of a mystery as to where and how most of the early sharp-built schooners ended their lives. On the whole, however, if a ship is not known individually and internationally for her greatness, it is not unusual that her final burial is passed by without notice; like birds of passage, who ever does know?

I have found two interesting, relatively well-preserved bits of knowledge about two vessels whose original identity is unknown, but both were unmistakably Baltimore Clippers. One, shown in a photograph in the collection of the Peabody Museum of Salem, simply identified as "Schooner Entering Havana Harbor" and dated 1860 (Figure 3-3), is most interesting. This vessel appears like a ghost of the past. The proportions of her rig and spars, and the rake of the masts, clearly show that she is not of 1860. Her low hull and flat sheer, her transom shape, in fact the entire image, is that of a Chesapeake-built schooner of 50 years before. She looks very tired and a little hogged in the middle, perhaps, but still moving along with a little pride in her bearing. I would say that she was a survivor in 1860, to appear as a brief image on a photographer's plate and disappear again, to be known only as an inter-island trader — and on to oblivion.

Another mystery schooner, also from the Caribbean, sailed among the islands in the eastern half of this American middle sea. Carrying local cargo, passengers, and mail, this schooner (Figures 3-4 and 3-5) was well known among the islanders. She was last photographed in

1903 and appeared in a newspaper article in St. Thomas, Virgin Islands. As reported then, at the beginning of this century, when half of the Virgin Islands belonged to Denmark, this schooner sailed under the name *Vigilant*. One photograph from 1879 shows her approaching Christiansted with the Danish Prince Valdemar aboard. Another photograph shows her in Christiansted harbor in "dress ship" condition, with the Danish national flag on her stern flagstaff. There is a large ceremonial party on board under an awning from bow to stern;

Figure 3-3. A late survivor is photographed in 1860 entering Havana harbor. Her stem head profile seems too heavy for a Baltimore Clipper, but close examination of the original indicates the starboard anchor obscuring her actual stem head. She is an old and unknown topsail schooner looking very tired, but still with a bit of dignity.

the celebration was said to be the centenary commemorating the schooner's reported participation in a battle in 1801 against English warships, although this is questionable history. Finally, the article reported that her former American identity was *Nonsuch*, a Baltimore Clipper, and that she first appeared in St. Croix, Virgin Islands, in

Figure 3-4. Vigilant, *formerly* Nonsuch, *as she was seen in 1903, operated as an inter-island trader among the Danish Virgin Islands. She is showing some few signs of her long life, which began nearly a century before.*

1824. Her previous existence was obscure, stated Battandier, her owner (at that time), who had no registration or documentation papers for her. He speculated that she may well have been a smuggler, privateer, or pirate vessel before 1824. Quite likely—such history would fit the stories and fate of a number of her sisters.

Figure 3-5. Deck scene on Vigilant. *The original caption on this photo when it was published in a Caribbean newspaper read: Deck interior of Schooner "Vigilant" 1903, which for many years plied between St. Croix and St. Thomas with post and passengers.*

According to Baltimore customs records and documents of 1812, commission applications, and navy privateer records in the National Archives, a Baltimore Clipper named *Nonsuch* was awarded Commission No. 1 as a privateer on June 29, 1812. She was owned by George Stiles of Baltimore, with no part owners. There is no record of her builder, but it is quite likely she was built before the war, having been given Commission No. 1 early in 1812, before hostilities, and readied and fitted for such purpose. The record also shows that this Baltimore Clipper was sold to the Navy and sailed as the USS *Nonsuch* in 1813—a bit surprising, because the records indicate that George Stiles as sole owner earned nearly $120,000 by *Nonsuch*'s prizes in 1812-1813.[1] If that represents only one year's earnings for one vessel, she was among the most profitable of the privateers.

Although research indicates a number of vessels named *Nonsuch,* there is only one other topsail schooner of that name, and she was British, having been built in 1840. She is described as a fast vessel with raked masts, able to sail from Aberdeen, Scotland, to London in 49 hours. Except for her raked stem, a fixture of the so-called Aberdeen Clippers (she was built in Aberdeen), her profile is that of a typical Baltimore Clipper; this feature does not agree with the photograph of the Virgin Islands schooner.

The *Vigilant* (ex-*Nonsuch*) could be traced through five owners from 1824, except for her original (or the U.S. Navy) sale, if that was the schooner. The sparse records do not indicate that the Navy ever used the USS *Nonsuch* in active hostility or commerce raiding after purchase—a pity. It is believed that sometime after the 1812 conflict, this vessel somehow fell into unknown ownership in the Caribbean volatility between 1815-20. She was almost certainly an original Baltimore Clipper, and as such she lived longer than any other. Owned by the widow of her last purchaser in 1873, Captain P. Pentheny, the *Vigilant* disappeared in 1917. She would have at that time been 116 years old—not bad for a Chesapeake-built schooner.

There is no knowledge of which or when was the last Baltimore Clipper—there is no record, nor is it a definitive matter. The extreme examples and the purest of those originated in the first decade of the 19th century. This is a rather narrow band in the spectrum of American shipbuilding, but at the same time, it is the brightest of all the multicolored bands, not only for American schooners, privateers, and fast vessels—it is the brightest and most significant of American shipbuilding history!

This may sound self-serving and chauvinistic, but look again at the facts. This period of history reflects the early struggle to stand alone not only politically but economically, as a new nation embarking toward a brave yet unknown destiny with a new form of government. With experimentation, there was a good deal of stumbling, flailing about, and moving into deadend by-ways in our first 30 years or so after declaring independence. But shipbuilding was one of the things this young nation could do, and much of it was for European markets, before and after our independence. As described in Chapter 1, this shipbuilding market was mostly merchant-ship types going to Britain and northern Europe. Many from New England and a good number from the Chesapeake yards were built on European lines and style, according to the market demands. Most of the domestic vessels for fishing and coastal trade were also built to European practice and doctrine, particularly in the New England yards and those of Delaware and New York. In the Chesapeake, the builders were living in a much less sophisticated environment. The people were more independent, and this was necessary for their sustenance. Such a climate and philosophy conceives creative skills, and thus their own boats for fishing and piloting—and, with political instability, the smugglers—were created along individual lines. As a type of vessel, those topsail schooners and brigs coming out of the upper Chesapeake in the early 19th century and fully prepared for privateer and letter-of-marque commerce were the first truly "all-American" ships, unlike anything else in the world. They were readily recognized, praised, and envied in the maritime world where they emerged. Their peculiarities and physical characteristics carried on to influence the naval architecture of sailing ships for the rest of the century. So, this was a very bright light in our early history.

A persistent imprint

We have contemplated the demise of the Baltimore Clippers so darkly and without any noticeable eulogies or farewells. It was something akin to the fall of a popular and successful personage: once rich and famous with financial gain, the "belle of the ball," and then suddenly the party is over. The path leads down the road to lawlessness, poverty, shame, and oblivion—but not quite.

This species of sailing vessel was honestly conceived and built, was usefully and brilliantly employed, and its particular character in design did not fade away. It left an imprint that was persistent. True, its place of origin was largely forgotten: there was little to commercially sustain such vessels built and owned in the Chesapeake in the years following 1815. The owners and captains could see only their continuance in rewarding revenues, but the financial slump of 1819 ended such hopes. The owners who turned their ships south to exploit questionable and volatile Latin American adventure fell into disrepute, as did their ships. The more non-speculative and conservative Baltimore shipping population turned to large-bottomed and slower trading vessels. In this, most shipbuilders clearly abandoned the old Baltimore Clipper model—because it was not profitable in peacetime. There was one bright exception: One longtime owner and financier who had invested in many a privateer and blockade runner out of Baltimore was not completely ready to walk away from their fascination. After helping fund and establish the first railroad system in the 1820s, the original Baltimore & Ohio Railroad, John McKim returned to the shipping industry.

In 1832, when the typical sharp-built topsail schooners had been long gone from the builder's yard and had become only the subject of talk and memories, there was a new keel laid down in the Fells Point yard of Kennard & Williamson. Since before the War of 1812, the McKim family had actively and heavily invested in sharp-built ships. One of the few shipping investors who did not go under in the panic of 1819 nor turn away from the risky presumption that fast ships could also be profitable, John McKim led the owners of this new ship, named *Ann McKim* (Figures 3-6 and 3-7).

There were and are some noteworthy historians of the Clipper Ship Era of the 1850s-1860s who will argue that the *Ann McKim* was not the first clipper ship to be launched. It is difficult to understand this argument; the *Ann McKim* was most certainly a *ship* by all nautical and international definition and understanding. She had three masts and was square rigged on all three. She was 143 feet between perpendiculars, 31 feet molded beam, with a draft aft of 17' 6". These were impressive dimensions in 1830-period shipping—certainly greater by far than those of the old-style Baltimore Clipper, privateer and blockade runner.

After the Treaty of Ghent settlement in 1815 and the resultant consolidation of the political establishment, there remained a great need for economic growth. This essentially meant foreign trade, together with expansion of resources—not only in the United States, with its unrealized resources, but in western Europe and Great Britain. The western world was literally on the threshold of the great Industrial Revolution. By 1830, the newly invented steam engine had quickly found applications on land and water. From Baltimore, the first great railway was pushing its way westward. During the 1820s, many of the same investors who backed Baltimore Clippers transferred their hopes or expanded them to the Baltimore & Ohio Railroad; among these were John and Isaac McKim. Steam-powered watercraft had already proved successful in a limited way with John Fitch's ferry on the

Figure 3-6. Ann McKim, *designed and built by Kennard and Williamson, 1832. Her hull design, dimensions, and three-mast ship rig qualify her to proper recognition as the first clipper ship.*

Potomac and Fulton's Hudson River experiments. This promising expansion was a time to look for larger sailing vessels. If they could be fast as well, this was desirable, too, but quantity and volume were the key to profitable expansion then. The more farsighted investors realized that greater size, together with speed, would put them on the cutting edge of the competition sure to come. This factor was uppermost in backers of the new type of vessel named *Ann McKim*. What else could she be called but a clipper ship?[2]

Those who have judged otherwise have been, understandably, regional supporters from the great metropolis of the North. New York's gifted shipbuilders came along nearly a dozen years later to develop some nicely modeled and even larger ships; John Griffiths was first with *Rainbow*. A resourceful ship designer, Griffiths introduced his design first with a half-model exhibited in an industrial fair in New York. His model embodied the compromise that the *Ann McKim* lacked: a fuller bottom combined with sharp ends. That, together with her greater waterline length, provided the necessary speed capability. It seems apparent that this vessel, when built in 1845, became a second clipper ship. Her greater capacity, her speed, and her resultant earnings opened the floodgates, even though she had met with a deluge of criticism by "nay-sayers" while being built. The

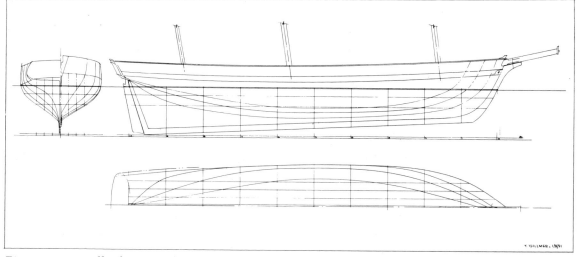

Figure 3-7. Hull, sheer profile of Ann McKim *drawn from reliable but limited source.*

Rainbow was 154 feet waterline, a large vessel for the time, with a displacement of 1,043 tons. She was closely followed in 1846 by another elegant clipper by Griffiths, the famous *Sea Witch,* 168 feet waterline and 1,250 tons displacement. Observe the accelerating growth in the first year: The formula had been set. The designers compromised on the clean, sharp deadrise built into the *Ann McKim.* While aware of its added sailing performance factor in upwind sailing, they could not resist the pressure of the ship owners for carrying capacity, so they gave their hulls nicely rounded bellies.

It is interesting to look at the claims for the primacy of clipper ships and the times identified as the Clipper Ship Era, and to finally inquire what specific peculiarities define a *clipper ship.* Actually, under the cold, bright light of honest scrutiny, the "authenticity" arguments become much like the science of the Wizard of Oz: They all fall away into hollow, unspecific, and unsupportable rhetoric. There is no mystery, nor any solid factors, nor technical definition that draws the line between a so-called clipper ship and one not so called. The whole matter reduces to very simple geometric factors in a reasonable analysis.

With the *Ann McKim,* a trend was begun in Baltimore in 1832 by a consortium of investors, predominantly of the McKim family, to build a larger vessel with three masts: a fully square-rigged ship identity. Not that the Fells Point shipyards had been limited to the smaller topsail schooners or brig-type vessels; many larger three-masted ships had been launched here, and some were moderately sharp-built during the 1812 era. It was simply that this different and extended hull shape supporting a three-masted ship rig began a new and contagious style.

So, let us examine the *Ann McKim* more closely. What made her so different from other ships? She was a larger sharp-built vessel with many characteristics of the privateer-schooner pattern established so long before her. Being larger and heavier, she consequently had to separate her sail plan into the manageable units on three masts. Her hull exhibited some basic characteristics of the old type of fast schooner but was not so extreme. Her keel was not parallel to the waterline, as was common among most contemporary merchant ships and as was customary from centuries past; it was raked down aft from the stem to her sternpost. Her body sections were not flat and full, and they rose with an appreciable angle from the keel; this *dead-rise* or *rise of floor* was a notable and identifiable feature of the ancestral Baltimore Clipper form. While these features were clearly present in the hull of the *Ann McKim*, together with the sharp-ended waterlines, there was also a noticeable modifying shape. In being longer and broader, she had less proportional depth and breadth. The lines were more gradual in change of direction. Nor did her masts show the old extreme rake. Essentially, she became a new type, with her increased size and ship rig, retaining the best features of the successful Baltimore Clippers without emphasis, but modifying and softening them to suit her purpose as a fast carrier of merchandise.

Her first employment was in the South American trade, where she made several successful and notably fast voyages. However, the trade to the developing and as yet unstable countries of South America was not of sufficient growth to induce or attract fast and expensively built ships. And the *Ann McKim* was expensively fitted out—much like a yacht. She had Spanish mahogany hatch coamings, her frames were of Southern live oak, and her bottom was sheathed in imported red copper. All of the rails, skylights, and companionways were of bright Spanish or Honduras mahogany, and she mounted 12 brass cannons, mostly for show.[3] The brass fittings on the *Ann McKim*, such as capstan heads and other deck hardware, gave her a very smart and yacht-like appearance.

She remained in the South American trade until she was sold to a New York shipping firm after the death of Isaac McKim. The ship owners Howland and Aspinwall took her over in 1837 for the China trade. "Although the *Ann McKim* was the first clipper ship ever constructed, it cannot be said that she founded the Clipper Ship Era." This is quoted from the well-known volume by Arthur H. Clarke, *The Clipper Ship Era*, published in 1910. The author, Captain Clark, was himself in his youth a captain of medium clippers (1863-1877) and a close friend of Donald McKay, the designer and builder of the well-known great clippers of Boston: *Flying Cloud, Lightning,* and *Great Republic.*

My intention is not to dwell on the history of the great clipper ships of the mid-19th century, but rather to illuminate the impact of the Baltimore Clippers on the clipper ship story. The role of the *Ann McKim* has been, in previous treatments, falsely minimized, largely by the fact that the great clipper ship yards were in New York and New England. The benefactors and the historians of these remarkable ships, in their enthusiasm and pride, have disconnected themselves with the progression of ship design and development, and have largely ignored the historical importance of the Baltimore Clippers. It is not too late to pull it all together and remind our friends in New York and New England that these vessels existed, that they were welcomed when they were needed, and that they were significant.

The *Ann McKim*'s relationship to the subsequent maximum clippers—the extreme clippers whose story in seafaring is so overwhelming—is clear in the unfolding evidence. She was built as a clipper—a Baltimore Clipper *ship*. She proved herself as a fast merchant ship: she was recognized by the New York shipping firm Howland and Aspinwall, who bought her and placed her in the China trade, where her consistently good passages were impressive. The owners, being merchants, concluded that she was a fast ship and vowed to build "another that is as fast but larger to carry more"—which they did, with the ship *Rainbow* mentioned earlier, designed and built by John Griffiths a few years after their purchase of the *Ann McKim*. The larger *Rainbow*, 11 feet longer on the waterline, was designed for greater carrying capacity by filling out her sections below the waterline and providing a much rounder bottom or belly with very little dead rise. This would increase her wave-making drag, but she would make up for that by her longer and even sharper waterline. So, this was the basic compromise that began the great clipper trend and growth.

On the question of comparative speed between the Baltimore Clippers—those sharp-built schooners of the 1810-1815 period—and the great clipper ships of the 1840s and 1850s, there is really very little difference. The difference in the finite speeds through the water lies only in the difference in size: the difference in waterline length between the two types. The Baltimore Clippers varied somewhere between 75 feet and 95 feet on the waterline. The larger schooners, such as Kemp's *Chasseur* and *Rossie*, were nearly 90 feet, and this, according to the hydrodynamic laws developed by William Froude in the 1870s, would mean a hull speed of nearly thirteen knots. The typical record-setting clipper ships of the 1850s were nearly 220 feet on the waterline, which by the same hydrodynamic laws means a hull-speed capability of 20 knots or better. But the captains of the earlier Baltimore schooners were not prone to checking their speeds through the water, as were the clipper ship captains of nearly 50 years later; there are no records to allow any direct comparison. But with the recently built reconstructions, we know that the sustained speeds measured with 20th-century instruments could exceed 13 knots. This is comparable to the best speed records of the fastest clipper ships of the great Clipper Ship Era.

The Clipper Ship Era of the mid-19th century was a spectacular showcase, and it was in full flower during the decade of 1850-1860. There were what have been called the Yankee Clippers, but let us not perpetuate this inaccurate generalization. There were the so-called "California Clippers," which were inspired and fired by the California Gold Rush fever after 1849. That national contagious greed was the engine that caused the first extreme clippers to be built, that moved Webb of New York and McKay of Boston to launch their largest and most successful and beautiful ships. Other ships built during the same and later period were so many that separate identities of the breed are almost lost. Many vessels called clipper ships really were not, and when history mellowed and the gold was all panned out, the most spectacular years of the Clipper Ship Era were over. Most of the unbreakable sailing records had been made. The vessels that had sailed from New York to San Francisco in less than 90 days, such as *Flying Cloud* (twice), were the greatest of the clipper ships. Those that had exceeded 20 nautical miles in one hour (*James Baines*) or had sailed more than 430 miles in one day (*Lightning*) were also the greatest of clipper ships. Actually, one of the greatest yet tragically unproved was not a three-masted ship, but a four-masted bark. *Great Republic*, built in Boston by Donald McKay, was built as the clipper to outsail all others. She was 325 feet long, 53 feet beam, and 4,555 tons—the largest ship ever of her time. Other great clippers were, when launched, also the largest to that date.

"Large" is the hidden factor in both their commercial attraction and speed potential: The clippers were large in both volume and waterline length. The first dimension, *volume*, was pushed by their merchant identity; the second, by *hydrodynamic* (Froude's) law. Length on the waterline, other things being equal, determines the hull speed. The designer/builders were aware of this fact but not of the supporting theories.

Relatively few Baltimore Clippers were built to the investor's blueprint for a bigger, faster commercial carrier; in fact, commercial bulk carriers preferred slower, cheaper, and bluff-ended ships. However, in the fast lane, there were investors who had been impressed by the swift maneuverability of the Chesapeake schooners.

Smaller working vessels, particularly pilot boats, need speed as well as ocean ability. The traditional fast Virginia pilot schooners, which patrolled the waters of the Virginia Capes at the entrance to the Chesapeake Bay, had developed very closely alongside the larger Chesapeake schooners. They were a notable type as early as the Revolutionary period. In many respects, these pilot schooners bore a strong family resemblance to the Baltimore Clippers—not surprisingly, both having originated in the Chesapeake. The primary difference: The Virginia schooners were a bit smaller, running from 50 to 60 feet on deck at the most. They were also simpler in rig and fittings. The masts were most often without stays or shrouds, and the jib was set flying—the cleanest and most essential rig for pure sailing. The decks were completely clear, and there were no bulwarks. The transom projected above the deck aft, and the bowsprit heel fitted between the knightheads at the stem. The hulls were beamy, but the waterlines were sharp, and the keel raked deeply down aft under a finely rising counter, typical of all early Chesapeake craft. These basic features, of course, were those of the Baltimore Clippers—except that, the clippers being larger, their masts required staying, and their decks needed the bulwark protection. The fundamental characteristic of both types was simplicity. The characteristics of these fast Chesapeake sailing craft were not lost as their reputation spread; they were soon adapted by the designer/builders of New York, in their own version of hardworking, all-weather pilot boats.

In making judgments on the apparent spread of Chesapeake-type characteristics, I must say that there is no direct documentation of transference. While nothing (such as old building contracts between New York's pilot boat owners and Chesapeake Bay builders) has been found for the period after 1814, there were many purchases by New York buyers of boats built on the Bay. Inasmuch as an awareness existed, not only nationally but internationally, of the high-performance characteristics of Chesapeake-built vessels, it would be helpful to briefly review the state of the art of ship design and shipbuilding in the 19th century from 1800 to 1840.

At the turn of the century, there was no separate profession for naval architecture; a ship designer was also the shipbuilder. This was true in the most advanced and cultured countries of Europe as well as in developing countries, such as the United States. This is not to say that the art and science of naval architecture was not then reasonably advanced, nor that all shipbuilders were simple wood-crafters. Indeed, by the latter half of the 18th century, some shipbuilders in Europe were using in their calculations Newtonian mathematics and the highest physical theories of contemporary science, still used today.

Figure 3-8. The yacht America *showing her heritage of the Baltimore Clipper type. This is a very early photograph (circa 1868) of this famous racing yacht and Civil War blockade runner. Note her very large fore triangle with the fore staysail hanging in a loose furl.*

Their mathematical theories for stability, hydromechanics, and form computations that feed our computer programs today were available at the end of the 18th century.

However, in all advanced scientific technology, the adaptation is most often slow. On the American frontier and in the geographically remote locations, including shipyards on the Chesapeake Bay and the rocky inlets of the Maine coast, the use and appreciation of the higher scientific tools was not very evident. This makes it even more remarkable that the characteristics of the sharp-built, Chesapeake-built boats were taken up by the more sophisticated centers of shipbuilding. The shipbuilders of New York, Boston, and the Thames and Portsmouth shipyards in England had the knowledge to create fast sailing hulls. They were aware of the advancements in stability set forth by Fredrik Henrik af Chapman and the French ship designer and author duClair Bois. By 1800, there had been model towing tests in France as well as in England. The ship designers of these shipping and building centers had been drafting their hulls' lines and structure on drawing boards, calculating their displacements, and plotting curves of displacement variation with drafts. All of these procedures make up basic naval architecture.

So, why then did the Northeastern shipyards not build their own fast vessels earlier, rather than follow the lead of the unsophisticated Chesapeake builders? The answer is found in economics and international relations. The engine that moves the shipbuilding industry, like other industry, is the financier—the moneylender and the funder. The product must prove itself first. When these early fast vessels finally attracted the attention of the big investors, their characteristics were capitalized upon and enlarged.

Not that the New York pilot boats were identical to the Virginia pilot boats or the upper-Chesapeake sharp-built schooners. However, they embodied the features most significant and appropriate for their own locality: deep draft to the keel; the raked and rounded stem profile, with its sharper entrance; and the broad, flat quarters running aft into a finely modeled transom.

This form was quickly recognized also by the designer/builders of a growing number of private yachts in the New York area. The most notable and famous of these yachts was the *America*, built by the son of Baltimore Clipper designer Henry Steers. George Steers was himself a designer/builder of several extreme clipper ships, and when he built the yacht *America* (Figure 3-8) in 1851, she was the embodiment of the best features of the Chesapeake schooners of nearly half a century before: the deep drag to the keel, extreme deadrise, flat run, and sharp entrance. Indeed, Steers' vessels, clipper ships and schooners alike, were notable for their extremely sharp entrances. This feature, hydrodynamically, can be easily carried too far, as in Steers' designs: His vessels, like some other clippers, had overly hollow waterlines at the entrance. Such a form results generally in the development of a concave surface before the hull swells into reverse curvature, making for "shoulders." When the hull moves through the water, these shoulders resolve into barriers, creating an unnaturally deep wave train and greater resistance to the hull.

A difference in cloth

No objective analysis of the unique and spectacular victory of the yacht *America* has been made. There have been innumerable speculations on her remarkable superiority to the best of Britain's yachts, hundreds of glowing reports in contemporary news media, much evidence of stupefied English observers; but there have been few serious, technical comparisons between the *America* and her competitors.

In reviewing the race and the rather indifferent preparations by the American crew, it is interesting to observe that their boat, with her stylishly raked masts, was originally rigged with a jib plus an extra-long jibboom beyond the large forestaysail. This apparently was a bit too much foretriangle sail area, and it was dispensed with just prior to the race, leaving her with the simplest and most spartan of sail plans. Her sailcloth was of most carefully selected cotton weave, a material that was not yet accepted in Europe and particularly in England, where tradition—flax—was the prevailing order. The British sails were made by Ratsey, a firm that had been in the sailmaking business for nearly 100 years and had outfitted Nelson's ships before Trafalgar (and is still in business). The difference between the texture and weave of cotton sailcloth, which is hard and firm, and that of the traditional soft and yielding flax sailcloth is vastly important, particularly so in fore-and-aft-rigged sails of schooners. The cotton cloth remains hard and retains the shape as the sailmaker's skill molds it, despite the wind and weather conditions or even reasonable age, when the sails are well cared for. The technical sophistication of yachtsmen in the mid-19th century is relatively unknown, but whether or not they were aware of aerodynamics, cotton cloth produced ideally shaped airfoils. For this reason, together with cotton's smoother surface (than that of flax), the choice of cotton sails proved to be a most significant and winning factor for the *America*. I believe that the greatest advantages the yacht *America* had over the British yachts were not only her hull configuration, but her sailcloth and the accompanying superior aerodynamic flow.

While most of this discussion has centered on the Chesapeake vessel's distinctive hull structure and rig configuration, I should mention also that the Baltimore-built privateers and blockade runners spread hard woven cotton sailcloth woven in the mills of Ellicott City, Maryland. Not only was America the source of raw cotton; by the mid-19th century, American looms were consistently producing a hard and fine woven cloth, because they were engine power driven. The marked difference in hull forms between the American yacht and those of her English competitors prevailed historically for another half century: The American hulls were generally beamier, with flat runs beneath their quarters and a down-raking keel; they were not deep through the body of the hull but of great deadrise in the sections, and this form was typical of American sailing vessels, where there were no pressures for built-in cargo tonnage. The British yachts, pilot cutters and other comparable working craft were traditionally narrow and deep, with little evidence of support under the quarters; as a matter of fact, there was little evidence of the quarters existing at all. This characteristic difference between the two generic yacht styles prevailed into the 20th century among the racing yachts of the two countries.

However, aside from the complete humiliation of the British fleet of sailing yachts in 1851 by the yacht *America*, English merchant shipping was thriving during this whole fast-ship development period. During the great building boom of these ships in America, the British ship owners were good customers of the best New York and New England shipyards. And later, with their great, fast trading ships, the

British would move into a vacuum left by the diminished American clipper-ship trade after the debilitating Civil War of 1860-1865.

The quest for speed

As a British Royal Navy captain admitted to a contemporary American captive during the War of 1812, ". . . You Americans are a singular people as it respects seamanship and enterprise. In England, we cannot build vessels as your Baltimore Clippers: we have no models. And even if we had them, they would be no service to us, for we never would sail them as you do. We are afraid of their long masts and heavy spars and soon would cut down and reduce them to our standard. We strengthen them, put in bulkheads, after which they would lose their sailing qualities and would be of no further service as cruising vessels." Whether or not this Britisher may have been selling his people short, it seems that there was something to his statement. The British never did seem to understand our fast vessels, at least during the maritime conflict of 1812-1815.

But there was time later for them to contemplate this whole matter. During the 1830s and after, Great Britain was increasingly involved in the Orient and ultimately China—and in the growing tea trade, speed was important. Tea, an important ingredient in the daily life of British people even to this day, was in the mid-19th century a developing commercial bonanza—and the largest, fastest sailing ships were needed for the longest of ocean passages. As with the pilot boats, the prize went to the vessel that could get there first. It was some time in the 1830s that the images of British vessels began to noticeably change. The documentary evidence—the drawings and paintings of shipping—reveals topsail schooners with raked masts and other, un-British sail plans on hulls with flatter sheerlines.

A very interesting profile drawing appears in the British volume by David MacGregor, *Fast Sailing Ships*. This illustration, reproduced from an Admiralty plan in the National Maritime Museum in Greenwich, England, pictures a topsail schooner, *Jackdaw*, of rather moderate dimensions, said to have been built in Chatham, England, 1829-1830. The image portrayed in this profile is of an extreme type of Baltimore Clipper schooner of 20 years earlier. Her sheerline is flat; her extensive bowsprit-jibboom is very long and carries four rather than three headsails. Her foremast is complete with the schooner's gaff-rigged foresail and four squaresails from its lower fore course up to a fore royal, with stun'sails on all but the royal. Her main is conventionally large but surmounted with an oversized jack-yard gaff topsail and finally trimmed out aft with a good-sized ring-tail; the stun'sail shown on the fore course is also unnecessarily large. It would be understated to say that this rig is oversized or overcan-vased. This *Jackdaw* is almost a caricature of a Baltimore Clipper. It is an exaggerated, over-rigged example, but it does mark a strong statement of change in sailing philosophy.

There are other graphic examples of this change. A more realistic picture is a contemporary lithograph of three topsail schooners sailing inshore on a brilliant sailing day (Figure 3-9). Two of the schooners in this illustration are on closing courses — one on a broad reach,

Figure 3-9. British fruit schooners similar to earlier, sharp-built Chesapeake schooners: They were smaller and inhibited in their rig. No doubt they were an 1830s British attempt for speed to bring back fresh fruit from the Mediterranean.

the other on the wind on a starboard tack; the third is in the background on the right with her fore topsail and topgallant aback. They are identified as all being built in 1833 at Shoreham, England, and are named *Alexander, Rapid,* and *Martha.*

This is a very interesting and excellent example of marine art; unfortunately, the artist is unknown. The sail arrangement on each of these schooners is a bit different and indicates some development of the typical American overall sail plan. The schooner on the left, presumed to be *Alexander*, shows a running fore course. This type of light-weather course would relate to the modern spinnaker for downwind and reaching work; it has an ancestral connection with similar use on some American Baltimore Clippers, specifically one named *Midas* (Figure 3-10). The sail is essentially a light-weather sail hoisted to the yard only at three points. The mid- and main halyard hoist is from a short pole attached to the center of the sail's head; the other clews are on the port and starboard tack corners. The center schooner in the foreground, *Rapid*, shows five headsails in her foretriangle. The inner headsail is basically the traditional fore staysail reduced to two parts. Beyond these inner and outer staysails are an inner and outer jib and a flying jib, but the latter is set inside the outer jib on the foretopmast stay rather than the fore topgallant stay. The third schooner, *Martha*, has the same headsail arrangement except for the "intermediate" flying jib. She seems to be in the process of having come about and not yet swung over the topsail and topgallant yards. All three of these schooners carry large jackyard gaff topsails on the main, but they are made in the British style, with the jackyard at an angle parallel to the gaff—more like a lugsail rig. The advantage of the nearly vertical jackyard carried by Chesapeake-built schooners seems to be lost here in the lack of the leading-edge dimension. The only one of these schooners showing a studding sail is the *Alexander*, which has a large foretopsail stun'sail out to windward on the starboard tack and is apparently taking in another above on the topgallant.

These three vessels are all flying the British red ensign: *Martha* flies a private pennant on her main in red, white, and blue, and a white courtesy flag at her fore with the initials "WM"; the other two schooners are flying indistinguishable private or owners' signals at the mast trucks.

Although all three vessels are very well detailed in the painting, how closely they are related to Baltimore schooner design is not readily apparent. We cannot very accurately speculate about their below water configuration. We can say, however, that their rigs and hull profiles do conform with a definite marine-design trend that was most evident in England in the 1840s. These are most definitely flush-decked foretopsail schooners of flat sheer and lower freeboard—

Figure 3-10. The Baltimore Clipper Midas *escaping to windward. This artist's drawing is according to a British navy officer's observation and his quickly drawn impression. It is now an excellent study in the use of multiple sails intended for great spread of sail area for running.*

lower certainly than was the conservative custom abroad, but not quite as low as the freeboards of their American Chesapeake relatives. Up to this period, the British were not known for this type. Their schooners of the late 18th and early 19th centuries were very rare, and when they existed at all were short and full-bowed, with high freeboard and very conservative sail plans. Although the sail plans began to be less conservative by 1825 or 1830, this may be ascribed to marine-design adventurism—something akin to whipping a donkey. British designers were more successful in developing their smaller coastal craft, such as cutters and sloops, which were generally patterned after the fishing and pilot craft of the Channel.

The development of faster types of British craft—first the schooners and later the ships—followed the lead of American maritime-design success. The British motivation to improve the performance of their sailing craft has several apparent origins—the first being their capture and conversion to naval service of some dozen of the original Baltimore Clippers during the War of 1812. Whenever it was possible, they returned the American prize to one of their dockyards and carefully measured and lifted the lines before refitting the ship for naval service. The clippers were most frequently down-rigged with a more conservative sail plan, bearing out the British Navy captain's remarks. Later in the 1820s and early 1830s, the Royal Navy's cruisers captured many slavers, a few of which were probably post - Baltimore Clippers. They were generally trapped in the process of taking on their human cargo on the African coast. These vessels, such as the *Black Joke*, were sometimes taken into the naval service if they were in sufficiently sound condition. In at least one documented case, where some five slavers were captured at one strike, one was returned for conversion and the rest were run ashore and burned.

But proceeding through the 1830s and 1840s with the English development of faster vessels, a builder in Shoreham named James Bailey had in the early 1830s developed a type of schooner (indicated in Figure 3-9) that he referred to as a clipper schooner or clipper brig. These vessels were most successful in trade to the Mediterranean. While we have no graphic evidence of their underbodies, their sail plans are most reminiscent of the Chesapeake topsail schooners and brigs of a quarter-century earlier. Their raking masts and stun'sails give them a very impressive appearance. Their measured tonnage, according to Lloyd's Register, reveals something of their hull shape: they are described as "sharp." These vessels, often called fruit schooners, traded mainly in the Mediterranean, sometimes as far as the South American coast. It was during this same time, in America, that Baltimore and Chesapeake builders were turning out a number of sharp-built schooners for the fruit trade to Florida and the Caribbean—some of which, unhappily, were sold into the slave trade.

From the topsail schooners of the 1830s and 1840s, the British found their way to larger, faster sailing vessels. After the "clipper schooners," they developed a type called the "Aberdeen Clipper," generally identifiable by its long, forward-raking stem and low length-to-beam ratio. However, with the success of the American clipper ships in the 1850s, the British shipping interests bought a number of the fastest and largest of the American vessels. The great *James Baines* and *Lightning* from Donald McKay's East Boston yard went directly into British ownership, as did other clipper ships from American yards.

With the end of American clipper construction due to the Civil War, England ventured into the creation of some fast and famous clipper ships worthy of their name. These great composite-built ships (iron or steel frame with wood planking) continued in world trade with China and Australia into the 1870s, competing with and often bettering long-passage records of the early steamships. But it was a losing battle, preordained as such. These ships and their stories ended the Great Age of Sail. They will never be forgotten, nor will, we hope, their predecessors, which engendered their kind.

CHAPTER FOUR

The Renaissance

It was during the summer of the bicentennial year 1976 that the City of Baltimore was host to six "tall ships" from Europe and South America. Moored in the Inner Harbor over the Fourth of July, they were received with many grand ceremonies and celebrations, including an official visit from then-President Ford as well as from many foreign ambassadors. Holiday flags flew, bands played, and crowds of people came from far and near.

At the same time there was, in that most remote corner of Baltimore's Inner Harbor, a small, unimpressive shipyard, almost unnoticed among all the festivity nearby—just a modest work place in the southwest corner of the harbor behind the esplanade. A semienclosed shed (open except at one end) held a blacksmith's forge, his coal bin, and his anvil on a heavy log. Crude workbenches were set up, together with sparmaking space, frame-assembly platen, and rigger's benches. A large ship's saw stood in the open between the shed and the building stocks and shipway. There were no flags or Fourth of July decorations, but nonetheless this shipyard seemed to overflow with activity—probably no more than 15 men, but all of them working and sweating. The tools were mostly hand tools: block planes, adzes, handsaws, mauls, and chisels.

The work was focused on the partially framed backbone of a wooden vessel. It did not seem impressive; there were but six frames (ribs) standing. However, this was to be Baltimore's "tall ship." She was rising modestly from stacks of yet uncut timber to become the first Baltimore Clipper to be built in more than a century and a half.

◀ 115

She would, within a decade, become one of the proudest and most popular symbols of both Baltimore's past and its present. This 1810-type sailing machine would be taller for her size than any of the so-called "tall ships," made of steel and wire, assembled in the Inner Harbor in 1976.

The story of the *Pride of Baltimore* began with a decree by the mayor and city council that a topsail schooner should be built on the shores of the newly refurbished Inner Harbor of Baltimore's downtown; that it should be "an authentic example of an historic Baltimore Clipper . . . fully operable and capable of being sailed . . . construction to start during the spring or early summer of 1976." This pronouncement (Figure 4-1), published in the *Baltimore Sun* as an invitation for interested contractors to submit bids by September 24, 1975, was the first real step. It was no big surprise that the bid accepted was from the International Historical Watercraft Society, a corporate designation of Melbourne Smith of Annapolis, Maryland. Smith as the proposed replica's builder, together with myself as designer, had discussed and prepared for this day for some weeks; the acceptance was very nearly a foregone conclusion.

To build an authentic reproduction of a Baltimore Clipper, you must first consider the past nautical performances of the predecessors, and believe that one can be reproduced—that the uncountable parts can be assembled to the prescribed shape to create a vessel that will sail again in the same old way. Assuming that the "shape" and all of the design plans can be adequate, where will the skills come from to put it together? Where will the wood and iron come from, and the sailcloth? Where and how will all of this—the skills, the wood, the iron, the rope, the sailcloth—be worked? The thoughts were enough to cause a sleepless night or two, but the question of basic materials was soon resolved, the few necessary skilled shipwrights and blacksmith were soon enlisted, and the building location was designated by the city—a small piece of property, less than an acre, at the south end of the esplanade along Light Street. Here the building stocks were laid out, and the open shed, whose roof was supported by barked sapling posts, was built during a weekend—all within a 10-foot-high chainlink boundary.

Melbourne Smith left for Belize (formerly British Honduras) to buy tropical hardwood timber for the vessel's backbone; he arranged for spring delivery. Meanwhile, I went to work at the drawing board to flesh out the drawings, already begun.

She was to be (according to the city's designation) an authentic, fully operable Baltimore Clipper "85 to 90 feet length on deck." It was agreed that she should also be a fore-topsail schooner, because the schooner rig was by far the most popular historic rig. According to ship registry records from 1810 to 1815 for sharp-built vessels, schooners numbered 10 to 1 against brigs and 50 to 1 against sloops and any other rig. The foretopsail rig was a bit more workable, produced a quicker vessel in performance, and was essentially as fast as the double-topsail rig on all points of sailing.

CITY OF BALTIMORE
BUREAU OF PURCHASES
SOLICITATATION FOR PROPOSAL
BALTIMORE CLIPPER SHIP
BID CONTRACT NO. BP—18876

The City of Baltimore wishes to have built as a public attraction on the shores of the Inner Harbor an authentic example of an historic Baltimore Clipper ship. The ship is to be between 85′ and 90′ length on deck, fully operable, capable of being sailed, and equipped with replica cannon. Wherever practicable, the construction materials, methods, tools, and procedures are to be typical of the period, and construction is to start during the spring or early summer of 1976. Responsibility for all design, construction (including mold loft and other temporary structures of the shoreline), launching and sea trials will rest with the design-build team.

Anyone interested in performing the work as stated above should submit a written proposal of interest to the board of estimates of Baltimore City, in care of City Comptroller, Room 700, 26 South Calvert Street, Baltimore, Maryland 21202, so as to be received no later than 11:00 A.M. daylight time, September 24, 1975. The proposal will be submitted in a sealed envelope with the contract number "BP-18876" and "opening date September 24, 1975" shown in lower left corner in large print.

Said proposal shall include full details on the design and construction capabilities and experience of the design-build team, and shall certify that the team is willing to build the ship as a public attraction during construction on the shores of Baltimore's inner harbor, utilizing wherever possible, construction materials, methods, tools, and procedures which are typical of the period. Said proposal shall also indicate the approximate date by which the construction activity on the shoreline would commence and the length of the construction period.

After receipt and review of said proposals, the city will notify those design-build teams, which on the basis of the submissions received, are determined to be qualified, and shall offer these teams an opportunity to make a design-build price proposal. The finally selected contractor must post a performance bond in the total amount of contract price. If there are questions regarding technical details of this requirement, you may contact Mr. J. H. Scattergood, (301) 837-0862.

S. D. EMANSKY
City Purchasing Agent
se.11,12-4t

Figure 4-1. Classified advertisement by City of Baltimore, September 1975.

While the timber shipment was being arranged and taking place, I proceeded in designing the vessel. In preparing the lines drawing, the first in the sequence of drawings after the preliminary design has been accepted, the designer must provide for the later transfer to full-size frame patterns, for it is the builder's responsibility to loft these lines to full size from the table of offsets that accompanies them—a tedious process. As described in Chapter Two, the alternative of the builders of the original Baltimore Clippers, as well as the builders of other vessels of that time, was to build a half-hull model of the proposed hull, and to build it adequately large and to a scaled or proportionate ratio. For some builders, a half model is easier to visualize and understand. At any rate, the building of one is a historical procedure, for it was the half-hull method that liberated the creativity of the 19th-century builders of the Baltimore Clippers. It avoided both the dogma of the European practices as well as the need to understand descriptive geometric projection. In the case of this authentic reproduction of a clipper being built for the City of Baltimore in 1976, the builder followed the historic route, and a large half model was constructed from the designed hull lines.

It was built in lifts—horizontal layers of wood whose thickness was identical to the space between the regular waterline levels and the shape of those on the design. After the model, with these lifts pegged or temporarily fastened together, was smoothed and faired to shape, the location of the frames was scribed on. With these frame lines in place, the model could be taken apart and the offsets for the frames measured and scaled up to full size. They were then, on a floor surface adequate for their size, located and drawn full size. The accuracy of the half model, and from it to the lofting surface, was checked and confirmed by the designer, to ensure accurate correlation between design calculations and the actual vessel. Although this was the old method, followed for this new schooner, no Baltimore Clipper was ever processed in design so thoroughly and to the last detail as this one, at this time.

In the autumn of 1975, a meeting had been held in Annapolis, followed by many other meetings, by the principals in planning the design and building of this early-19th-century "replica ship." The first drawings of the ship's hull configuration (Figure 4-2) as well as her profile (Figures 4-3 and 4-4) were prepared before the year was out.

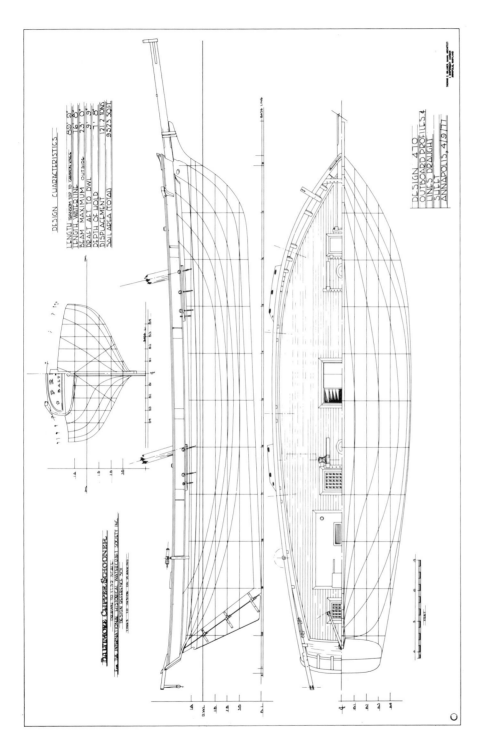

THOMAS C. GILLMER, NAVAL ARCHITECT
ANNAPOLIS, MARYLAND

DESIGN CHARACTERISTICS

LENGTH TRANSOM TOP TO COMMON KNEE	89' 9"
LENGTH WATERLINE	69' 8"
BEAM MAXIMUM OUTSIDE	23' 0"
DRAFT AFT TO DWL	9' 3"
DEPTH OF HOLD	9' 8"
DISPLACEMENT	121.2 TONS
SAIL AREA (TOTAL)	9,523 SQ FT

DESIGN 470
OUTBOARD PROFILES &
LINES DRAUGHT
SAIL
ANNAPOLIS, 4/9/77

BALTIMORE CLIPPER SCHOONER
DRAWING TO 1:1.32 SCALE
for THE INTERNATIONAL HISTORICAL NAUTICAL SOCIETY INC.
LINES 16 DESIGN 470 DRAWING

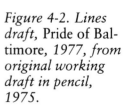

Figure 4-2. Lines draft, Pride of Baltimore, *1977, from original working draft in pencil, 1975.*

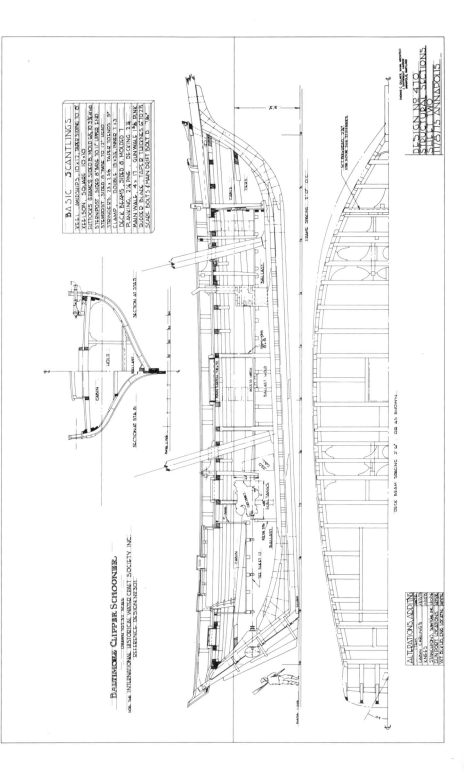

Figure 4-3. Structural profile and plan of Pride of Baltimore, *1975, showing modifications, gun ports, 4 to 5 per side, propeller aperture, collision bulkhead forward, etc.*

The Renaissance

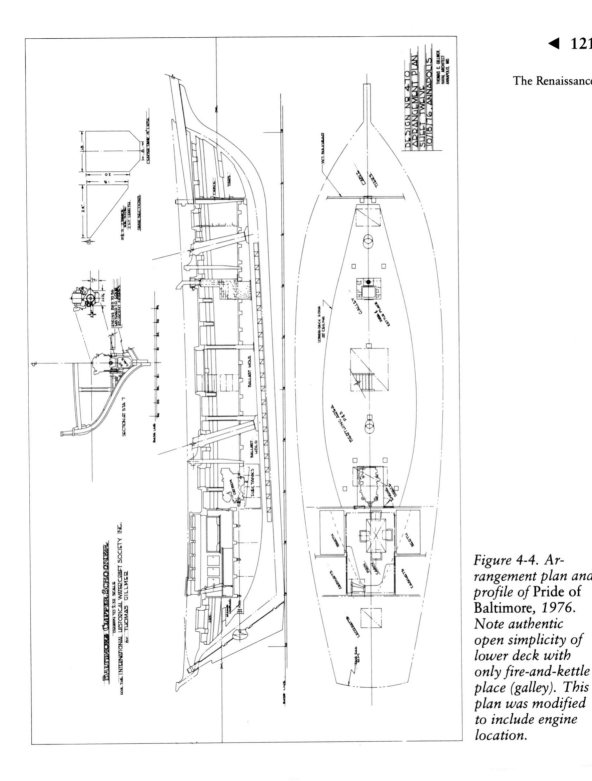

Figure 4-4. Arrangement plan and profile of Pride of Baltimore, 1976. *Note authentic open simplicity of lower deck with only fire-and-kettle place (galley). This plan was modified to include engine location.*

These were determined after studying about ten original drawings of Baltimore Clippers—captured privateers—done in British dockyards during the War of 1812, as decribed in Chapter Three. Prints of these antique drawings were sent to me from the National Maritime Museum in Greenwich, England. The final configuration for Baltimore's replica was an amalgamation of the selection—not without some favoritism, but it was an honest attempt to produce a vessel that would be typical and retain the best historic features within the size limitation.

The size frame of the new vessel was first considered to be 90 feet hull length (from the top of the transom to the end of the gammon knee), 79 feet waterline length, 23 feet breadth of beam (maximum, outside of planking), and a little less than 10 feet draft at the heel of the sternpost. Her displacement was consequently to be around 120 tons, and this would place her in the category of moderate to average size. As the design developed, the replica's dimensions were to be 89 feet on deck, 76 feet 8 inches on the load waterline, 23 feet beam, extreme draft at after end of keel 9 feet 9 inches, depth of hold 7 feet 8 inches, displacement at load waterline 121.2 long tons,[1] with an estimated sail area of 9,500 square feet in all plain sails.

I have described how, visually, the Baltimore Clippers were recognizably different from other vessels, but little has been said here or elsewhere about their different technical character. I would like to point out how certain numerical substantiations that develop in the design process specifically set the Baltimore Clippers apart.

In naval architecture there are some useful terms called *coefficients*, dimensionless ratios or numbers that can be used to compare vessels regardless of their difference in size. Some of these coefficients can be applied to hull forms and some can also be applied to sail plans.

Upon analyzing the available records of Baltimore Clippers existing during the first decade of the 19th century as well as during the War of 1812, I came up with the following coefficients, which I believe reveal definitive identity. Using total sail areas, the sail area/displacement ratios[2] of this group, when averaged, are above 31.0. The displacement/length ratios of these (where the dimensions have been recorded) are between 260 and 310. The numerical values of these coefficients for the *Pride of Baltimore*, when commissioned in 1977, were 32.0 and 271, respectively.

There is a third coefficient that applies as well. While it is not as definitive, it provides a measurement showing the vast differences between the contemporary vessels of 1800 and the sharp-built Baltimore Clippers. This dimensionless measurement, called the *prismatic coefficient*, shows the disposition or distribution of the displacement toward amidships or the ends of the ship. For the average late-18th- and early-19th-century commercial vessels with bluff bows and rounder sterns and fat bellies, the prismatic coefficients were approximately .70 to .80. Smaller vessels of fair-to-good sailing characteristics — such as packet vessels and warships, frigates, corvettes, sloops of war, brigs, and the like — had prismatics between .65 and .70. The sharp-built schooners, Baltimore Clippers, and pilot boats had hull forms whose prismatics were generally less than .61. On the *Pride of Baltimore*, this coefficient was .58. In a few Baltimore Clippers and Virginia pilot schooners it was as low as .50, and such figures indicate extreme sharpness. The *Pride*'s hull could be described as conservatively sharp, with her center of buoyancy slightly forward of her 'midship section (the transverse section midway between the forward and after limits of a vessel's waterline).

The construction begins

The first load of timber arrived in the shipyard early in April 1976, and the workmen were ready and waiting. The piece of timber selected for the keel was the longest and heaviest in the load — a beautiful specimen of wood from Central America, a species of lignum vitae called Cortez. Important for its use in the keel, this wood does not float, as do most deciduous woods of North America, nor does it absorb water; it is very dense, at 78 to 80 pounds per cubic foot, compared to salt water's 64 pounds per cubic foot. Cortez is a very deep red-brown in color, with close, fine grain — almost imperceptible — and, after planing, rubbed with a little abrasive and a cloth, looks as smooth as polished marble. Possibly it was overdoing it a bit to use this sort of tree in a keel for a schooner, but considering the schooner and the disposition of much of the timber being cut from the rain forests of Central and South America (more on this in Chapter Five), it seemed a far better use than any other.

The keel timber was moved into place in early May, and master shipwright Simeon Young and his helpers from Belize began dressing it down. The annular rings were visible on the ends of the undressed log: a test count of these added up to a bit over 1,000.

The keel was sided down to 10 inches and molded to 12 inches; it was then notched with shallow ³/₄″ cuts for the frame placements— more as a ceremonial activity on the part of the builders, rather than a necessary step. The frame spacing (see Figure 4-3, the structural profile of the *Pride of Baltimore*), set at 24 inches, appeared to be close, but this is historically correct, for the Baltimore Clippers were more open in frame than many of the contemporary merchant vessels in the early 1800s. The USS *Constitution*, by comparison, has frame spacing of ³/₄ inch, which amounts nearly to a continuous wood surface (although the gaps are a little too wide for caulking). The planking laid onto a surface of this sort, together with the inner ceiling, provides a total hull thickness of nearly 3 feet. I mention this to emphasize that a Baltimore Clipper schooner in its time, with 22 to 24 inches between frames, was considered an especially lightly built vessel.

Master craftsmen

The question often arises, during the planning and the building of a wooden vessel nowadays, in the age of steel, aluminum, and fiberglass: "Where do you find the skills and the craftsmen to do such work today?" It is a most legitimate question. The employment of one Simeon Young was rather prearranged. He had been a former associate of Melbourne's in a small shipyard in Belize, building and repairing workboats for the Caribbean trade. A master craftsman, Simeon proceeded decisively with the dressing down of the heavy timbers for keel, keelson, and deadwood. He needed only to know the dimensions required and whether there was to be tapering or scarfing or other shaping. His adze work, when finished, appeared to have been surfaced by a continuous movement of the blade. He moved about the timber assemblies and framework of the vessel as though in a familiar room, and all who worked with him followed because they knew he had been there before.

When the backbone, keel, and frame timbers are coming together (Figure 4-5), the whole concentration is limited to but a few hands. There is a most fundamental transition of thought, planning, measuring, and checking. It is truly the start of a transition from concept and design to material, which comes together very deliberately. Work proceeds quite slowly and shapelessly, led by a master shipwright such as Simeon, who takes his cues from the contract builder. There are a few workmen, and their numbers grow as the assembly grows.

The blacksmith—or, correctly, shipsmith—is an independent worker, a rather lone worker, but his work must be integrated with the sequence of construction. It begins with the heavy fastenings, the long, wrought-iron bars, steel rods, or both—the temporary holding-and-positioning spike-ended spanning bars that are forged for specific jobs, as well as the permanent drift rods that are driven through the heaviest timber assemblies in holding the deadwood together, the keelson through frame and keel. The master shipsmith for this job was Jerry Trowbridge.

Jerry is a large man with a snow-white beard and a muscular body. Early on in the project, he moved his tools, his forge, his coal bin, and anvil into a small, square space at the south end of the builder's shed. He was ready to work at anything within his scope of talent, which was considerable. Jerry was professionally an electronics engineer, but his employer would have to get along without him for awhile.

Figure 4-5. Framing up, spring 1976.

Nor was Jerry without experience in maritime things. Some years before joining the shipbuilding team, he had built his own boat, in steel, launched it, and sailed away with his wife on a round-the-world voyage. They had moved back to their farm west of Baltimore, a wonderful pastoral setting; but the sea was still with Jerry, and so he came to help build this "old-style" ship. A most skillful artist with metal, he would forge such things as large and heavy iron-strapped pintles and gudgeons for the rudder, the channel chains for the deadeyes, cannon trunnion holds — a nearly endless variety of small and large "tailor-made" fittings. Jerry's good humor infiltrated all who worked with him. He was irreplaceable.

One day later in the summer, a young man — he could not have been more than 19 years of age — presented himself at the shipyard. By then the ship was growing, looking more like the antique sharp-built schooner she was to become, and was attracting more and more attention, with increasing curiosity. This young man identified himself as Peter Boudreau. A fine-looking lad, he was dressed in a casual

Figure 4-6. Deck framing, beams and carlings.

but trim outfit bespeaking the sea and much sun. He said he was a crew member of a charter schooner presently in Annapolis from the West Indies, but he wondered if there was an available job in the shipyard. He was most anxious to help build this vessel — and he did. Peter began work directly under Simeon, who was then completing the frame and beginning to place the deck beams and carlings (Figures 4-6 and 4-7).

Planking (Figure 4-8) began in early autumn, with some difficulty: the garboard strake was giving trouble at the rabbet line, and Simeon Young was slowing down. Simeon had contributed much in setting up this solid frame. With his adze, he had skillfully created other elements, such as the rudder and finely curved tiller of rosewood, while watching over the hull framing. But he dreaded the northern winter and yearned for the tropics. In November, Simeon returned to Belize, together with his friend Sandoval, who had accompanied him as a helper. At this point, Peter, whose skill and ingenuity were clearly evident, was ready to move up to more responsibility. He was soon heading the deck assembly, and his upward march had begun.

There were many in the building crew by this time, and I do not

Figure 4-7. Completely framed, ready for stringers, clamps, and beams.

intend to biograph them all; that is another story. But these few cannot be overlooked in the work of building this vessel.

From the start, several fine, historically motivated citizens of Baltimore were working on the project as well. Most prominent among them was one "Mr. Jerome" (we will ignore his real name, because it would most likely embarrass him), a retired bank officer, formerly vice-president of a well-known financial house to the north of the harbor in central downtown Baltimore. Jerry was most knowledgeable in nearly every urban respect, particularly of the workings of Baltimore—its finances, politics, good and bad elements—but he was especially helpful in directing us where to find difficult building supplies and who to see when problems arose. Mr. Jerome's job description in the shipyard was "gatekeeper and accountant," but his services were vastly greater. And in rare moments when things were quiet and slack, he was a great lifter of morale and teller of stories.

There were many other masterful craftsmen, including Allen Rawl, a Baltimore contractor who dropped his regular work to devote all his time and skills to the *Pride*; Michael Kozma, who was naturally adept in all manner of sea craft and rigging; and Andrew Davis, who had

Figure 4-8. Hull being planked.

nothing to offer in experience but a great deal in dedicated, quality work and acquired skill. After the *Pride* was completed, Andy went on to direct the building of the *Spirit of Massachusetts* in Boston, a replica Gloucester fishing schooner. With this finished, he decided to become a naval architect and enrolled in the University of California at Berkeley, where he is obtaining his master's degree in naval architecture.

At this point in the narrative, the growing schooner can no longer be "it" or "this vessel." Sometime in late 1976, her name was designated and approved by the city officials. We were creating the *Pride of Baltimore*.

It was this sort of random and varied selection of devoted people— totaling some 15 toward the end, at launching—that made up the building crew. They came willingly, enthusiastically, and voluntarily, because they were attracted to a seagoing replication and all that it suggested. They will always remember and be remembered. The *Pride*, when she sailed away, was the assembly of wood and iron and rope and skill and muscle that they put together, piece by piece and day by day—the ordered and organized progression of structure so sparingly described here.

The Pride takes shape

In the building of a traditional wooden ship, the assembled frame takes its shape symmetrically above the keel, port to starboard, and is held together temporarily until permanently fixed by longitudinal stringers inside and the planking of the hull outside (Figure 4-9).

The heavy timbers for the backbone, hull, deck framing, planking, and trim were primarily tropical hardwoods from Central America. In addition to Cortez for the keel, there was bulit tree for other parts of the backbone assembly, bulit tree for frames and deck beams, yellow pine for hull planking and decking, and Honduras mahogany for furniture and trim. These woods and their specific qualities and uses are described more fully in Chapter Five.

As the vessel went together, there came a growing confidence in the authenticity of the old techniques and their rebirth. Those skills had not really died; they were being reawakened. There were also discoveries about wooden vessels. As the construction materials were delivered from various sources—the heavy timbers first, then the planking stock, the hardwood, the boat nails, the heavy wrought-iron rods and flats, the long bolts—they were individually worked to shape, then brought together piece by piece. As in any traditional vessel, some pieces went into subassemblies, while some pieces moved directly to the growing structure. In all of this, you can imagine the sounds of the shipyard—a cacophony of chunking, banging, and sawing, with the blacksmith's hammering backed up by a growling, open, blazing forge.

For over half a year at the Light Street shipyard, the ship was just a structure of parts and pieces and subassemblies surrounded by staging and scaffolds, crawling with shipwrights and skilled help—until one day in December, the sound of banging hammers and mauls inside the growing hull changed their tune to a vibration, a ring, of higher frequency, such that a heavy blow of a maul at one end of the hull could be felt in a timber at the other end. If a ship is, as many believe, a living thing, then it was at this point in the *Pride*'s construction that she was born. In any case, there was no doubt among her builders, when the *Pride of Baltimore* was nearing her launching day, that she was of a different time and that she was closely authentic.

By December 1976, the schooner's hull was completely planked in,

Figure 4-9. Hull planking, completed.

the deck was laid, the hatches were framed, and most of the gunwale rails were finished. She was beginning to look impressive. But December and January were very cold months; it was a bitter winter. Nonetheless, the work was hurried along. The ship's brick "fire and kettle" place had been rushed into completion, and a daily fire was kept there below the heavy iron griddle plate. It helped to dispose of considerable wood scraps and at the same time provide some warmth for the workers.

When the hull was completely caulked with cotton and oakum and the seams payed with a mixture of hot pitch and thickening, her topsides were painted black, with green antifouling bottom paint below the waterline. She was completed with a broad white "stripe" (the exterior gunwale) and a narrow red "stripe" (the deck covering board, protruding outside). Once the seams of her natural pitch-pine deck had been filled with black pitch and her wide mahogany caprail had been varnished, she was quite ready for the water.

Launching

The ship upon launching was a bare, empty hull, with only the heavy work accomplished. She was as light as possible for safe lifting; the crane operators' instruments showed that she weighed 65.2 tons, which checked reasonably closely with the calculated weight of 64.5 tons. She had none of her permanent ballast aboard; no masts nor machinery nor rigging. However, her bowsprit was in place, her fore and main channels and chainplates with deadeyes were installed, and she was ready to have her masts stepped and lower shrouds and stays rigged as soon as ballasting permitted.

On a cold, damp, overcast day in February 1977 (the 27th), *Pride* was launched in Baltimore's Inner Harbor adjacent to the Light Street shipyard. The mayor was there to commend her, and the district's congresswoman to christen her, and there were some 10,000 citizens to cheer her as she was lowered into the water (Figure 4-10) by "Big Red," the largest floating crane on the Bay, from Bethlehem Steel's shipyard. She made a pretty sight hanging above the water like a very large ship model without her rigging.

The schooner's hull hung over the speakers' platform where the city and state officials sat as Congresswoman Mikulski hammered a bottle of champagne against the stem. The champagne bottle finally submitted, and the hull gradually and gracefully descended into the water, to the cheers of all. It would be another eight weeks until the *Pride* was rigged, ballasted, and finished out.

Ballast and rigging

The first work to be accomplished afloat was to put aboard her 40 tons of fixed ballast. This weight was composite. First, 15 tons of lead in 50-pound pigs were fitted in the lowest part of the hold, aft of amidships, on each side of the keelson. Above this, in layers, were 15 tons of iron cubes, roughly 8 inches on a side, these being aggregate castings of iron particles held together by a polymer resin, with a den-

Figure 4-10. Launching of Pride *by floating crane "Big Red," February 27, 1977.*

sity of 95 percent solid iron. This sort of ballast was chosen because the cubes could be handled more easily and stacked together more closely than iron pigs; also, they were not subject to rusting or other forms of corrosion. Finally, there were the traditional and historic ballast stones: a total of approximately ten tons of washed Belgian paving stone that had been part of the old streets of Baltimore. These stones were fine, glistening, gray granite, each stone measuring approximately 6 by 6 by 9 inches. Putting the ballast in place involved all hands of the building crew in a day and a half of back-straining work.

Next it was time to step the masts, both of which were ready and finished, with standing rigging. The main lower mast was $17^{1}/_{2}$ inches in diameter and would reach 62 feet 9 inches above deck; the fore lower mast was $18^{1}/_{2}$ inches in diameter and would reach 60 feet 9 inches above deck. The rigging crew had begun some months before to dress down the two Douglas-fir spars from Oregon. The portion of each mast to reach below deck to the keelson was trimmed to eight sides. This octagonal surfacing was extended approximately 20 inches above deck, where the mast hole was also octagonal. Once the masts were stepped, and after a silver coin dated 1812 was placed beneath the mainmast, wedges were fitted flat against each mast and driven tight; canvas boots were later fitted over and the covering made watertight.

A logical process

Naturally, during the construction as well as the design of the *Pride of Baltimore*, there were difficult phases. We were regenerating something that had been laid to rest long past. Consequently, there were questions that could not be answered as to her structure, shape, and rig. These questions were not critical, but they were important—yet there was no source to go to for the answers, for it had died with the building of the last Baltimore Clipper, at least 160 years ago. So, in these gaps of design and building knowledge, the only course was to fall back on logic and pragmatism. It was rather like reading a book or a manuscript in which every so often a word is missing, so one must replace the missing words with some of one's own that will result in a sensible statement.

One example of this was in the overall rig arrangement. Among the original plans obtained from the National Maritime Museum in England, there were no two-masted topsail schooner sail plans. The lines and structure were clear in the old hull drawings, showing spar dimensions and contemporary rigging details—but there were no overall assembly views of these parts. How much to rake the masts was one important question. Old paintings and iconography by artists of this period, good or bad, were always consistent in showing that Baltimore Clippers had extremely raked masts. There was no quickly apparent functional purpose in this characteristic, so engineering solutions were useless. The most practical course, as usual, was the most direct: locate the mast step, or at least a position for it or its center, then transfer it to another view or projection showing the deck, and locate the mast hole or mast partners for its center. These two points and their separation generally established a common angle of mast rake between 17 and 15 degrees. The rake of the foremast, of course, was generally about $2^1/2$ to 3 degrees less than that of the main.

The rigging of the *Pride* took approximately six weeks; and after two or three builder's trials, she would be nearly ready for sea. It was decided to change her basic standing rigging before her summer sailing program toward New England. The synthetic Dacron stays had too much elasticity, and they were replaced by steel-cored, hemp-covered wire. This was a strategic decision and a departure from authenticity forced by the unavailability of the natural hemp. Such rope had been made by hand in the early 1800s on the ropewalks of South Charles Street, Baltimore, long since closed down.

There were one or two other compromises with authenticity. She had an auxiliary propulsion plant: an 85-horsepower Caterpillar diesel engine. This engine was too underpowered to drive the hull as a powered vessel and too large to fit properly into the small space available. Her single propeller had to invade the sternpost and rudder area by way of a central aperture. This aperture reduced the rudder's effectiveness to an extent that was not measurable, and therefore a somewhat greater rudder angle was required for sailing some upwind tacks. The engine was not originally in the design, but was insisted upon as a 20th-century necessity in busy harbors that the *Pride*'s predecessors did not encounter.

The sailcloth was as close to the correct kind for the 1810 period as could be obtained, using several grades of cotton weave and some of flax. The flax sailcloth was used originally in the forestaysail and fore topsail; however, not too much later in the *Pride*'s active seagoing career, the flax sails were replaced by cotton sails. As noted in Chapter Three, it is known that a singular winning advantage of the Baltimore Clippers over foreign vessels, in addition to their hull form and sail plan, was their fine American cotton cloth, which can be more firmly woven and sets harder, with less distortion, to better aerodynamic curvature than any other natural fiber.

The *Pride*'s sail plan (Figure 4-11) had been modified to not show any fore course, which is a large squaresail below the foreyard—essentially a light-weather sail used as a spinnaker or downwind running sail by most square-topsail schooners (see Figure 3-10). The sailcloth used was, of course, not as light as today's synthetic cloth, but normally similar to that used for the old stun'sails and ringtails.

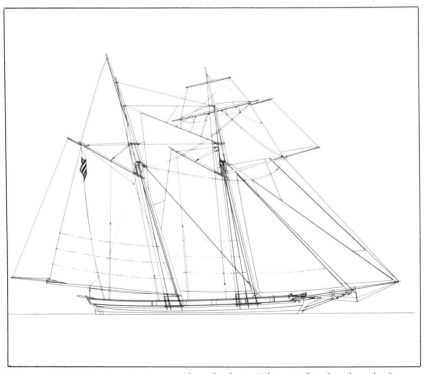

Figure 4-11. Basic rigging and sail plan. This is the final sail plan, modified to eliminate the fore course.

The fore course was often hoisted on a running block instead of a hal-yard, with tack lines at the yard's ends and outrigger poles from deck. If the *Pride* had used this course as first designed, she would have had a total sail area of 9,523 square feet.

The Pride underway

On May 1, 1977, with her sailing crew, many of whom had been her builders, the *Pride of Baltimore* was commissioned by Mayor William Donald Schaefer. Then, with a tooting of horns, the ringing of bells, and a feeble cannon salute from the old USS *Constellation*, she left the Inner Harbor of Baltimore amidst the water spray of Coast Guard fire boats, past the dipping flag of Fort McHenry, and sailed down the Chesapeake Bay to the oceans of the world.

During the watercraft parade in New York harbor celebrating the nation's 201st birthday, the *Pride* was recognized as the vessel with the most character and was so described in a favorable report in the *New York Times* as well as being officially noted in the awards cere-mony afterward at the United Nations Plaza.

The *Pride* sailed again during the summer of 1977 to Halifax, Nova Scotia, and to several other East Coast ports, returning on Au-gust 8 for a maintenance-and-repairs stay. It was during this latter op-eration that she was finally rigged with her square topsail, and what a difference! The first impact of this near completion of her historic rig was in her appearance (see Figure 4-12). It also made a notable differ-ence in her sailing capability—more than I had anticipated. In these early months, the career of this upstart Baltimore Clipper could be described as undistinguished—except for a humble lifesaving episode in lower New York harbor. Somewhere between Bedloe's Island (the Statue of Liberty) and lower Manhattan, the *Pride*'s crew sighted a frantically swimming animal. As they came near and fished it out of the water, it was discovered to be an oil-debris-soaked mongrel dog. Promptly dried off, cleaned up, fed, and given the name of "Deeo-gee," the dog quickly assumed the role of ship's mascot and protector and held this position for the next eight years of cruising, after which she was deemed too old to manage the ship's ladders and heeling decks (Figure 4-13). She was given an honorable retirement home ashore and bid a fond farewell.

Sailing characteristics

At this stage in the *Pride*'s story, it is important to record some of her sailing characteristics.

In late 1977, the *Pride* was fully rigged and operating at sea (Figure 4-14). For the next nine years, under various crews and rotations of captains and in all weather conditions, flat to extreme, she called on all of the major seaports in the continental United States and many of the minor ones. She sailed into the Great Lakes twice through the St. Lawrence Seaway. She sailed the eastern seacoast from Newfoundland to the Florida Keys, and the Gulf of Mexico to Galveston. She sailed the Caribbean from its southern and eastern limits, the Lesser and Greater Antilles, from Tobago and Barbados and Jamaica on to Panama. She sailed on into the Pacific and up the west coast of North

Figure 4-12. Pride *under sail, four tacks, water color by William Gilkerson.*

138 ▶

Pride of Baltimore

Figure 4-13. Pride *at sea.*

Figure 4-14. Working in main rigging, Pride *at sea, J. Lamb and J. McGeady.*

America, all the way to British Columbia. In calling on the ports of California, Oregon, Washington, and Victoria, B.C., she made many friends.

When she returned from all this, and after a winter's overhaul, the *Pride* sailed for European waters (Figure 4-15). She stayed away a bit more than a year while she cruised from Ireland through Scandinavia, into the Baltic Sea and out again, stopping in England, Norway, Denmark, Germany, Poland, Belgium, and France. She arrived in Spain in late fall of 1985 and wintered there, in Malaga. She was called home prematurely in April 1986, and the itinerary for 1986 was canceled because of the terrorism seemingly prevalent in the eastern Mediterranean at the time.

Figure 4-15. Return of captain and departure for Europe, 1985. The captain is returning by ship's boat with departure orders from the mayor of Baltimore.

These adventures are cited geographically, without mention of her detailed itinerary, simply to affirm her background as an active vessel, not a "pond lily" or a mere museum exhibit. In this time, just short of a decade, her log added up to over 150,000 nautical miles, which, put end to end, would wrap around the world at the equator six times!

This book is bound to include some valid data on the seagoing performance of a Baltimore Clipper. The *Pride* did not have a reliable pit log or electronic speed log of modern style; these instruments are not entirely reliable at best. She did, however, have some attentive captains whose observations both with navigational positioning and with a reliable taffrail log were noted and recorded.

In the earlier chapters on the history of the Baltimore Clippers, much was made of their windward ability. How close could they sail to the wind? Today's analysis does not expect that they were comparable to modern racing yachts or even to today's fiberglass cruising sailboats, with their smoothly molded hulls and airfoil-like Dacron sails. Instead, we must compare the clippers' performance to that of their contemporaries, as discussed in Chapter Two.

This is the experience briefly collected from the captain who sailed the *Pride of Baltimore* on the Pacific Coast as well as on her transatlantic passage to Europe (Figure 4-16): She could, in normal seas up to 4 feet and winds of Force 3 to 4, hold a course to 47-50 degrees of the wind direction, with a sail pattern of all plain sail (all lower sails plus fore topsail, topgallant, outer jib, and gaff topsail) or shortened to jib, staysail, square topsail, foresail, and mainsail. According to this captain, she could improve on this point of sailing about 2 to 3 degrees by reducing the windage of the square topsail. The latter observation is a bit controversial with captains and crew, some of whom felt that they could sail as close to the wind with the square fore topsail as without.

There is no question that in most windward work the square fore topsail added considerable drive to the vessel but may have contributed to some *leeway*. However, leeway, the component that contributes to *course made good*, is the result of additional factors.

Leeway, or lateral drift, is the penalty that all sailing craft must pay in moving ahead; some pay more than others. Technically, leeway is the difference between the course as steered and the course sailed in degrees. It also (and more discouragingly) is better understood as the downwind distance that vessel moves as it is set off its course; leeway occurs when the vessel is sailing across the direction the wind is blowing. There now are some fast-sailing craft of narrow and deep fin configuration and "high-tech" design that claim to be immune from leeway, but this is not so: all upwind and crosswind sailing involves itself in leeway as a matter of sailing dynamics. For some of these craft, leeway may correctly be negligible, but it is nevertheless existent. Other more worldly and common sailing vessels must face the inevitable, and hope that they can suffer less leeway than may be critical. It is nice to make that distant upwind headland around which lies the anchorage or home mooring before the setting sun leaves a darkened destination, to make it without tacking or only tacking once—no more than once, dear Poseidon!

There are many things that affect leeway. The most fundamental one can be seen in the force diagram, Figure 4-19. The theoretical vessel with one squaresail is sailing to windward with the wind forward of the port beam. This is the *apparent wind*—the wind one feels on one's face or is measured on the ship's "telltale" or anemometer as the ship moves forward into it. Apparent wind is the combination of

Figure 4-16. Good day at sea—transatlantic.

Pride of Baltimore

Figure 4-17. Deck scene, relaxed under fore staysail bonnet.

the real wind and the ship's movement through the air, the wind the sail "feels" on its surface and the origin of the force that moves the ship. This air, striking the sail from the direction shown, creates a resultant force, FT, which is made up of two components relative to the ship—the useful *driving component*, FR, and the *heeling force*, FH. Relating this to the sail's effectiveness, the total force, FT, is separated in the *lifting component*, L, and the *drag component*, D, perpendicular and parallel to the sail's direction. The drag is the necessary aerodynamic force component that cannot be diminished. It is the inevitable component—sometimes called, in technical circles, *induced drag*. If the curved sail, as an airfoil, is to produce *lift*, which is ultimately resolved to pull the ship ahead, the drag will exist in the direction of the wind to slow it down. This is the basic resolution of the wind forces—the sail's aerodynamics.

Figure 4-18. Hard on the bowsprit. At sea, 1984.

Beyond this, there are other forces that the shipboard hands—or, before them, the builder and the designer—are able to control, to some extent. In the case of the Baltimore Clipper, the nature of the hull and rig inherently combine to optimize the useful driving forces, and within the historic framework minimize the drag and lateral

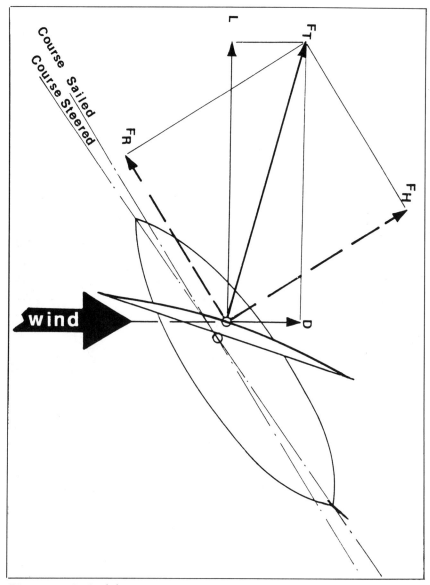

Figure 4-19. Sail force vectors.

forces. By the simple rig, lesser stays, and running rigging of the Baltimore Clipper, windage is reduced. The balance of the rig and the long, narrow rudder—which does not carry a rudder angle that drags excessively, further minimizes leeway. The profile of the hull, its more efficient movement through the waves, along with other considerations, reduce drag and lateral forces, making sailing more efficient.

Returning to the *Pride of Baltimore* and the captain's observations, it is difficult to determine very precisely the amount of drift that a sailing vessel is subject to; it is an inconstant thing, as noted above. Beyond the forces described and the detailed peculiarities of the individual vessels, there are the factors of the wind and sea, the trim of the sails, and other variables. The *Pride* was credited to be a good "upwind" boat, "holding to its mark" (in sailor's terms) with a reasonably predictable drift angle of less than 10 degrees, according to her captain. Her optimum sailing condition for best sustained speed through the water was wind Force 2 to 3, with all plain sail; sea state relatively calm, with 2- to $2^1/2$-foot waves; speed 8 to 10 knots.

Although this speed relates to neither her maximum speed nor her hull speed, it does reflect a slightly disappointing performance; as her designer, I cannot but feel that she was capable of better. The captain and crew must be absolved: they were most expert and generally were able to coax out all of the boat's capability under most conditions. However, it is felt most analytically, and from direct observation from photographs (both still and motion, in all angles of sailing), that there was fault in the sails. Made of heavy cotton sailcloth to specifications that were rather indifferently followed, the sails were not properly worked and were replaced by various sailmakers. They simply did not set as well as reasonably expected, producing myriad wrinkle patterns from clew to tack, and bulges and lumps in critical spots as well. I appreciate the difficulty of making heavy cotton canvas sails for gaff and square-rigged sail plans in this day and under modern sailing technology. It was perhaps a skill and an art that had not been recovered as much as the other wooden boat building techniques in this reconstruction. Sailmaking also is an item in the design and construction process that the builder and designer have less control over. The sailmaker in the 20th century is situated remotely, both geographically and philosophically, from the shipbuilding process. When one views the painting by the 19th-century marine artist

Thomas Buttersworth of a Baltimore Clipper hard on the wind with beautiful, smooth sails, one cannot help feeling envious and a bit deflated about the restoration of a Baltimore Clipper.

In the life of this schooner, there was more than simply cruising from port to port. In addition to observation of her sailing capacity—speed, windward ability, leeway—something of her weather endurance and conditions in seaways should also be recorded. Again, there are no precise yardsticks or instruments to measure these things; we have only logs and the credible recollections of captains and crews. First, a note or two from the writings of the *Pride of Baltimore*'s crew:

Very dark squall line approaching from astern—rain commences and wind increases up to 40K. . . . Sugar's at the helm while I call out the compass headings. Rain too intense for helmsman to see compass. Squall passes within an hour. . . .

Following seas and strong breeze off the quarter have *Pride* scorching along between 8-12 knots for the last 7 hours. Standing on deck gives you the feeling of riding a large surfboard on some big crests. The motion below is quite smooth.

In the trades (tradewinds), Captain Armin Elsaesser (Figure 4-20) wrote:

Figure 4-20. Captain Armin Elsaesser at helm, 1986.

Glorious sailing! Rarely has sailing on this ship been this exciting for this long. Now we are flying! We come off the foaming white crests in sapphire seas. *Pride* lifts her head 4-5 feet beyond the waterline. The jibboom points skyward and our ship rushes ahead, throwing spray and foam, and then settles back into the deep with a thunderous roar. The power! The energy! The giddy feeling of soaring through the liquid blue space . . . one must see it and hear it and sense it as *Pride* slices an ocean path to her destination.

In her time, the *Pride* encountered many bad weather conditions and handled them gracefully. There was much written and spoken of in the media in April 1979, when she was sailing for Norfolk from the south. She encountered a heavy storm—galeforce winds and high seas—off Cape Hatteras. She was overdue in Norfolk, actually not heard from for three days, and the press sounded an alarm for her possible loss. Headlines screamed: "Baltimore's Ship Missing at Sea," "Searching For *Pride of Baltimore*," and "Air Search Continues." When the weather had blown itself out and searches and distress were giving way to despair, a weak radio signal was picked up at the Coast Guard station at Cape May, New Jersey. It was the *Pride*, whose captain wanted a confirmation on his position. The storm-weary schooner and crew were about to head into Delaware Bay. They had run before the gale and seas nearly to Nantucket before turning back when the conditions subsided enough. The crew was in good spirits and they, together with the captain, were surprised to learn that they were missing; as far as they knew, they were not lost. Their weak radio, a standard yacht-type VHF whose range was no more than 25 to 30 miles, was their only voice at sea then, and had isolated them. The sea experience had been a wild ride, but well in hand and under control. The seas were, of course, high, 20 feet and above. The vessel had been boarded once by a following sea that smashed the ship's boat, which was lashed upside down on the stern davits. Otherwise, she had sustained no damage or strain from the storm.

The *Pride* had experienced almost continuously bad weather during the year she spent cruising on the West Coast. One storm followed another, and the Pacific Coast cities went on record with their worst weather season in memory. The *Pride* stood off the harbor at Eureka, California, for more than 24 hours in bad weather and high seas, waiting to run the entrance like a large surfing sailboard.

In her total sea experiences, she had seen the withering tropical heat of the Caribbean and Panama and the freezing cold of New-foundland. She had explored fjords in Norway, the islands of the Baltic, and the weather of the North Sea. After she had wintered in the Spanish harbor of Malaga over 1985-1986, she was ready for the eastern Mediterranean, but her owners back in Baltimore were more cautious in the face of possible terrorist activity from the contemplated Tripolitan shores. The *Achille Lauro* had been boarded by terrorists targeting Americans. Avoiding the eastern Mediterranean was probably a prudent idea.

The *Pride* sailed for home the end of March 1986, heading southwest from the Strait of Gibraltar, taking stores along the way at Madeira. After sloshing about in contrary winds for four or five days, they picked up the trades, as described in the above excerpt. I have a postcard from the captain postmarked Barbados, 15 April 1986, that reads:

> 4/14, we made it! *Pride*'s longest passage, Madeira / Barbados 3,000 miles, 16½ days, 7.6 knots average, downwind all the way with stunsl's flying! Cheers.
>
> *Armin*

Not bad, after a sluggish start and three windless days. A happy sailor and captain, with a happy crew!

The final voyage

The *Pride*'s arrival in Barbados—the Western Hemisphere again, after more than a year of Europe—was an opportunity for the crew to relax and enjoy a beautiful tropical island. She actually did not remain in Barbados very long. After replenishing some stores and fresh water, she moved up to the U.S. Virgin Islands, where she was back in American territorial waters. It was here that the crew enjoyed the early spring in the tropics, swimming and sailing the ship's boat, *Iree*. About 16½ feet long and patterned after a Chesapeake crabbing skiff with a centerboard and sailing rig, this small boat sailed well in the island breezes. Built with dedicated craftsmanship by Armin Elsaesser during one of his off-duty stints in Baltimore in the old Light Street shipyard, she was a handsome craft, and the crew kept her varnished interior and wales and her white hull clean and fresh.

The *Pride* was underway several times in Drake's Channel, British

West Indies (Figure 4-21), for the sheer pleasure of sailing in ideal sailing breezes of 15 to 18 knots, always prevailing from the east on a dependable bearing. The surrounding mountainous, verdant islands, deep blue water, and creamy fair-weather clouds in the clearest of blue skies made for exceptional photo opportunities, and many of the crew took advantage of such days. It was a happy and carefree time.

The total number of sea miles recorded in the *Pride*'s logbook—some 150,000—showed that in her waterborne life of little more than nine years, she had sailed more distance than the majority of sailing vessels ever travel—and now she was about ready to sail for home again. She was reprovisioned for the relatively short run from St. Thomas to the Chesapeake Bay. The *Pride* was due in Baltimore on May 22, and she departed from St. Thomas on May 11, setting a northwesterly course. The breeze was light, and to ensure her sched-

Figure 4-21. Pride *sailing a few days prior to loss, Drake's Channel, British West Indies, 1986.*

ule she ran on power-and-sail combination until she completely cleared the islands.

Early on May 14, the weather closed in and the wind hauled around to east-by-north. It picked up to about 28 knots, and the *Pride* was reefed down on her main to the second band of reef points. She was sailing then on a broad reach to an easterly wind and under double-reefed main, foresail, and staysail.

At this time, she was sailing easily with all five weatherdeck hatches battened down, except the after companionway to the captain's cabin. She was making a good 7½ to 8 knots at about 1100, when the captain came on deck and noted that the wind had increased to over 30 knots. He ordered the foresail to be taken in, and it was lowered, in response to the order, rather than brailed up. The captain had taken the helm, and the mate had called the standby watch to assist in reducing sail. In order to facilitate the taking in of sail, the helm had been eased off, changing the course about 25 degrees farther to the west.

It was just before noon, and all hands except the cook were on deck for the necessary sail reduction. Seas were on the starboard quarter and running about 4 to 7 feet in height. The wind velocity was about 30 knots or a bit more, and the *Pride* was sailing comfortably under her reduced sail plan (Figure 4-22). Only the double-reefed mainsail and the forestaysail were pulling her along at about 8½ knots. Captain Elsaesser and first mate Flanagan were aft at the tiller, and, because of her course change, the captain ordered the mainsheet eased. The rest of the crew were making up the foresail and securing the furled jib, and, as Flanagan was easing the mainsheet, the hopeless hand of disaster gripped the ship.

An intense blast of wind, building to hurricane velocity in seconds, struck. According to first mate Flanagan, the force was "unbelievable." It was estimated by several crew members to be of 80 knots or more, and it came from the starboard beam. Flanagan was forced to let go the mainsheet, and the main boom hit the water. The captain forced the tiller hard up to starboard to put the stern to the wind. The staysail sheet could not be cast off because it was underwater—as were, very quickly, most of the crew on the leeward side.

The cook was below deck at the foot of the after companionway ladder. As the open companionway hatch went underwater, he made three attempts to swim against the mighty flood of water cascading down into the ship. Before his fourth and last attempt, he was able to catch his breath in the starboard upper corner of the after cabin where a small pocket of air was trapped. He made it through and surfaced beside the nearly vertical deck near the helm. Others of the crew had climbed from the lee side to the starboard rail and observed the futility of staying aboard. The two canistered auto-inflatable liferafts were released, only to be fouled by the rigging above.

There is no collectively cogent memory of the sequence of abandonment of the vessel by the crew and captain. Elsaesser called for a head count in the water, but the response to this is not clear. One memory was clear enough to recall: that the last view of the ship was the main topmast going out of sight beneath a wave with the pennant still flat out with the wind, reading *Pride of Baltimore.* She sank upright, before the eyes of the desperate crew struggling in the wrought-

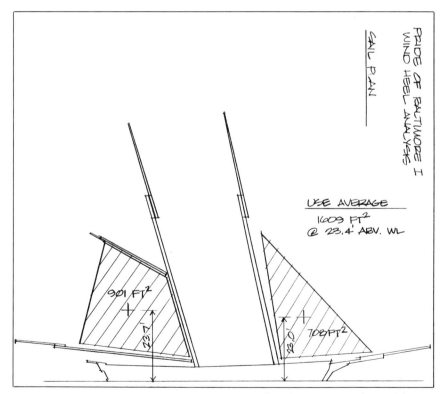

Figure 4-22. Sail configuration at time of sinking as confirmed by official investigation.

up ocean, with some 17,000 feet of salt water between them and the sea bottom.

The *Pride* took with her, besides her sundry gear and personal belongings, two ship's boats, two cats, and four human beings. In the water, the survivors were left swimming and trying to organize themselves, surrounded by chaos and desperation.

The names of those aboard the *Pride* before the catastrophe were as follows:

Captain Armin Elsaesser   Barry Duckworth, Carpenter
First Mate John Flanagan   Robert Foster, Seaman
Second Mate Joseph McGeady   Susan Huesman, Seaman
Boatswain Leslie McNish   Scott Jeffrey, Seaman
Vincent Lazarro, Engineer   Daniel Krachuk, Seaman
James Chesney, Cook   Nina Schack, Seaman

The following are those who were missing as a result of the casualty (so designated by the U.S. Coast Guard):

Armin E. Elsaesser, age 42, Captain
Vincent C. Lazarro, age 27, Engineer
Barry F. Duckworth, age 29, Carpenter
Jeannette F. (Nina) Schack, age 23, Seaman

Back in Maryland, it was May 19, in the early-morning hours before dawn, when the McGeady family's telephone rang in their suburban home in Severna Park. Their son Joe, the *Pride*'s second mate, was calling from some unbelievable place, on board a Norwegian freighter. His message was even more unbelievable: He and seven of his companions/shipmates had been picked up someplace in the Atlantic by this ship after a harrowing four-and-a-half days adrift in a leaky, crippled liferaft. The *Pride* was gone—sunk! Soon other telephones were ringing: the Pride of Baltimore, Inc., executive director Gail Shawe; the key members of the board of directors; Coast Guard headquarters. A press conference was called. The news was quickly spread. I was in the bathroom shaving when the telephone rang, prompted by an early-morning driver who had heard it on his radio. My response was disbelief—must be some nutty rumor. After a second call—same "rumor," I thought. Then I called the office in Baltimore; Pete Boudreau answered and simply said, before the question: "It's true."

CHAPTER FIVE

The Investigation, and
a Replacement Ship

On May 23, 1986, the U.S. Coast Guard, together with the National Transportation Safety Board, convened in Baltimore to open an investigation of the circumstances that caused the loss of the *Pride of Baltimore*. The witnesses subpoenaed for the investigation were logically chosen: the eight surviving crew members; the two relief captains of the *Pride*; the executive director of the corporation operating her; her builder and his yard foreman; and her designer. There were four who were designated as "interested parties": myself, as the vessel's designer; the operator/lessee (Pride of Baltimore, Inc.); the owners of the *Pride* (the mayor and city council of Baltimore); the representatives of the deceased Captain Elsaesser (father and brother). These interested parties were permitted and advised to be represented by legal counsel; they were also permitted to question or cross-examine all witnesses. As a matter of fact, the City of Baltimore and the board of directors of Pride of Baltimore, Inc., were represented by two and three lawyers each, with maritime counsel. Members of the board and the director were of course present, as were the principals of the others named above. It was a solemn occasion, and it continued with considerable media coverage for nine days.

The newspaper and television reporters were continually on the alert to discover some fault—lapses of performance, flaws in the ship construction, and especially design. It was, of course, precluded that there must be something wrong with the stability of a sailing vessel if it were knocked down by wind and could not recover. This presumption was further intensified and clouded by the sinking some months previously of a so-called "tall ship" carrying a number of youths on a voyage from Bermuda to Halifax, Nova Scotia. This vessel, the auxiliary bark *Marques* of British registry, was an old vessel of varied careers—as one or another historic ship in several movies and television documentaries, as a private yacht, and more recently as a school cruise ship. The *Marques* had been in doubtful condition, having undergone considerable reconstruction for her various roles. In type, condition, and circumstances, she was a most inappropriate source of comparison in the issue of the *Pride*'s loss.

However, another and most troublesome attack on the *Pride*'s credibility was deliberately introduced through the news media by an employee of a ship design firm in New England. This report charged that in a study prepared for the Coast Guard for certifying the requisite stability of sail training vessels according to certain criteria, the criteria of the *Pride of Baltimore* showed her to be the least stable of all sample sail training vessels selected for comparison, with a stability range of only 76 degrees. This was purely a contrived criticism, factually and technically incorrect, put forward for inexplicable reasons. The study was wisely marked by the federal investigators as not to be admitted into evidence. Its use as a reference of comparison was prejudicial.

The story of this federal investigation is now a matter of public record. There are still a few critics of the *Pride of Baltimore*, the vessel's concept, and particularly the perceived inadequacy of her seagoing capability, with the focus on stability. These criticisms are at this point academic and held to by people who seem to have an adversarial mind-set. The results of the investigation are available to anyone who will take the time to read the report. It is a realistic presumption that those who still criticize this fine American topsail schooner and her tragic loss have never read the final and official report and its conclusions. Here, in a brief summary, quoting only the pertinent paragraphs from the report, are the most significant of the findings and conclusions.

Washington, D.C.—February 11, 1987—G-MMI-1/24
U.S. Department of Transportation, United States Coast Guard

SAILING VESSEL PRIDE OF BALTIMORE—INVESTIGA-
TION INTO THE CAPSIZING AND SINKING WITH MULTI-
PLE LOSS OF LIFE ON 14 MAY 1986

◀ 155

The Investigation, and a
Replacement Ship

The finding of fact, conclusions and recommendations of the in-
vestigating officer, the comments of Commander, Fifth Coast
Guard District, and the Commanding Officer of the Marine Safety
Office, Baltimore Maryland:

Section 14—STABILITY

Par. 2, *Vessel Inclinings*. The *Pride of Baltimore* was inclined
three times by Naval Architect Thomas C. Gillmer. Vessels are inclined to determine the vertical location of the center of gravity at a
particular displacement. The location of the center of gravity is an
important factor in evaluating a vessel's stability or ability to float
upright.

Gillmer testified that he performed these inclinings for his own
information and not as a contractual requirement.

These inclining tests produced values to which the Coast Guard establishment could refer and use in making their own calculations.
They consequently produced for the investigation, done by their Marine Technical and Hazardous Materials Division at Coast Guard
Headquarters (among other things), deck edge immersion angles,
downflooding angles, and the *Pride*'s range of stability (at 87.7 degrees) port and starboard. They further determined righting-arm
curves for several values of center of gravity heights (KG). These
heights above the keel were 8.8 feet, 9.3 feet, and 9.8 feet.

Quoting again from Section 14, on pages 20 and 21 of the report:

These values of (KG) conditions were experienced on the *Pride of
Baltimore* over her lifetime. In a "schooner" configuration . . . with
four lower sails set (mainsail, foresail, staysail and jib . . . 4,227
square feet sail area), the *Pride of Baltimore* would meet passenger
vessel requirements for "partially protected" waters . . . for all three
KG values and would meet sailing school vessel requirements for
"exposed" waters (ocean) for a KG of 8.8 feet.

In reduced sail conditions such as mainsail and staysail or double-reefed mainsail and staysail, the *Pride of Baltimore* would meet
passenger vessel criteria when KG is 8.8 feet and *sailing school vessel criteria* for exposed waters when KG is 9.3 feet or less. With

double-reefed mainsail and staysail set, the *Pride of Baltimore* well exceeded deck edge, downflooding, and knockdown requirements at all three values of KG.

The *Pride of Baltimore* was also compared to Coast Guard-inspected sailing vessels in the schooner technical files at the Coast Guard Marine Safety Office in Portland, Maine. After comparison, the following points were noted:

· Hull proportions were not unusual;
· Light ship vertical center of gravity as a percentage of hull depth measured from fairbody to main deck was consistent with other vessels;
· The amount of ballast carried as a percentage of full load displacement was very high compared to other schooners;
· Downflooding angle, deck edge immersion angle, metacentric height, and freeboard were consistent with other schooners;
· Maximum righting arm and range of stability were consistent with other schooners.

The report finishes, of course, with "Conclusions," and there are 22 items in this section, none of them critical to the design and construction of the vessel. I will, however, quote those items that refer to the ship and her condition:

4. That the vessel was sailing with a double-reefed mainsail and staysail at the time of the casualty and that this was reasonable for the expected weather conditions.
6. That the aft companionway was open a sufficient amount to permit water to enter, flood, and sink the vessel.
7. That all other hatches were closed and did not contribute to the sinking.
9. That the *Pride of Baltimore*'s stability compared favorably with similarly rigged Coast Guard-inspected [certified] sailing vessels.
10. That there was no evidence of any structural failure or shifting of ballast.

The final and most satisfying observation of this official report on the investigation of this tragedy is in the last line item of "Recommendations": "That this case be closed."

The report was approved by the Commandant of the Coast Guard and signed by Rear Admiral J.W. Kine, Chief of the Office of Marine Safety.

An interesting fact in the investigation procedure was that each of the eight surviving crew members testified separately, and before they were called to the witness chair, they were not permitted to be present in the courtroom or hear any of the preceding testimony of their shipmates. They were individually questioned and asked identical questions; their answers were spontaneously given and were all very closely similar.

The crew members described the events prior to the wind burst as to their locations and what they were doing. They described the sudden wind blast much the same: "It was unbelievably strong, like a wall of wind" . . . "horizontal movement of cold air and water" . . . "sounded like a freight train" . . . "you just couldn't look into it, it hurt your face" . . . "water like stinging pellets." It—the storm blast—apparently subsided relatively quickly. It did not carry or build up big sea waves. Such sea waves that are associated with frontal storms or hurricanes build up over many hundreds or thousands of ocean miles—a distance called the storm wave's fetch. The *Pride* was overwhelmed and knocked on her side by wind alone—wind carrying much heavy water in particles picked up from the wave crests. But it was the dynamic energy of the sudden wind blast that acted like a hammer blow, a sudden release of kinetic energy that laid the sails down—and with them, the ship.

One witness at the investigation was Richard Biedinger, deputy meteorologist in charge of the National Weather Service forecast office in Miami, an expert on storm phenomena. With the help of weather records on the day of the casualty, he identified the cause as a "microburst." This is a fairly well-recognized phenomenon, particularly over land associated with frontal storms and semitropical conditions. Microbursts have been recorded over land areas and cited as having caused fatal aircraft crashes when the planes approached landing strips at low altitudes. Records of microbursts or downbursts over water are rarer, mainly because there are few meteorological stations and reports from ocean areas. Nevertheless, this sort of thermodynamics can occur over either water or land. It is described in one report:[1]

A microburst may come from a very innocent-looking storm. [Microbursts] can occur during any storm associated with cumulus cloud formations . . . they are difficult to predict or detect. Meteo-rologists estimate that the number of microbursts capable of induc-ing surface winds stronger than 70 knots can reasonably be as many as 13,000 a year in the United States.

Microbursts can best be defined as intense, short-lived down-bursts of wind which induce an outburst of damaging winds on or near the Earth's surface in a $2^1/2$-mile-or-less diameter.

Such high-velocity air is the result of moist, warm surface air that has been drawn up to stratospheric altitudes of 30,000 or more feet in developing cumulo-nimbus clouds, where it is chilled by the very low temperatures at that altitude. The air is then suddenly shrunk, becoming dense and heavy according to physical laws of vapor, and it begins to fall at accelerating rates. When this large "bubble" of frigid air mass hits the earth or sea, it flattens out horizontally and radially, and the result is an outburst.

So, the investigation concluded that the cause of sinking was "*a sudden and extreme wind that heeled the vessel beyond its range of stability and knocked it down.*"[2] It was not negligence, incompe-tence, faulty design, inattention to duty, lack of stability or certifica-tion, or replica inadequacy—not any of these reasons (or others like them) which, as the subject of prime speculation by the media, were spread inexhaustibly through networks and news syndicates from Boston to Texas to California and back.

After the summer and autumn of 1986, during which the Coast Guard investigating team as well as that of the National Transporta-tion Safety Board had examined all the evidence—traveling as far as Malaga, Spain, to check out the servicing of the *Pride*'s inflatable life-rafts, checking design calculations, recalculating design and stability criteria, subpoenaing further documentary sources, etc.—the report was finally written, submitted, and published (February 11, 1987). After all of this, it is surprising that so few people, particularly the passionate critics, ever read it. It consists of only 26 pages: less than a daily newspaper supplement.

Honoring a commitment

After the mourning and the eulogies and the memorials were held, the *Pride*'s survivors, builders, and designer returned to work. But nothing in their work or their world would ever be the same. The

Pride's loss was, and is still, a searing memory. However, the work of building wooden vessels is a commitment that is not easily abandoned (and going to sea can become a way of life); it is believed that only one of the surviving crew did not return to the same employment.

It is rather darkly humorous but it has been retold by those involved and retold again: When the sinking vessel had been abandoned and the crew was swimming in the storm-tossed sea, the first mate and the boatswain found themselves face to face in the water. The boatswain said to the first mate: "Sugar, if we ever get out of this alive, you and I are getting married!" And they did—the following September.

A response

This discussion of the loss of a contemporary Baltimore Clipper would not be complete or adequate if I did not address the criticism that has been leveled at the wisdom of building and/or operating replica ships. I realize that my observations may be somewhat biased, based on my experience as the designer of both *Pride*s and two similar projects, but they are a positive response to a negative argument.

I believe that the building and sailing of replica ships is a proper and honest inquiry into history. These are valid archaeological experiments and the sources of basic knowledge. From concept through construction and operation, the *Pride of Baltimore*, as well as the *Lady Maryland* and the *Pride of Baltimore II* and other similar historic vessels, are convincing examples of such inquiry and discovery. It is not for the critics of one loss to condemn the reasonable motives that build and sustain such ships. In the report of the official investigation of the *Pride*'s loss, no blame or fault was found with the vessel's replica status. The *Pride of Baltimore* was designed and constructed of the finest materials, by the most suitable methods.

Pride II

Not long after the completion of the investigation hearings, the decision was made to build a replacement ship. The two events had no relation, nor was the decision to build a spontaneous one. The matter had been considered since the loss, and while there was divided thinking, the force that moved it beyond debate was the popular reaction to the idea of building a replacement. People were responding by calling radio and television stations and sending money—all without solicitation!

As the board of directors of Pride of Baltimore, Inc., saw it, this unsolicited collection—nearly $200,000—was a public mandate. This amount of money would certainly not pay for a new topsail schooner of the sort that was in everyone's mind; it was, however, symbolic of public enthusiasm and hope. It was not ignored by the political world, either, since strong promises of support were forthcoming from that direction.

The first *Pride* had been insured for an original (not replacement) cost of $750,000, which was promptly paid by the insurer, Lloyd's of London. This, together with a $1 million grant put through by the governor of Maryland (former mayor of Baltimore), brought the amount raised for reconstruction close to $2 million. The actual cost of the new ship would be approximately $1.5 million, with the remainder used to start a support fund for the ship.

The actual replacement efforts—planning, design, and all matters relative to construction—were beginning to move by late summer of 1986. First to be decided on was the vessel's purpose and mission, followed by agreement on requirements and budget. In the meantime, I was named designer and supervising architect. Peter Boudreau was to be master shipwright and builder, and Gail Shawe was appointed executive director, which position she already held and agreed to continue on the board of directors.

The board had already named a small committee from their membership to coordinate the discussions on planning. It was almost unanimously agreed that the new vessel was to be larger, licensed by the Coast Guard for passenger carrying, with a greater cruising radius both under sail and under power, and that she must be a Baltimore Clipper as a design type—typical in size and historically identifiable in configuration. Her stated purpose was to carry on and extend the highly successful mission of her predecessor.

With these agreements and understandings well in mind, I began to design the new vessel—but the design process was quite unlike the customary approach to a new design. The board of directors had already requested a poster-like profile concept in color for promotion and media purposes; I had quickly drawn this up from a sketch in my file that seemed acceptable. During the preliminary discussions, the design was fleshed out with real dimensions. The length (approximately 110 feet, stem head to stern) was agreeable, with an appropriate breadth of 26 feet and a draft of approximately 12 feet. With a few basic coefficients and experience-ready relationships, her weight and cost could be closely approximated.

Since the original *Pride* had been the subject of considerable historical research, there was no need for further study. The first *Pride* had been acknowledged officially and privately among historians as a close replica of the original ship species. It was perhaps one element of authenticity in her design—specifically, her open space below deck—that had resulted in her rapid flooding and loss. This element was not to be repeated. At any rate, the configuration, the essential structure, and the sail plan of the new ship were to be authentic and identifiable as a Baltimore Clipper. These things being so, together with her blue-water sailing ability, the vessel would seem to be no less a true Baltimore Clipper.

Adherence to history

There has always been some discussion (and resulting contradictions) on what features in a reconstruction define a true replica. In the purest sense, there can be no genuine *true* replica; an identical reproduction would require too many unreproduceable properties in the basic materials and fabrication processes. There can be close duplication with considerable effort, time, and cost, but it is quite doubtful that, in a wooden ship of the size considered here, every item in its design and construction could be the same as the original. In the reconstruction of a type, there might be a bit more latitude, but there is still the further element of lack of precise knowledge in terms of minor details. We can only follow diligently, going by the existing few and incomplete plans of the original vessels from the British archives, with a composite prepared to requirements today.

I believe that the vessel built to the new design is no less a Baltimore Clipper because of her six watertight bulkheads, improved interior accommodations, and appropriate substitution of higher-quality materials. I further believe that the original owners and builders of the

Baltimore Clippers of the first decade of the 19th century would unanimously agree that the *Pride of Baltimore II* is a very elegant example of the fast schooners they first developed.

The design of the new Baltimore Clipper began with a preliminary 24-inch hull lines drawing (geometric configuration) to be examined for feasibility. This drawing was soon enlarged to a more workable scale, and, together with a trial sail profile, was shown to the board of directors' building committee; the basic design was approved with little or no discussion. The vessel's basic dimensions were thus set to be 109 feet overall hull length, 26 feet beam, $12^1/2$ feet draft, and 180 long tons *light ship displacement*—that is, empty weight, ready for crew and provisions.

It took a year to produce the design drawings, some 24 sheets altogether—four of which are reproduced here (Figures 5-1 through 5-4)—plus computer readouts for analysis. In the trade, these are generally called the working drawings, or the contract design. Although there is not space here to explain the process of ship design, I will, for the sake of understanding the sequence of events, point out what it is not.

It is frequently perceived that a naval architect can be employed for the planning process, to turn over, in due course, a package of blueprints called the *design* to the prospective owner and then walk away, leaving the rest up to the builder. Realistically, this is not the way it works.

A ship is a most complex system of engineering, intended to be a mobile habitat in an often hostile environment. Its mobility is unique: through an ever-changing medium it must propel itself, at controlled speeds and directions, its motion never in a two dimensional orientation. Regardless of modern sophisticated technology to assist in its requirements, a ship must be, in the end, self-sufficient. Consequently, the designer of this system, in order to meet these obligations and to ensure (as much as possible) a successful result, must closely follow the construction process, interpret his intentions to the builder, and continue the design work with detail drawings and analyses of the prospective operational characteristics. Much of this progresses with the building.

And so, it is often contemplated: When does a ship begin to be? Its origin, particularly a wooden ship's, does not seem to really happen at one time and in one place. Universally, a ship is officially begun

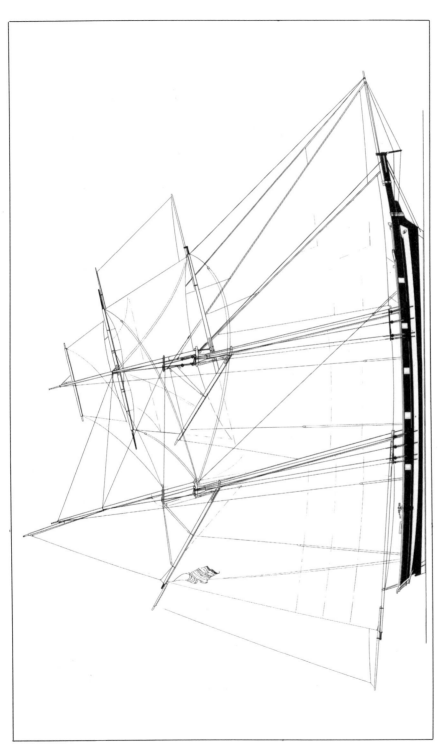

*Figure 5-1. Sail
plan of* Pride of
Baltimore II.

Pride of Baltimore

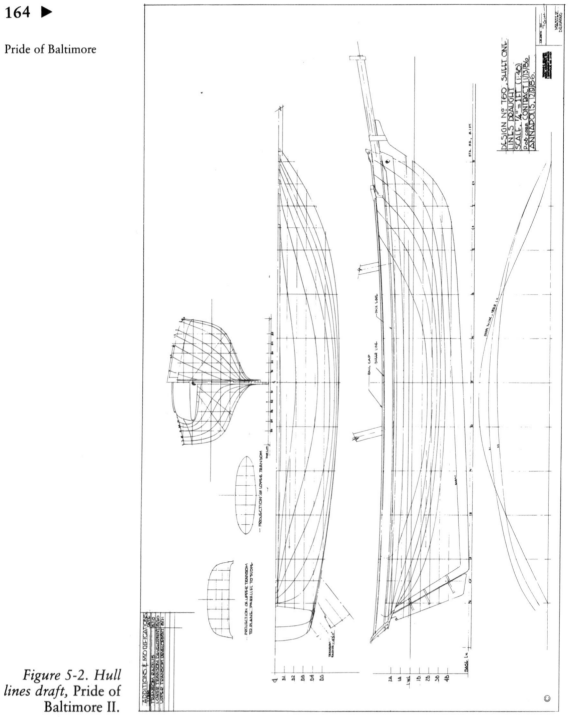

Figure 5-2. Hull lines draft, Pride of Baltimore II.

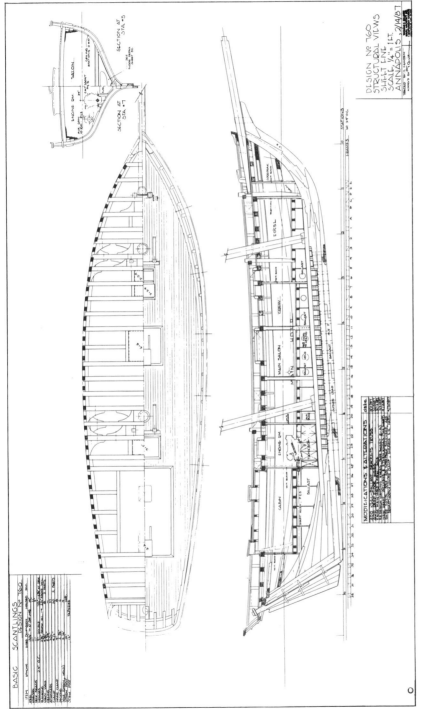
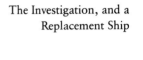

Figure 5-3. Construction profile and plan, Pride of Baltimore II.

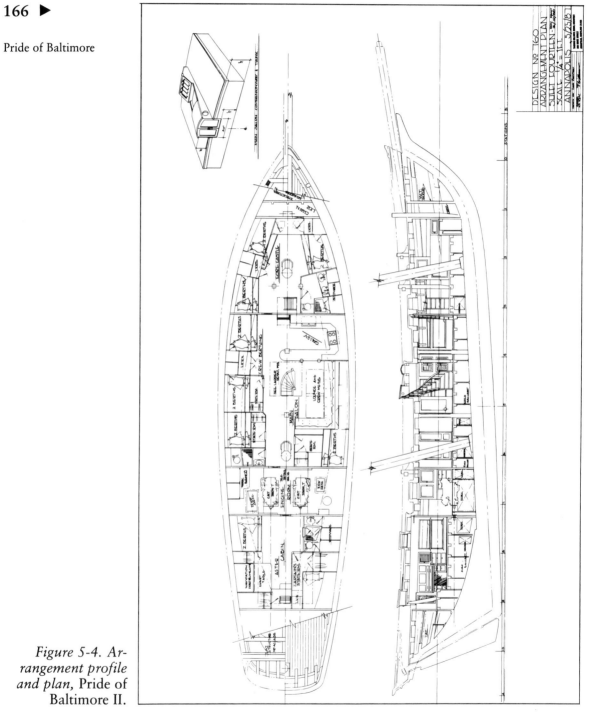

Figure 5-4. Arrangement profile and plan, Pride of Baltimore II.

and celebrated at the laying of the keel, that long, vertebrae-like assembly of timber. But once the backbone is complete, there are still a great many parts and components to be put together. In the oldest wooden ship known, the 6,000-year-old burial ship of the Egyptian pharoah Cheops, which has been reassembled, there are known to be 1,224 individual pieces of wood. This is but a small fraction of the number of pieces that make up a historic topsail schooner like the one we are discussing here. It is interesting, on the other hand, to consider the basics of a wooden ship from the standpoint of its parts. The keel is not only the most important single part of the ship, it is also perhaps the most carefully selected member.

Shipbuilding wood

Because of the scarcity and high cost of shipbuilding-quality wood in the United States, it was necessary to turn to other sources of hardwood for both *Pride*s of Baltimore. It was decided to use the same source for heavy hardwood timbers and planking wood for the new replacement as had been used for the original vessel—the tropical wood that grew in Central America, specifically in Belize. In fact, there is no better shipbuilding wood than well-selected tropical hardwood. Peter Boudreau, the builder, flew to Belize in October to meet with the timber dealers and begin the selection and purchase of wood.

There is no historical record of the use of this type of timber, because since early colonial days American ships had taken advantage of the abundant local supply. The great white oaks, the cedars, the longleaf Georgia pine—all in the Eastern states—had seemed inexhaustible. The British Navy during the colonial period depended almost entirely on New England timber for building their great ships-of-the-line and other naval vessels. Some 3,000 mature trees were required to supply the wood for one 100-gun ship such as Nelson's *Victory*.

There were no agencies or ecological societies for conservation in those days. Shipbuilding woods, even the inferior, fast-growing types, were always a problem among expansive nations. The Greek islands were denuded of trees in the building of their great trireme fleets. Such forest devastation went on throughout the Mediterranean region to supply wood for Roman warships and the great Roman grain ship fleets, followed by ships for the maritime city-states Genoa and Venice. During the ages of discovery, Spain and Portugal built thousands of ships of wood from their now devastated hills.

The designer and builders were not unaware of the large amounts of valuable timber required in building this second *Pride of Baltimore*. But good wood was and is being harvested in Central America — most of it wasted shamelessly, some of it sold. If not purchased for this project, it would go randomly for railroad ties, furniture lamination veneers, or even remain in the local countries for use as scaffolding to help build condominiums or expansive developments. It is my feeling that the best use for already felled, sound trees is to build a handsome ship!

The keel timber was to be of Cortez, as was used in this schooner's predecessor: a species known traditionally as one of the hardest, strongest, densest, and heaviest woods in the Western Hemisphere. As described in Chapter Four, Cortez is a beautiful, fine-grained wood, dark reddish-brown in color. Like other high-quality materials, it is difficult to work. Cortez is hard enough to turn the blade of a sharp knife, and its longevity is not definitely known.

The second species of hardwood used for the central timber backbone assembly is a wood named bulit tree, almost as good as Cortez and less expensive. It is only a little less dense and hard but a bit more workable with hand tools. Gray-brown in color, bulit tree shows some disuniformity in the grain structure and cannot be used in long lengths, as can Cortez. It is used in the stem- and sternpost assemblies as well as for the rudder.

Wood for the frames and frame assemblies was chosen from Santa Maria stock. This wood is a handsome hardwood that, when sawed and sanded, looks much like light-colored mahogany. Santa Maria is hard and tough — ideal for framing and also for the large deck beams — yet relatively light, more like oak in density. This weight factor between the ship's bottom, sides, and deck is important: the heavier woods must be kept low and the lighter ones scaled upwards.

All of the wood species described above are extremely resistant to decay and dry rot, much more so than any North American wood.

They are also resistant to ship worms (teredos). In fact, they are ideally suited to building the most durable of wooden ships. (There are other species in South American rain forests and coastal jungles that have only recently been discovered, and I hope they will stay there.)

The hull planking, which would total the greatest number of board feet of any woods used in this schooner, was first planned to be of Caribbean pine, sometimes called pitch pine. This was also supplied by the Belize timber merchant. However, when the structure had reached planking stage, it was determined that the quality of the Caribbean pine was not comparable to that of native Maryland white oak, the substitution of which was happily made. This wood had suddenly made itself available—and for only the cost of trucking and milling—through the kind officials of the State of Maryland's highway department, for the white oak trees had been cut in the course of new road construction. When the planking process was completed, it was tallied up that we had consumed 65 oak trees!

Wood for the decking in yachts (and, at one time, in warships) is traditionally teak from the Orient. However, for most Chesapeake working schooners it has been pine—pitch pine or long-leaf Georgia pine, a very heavy, resinous wood. When it seasons or ages, the resin hardens, and so does the wood. It had been considered for the deck planking, but it was becoming difficult to obtain, and after seeing the poor quality, with excessive knots, in the first order from Belize, we decided to seek another wood. Douglas-fir was the choice; this wood, primarily from Oregon, is still one of the great resources from our own country. Douglas-fir was to be also the wood for the tall masts and spars.

And, finally, there was to be a generous use of Honduras mahogany in the hatch frames, the deckhouse trunk, the companionway slides, and the caprails surrounding the deck on the bulwarks. Also, the trim wood and paneling in the main saloon were to be selected of Honduras mahogany.

Consequently, the wood for this wooden ship was to be very special, not simply that which was most immediately at hand. The *Pride II* is neither a yacht nor a working commercial vessel, nor is she finished like either. She is what she is: a refined Baltimore Clipper.

Design considerations

As the design progressed beyond the hull configuration and the selection of wood, there were other, most fundamental decisions. The vessel's resistance to the forces of the weather and the sea must be strengthened. This robustness must be augmented without decreasing her other seagoing qualities, namely buoyancy, able performance, responsiveness, and easy motion in a seaway, and so it was thus also a part of extending her stability.

Normally, in everyday considerations of mobility and locomotion, it would be nonproductive to add weight in the form of lead to a vehicle. This is not necessarily so with a sailing vessel. In fact, lead ballast will enhance the speed of most displacement sailing hulls by increasing the power to carry sail. All other things being equal, the name of the game in sailing design is to lighten the hull in order to increase the weight in the ballast. It was decided early in the design process that the new *Pride* would carry a substantial percentage of lead ballast on the bottom of her conventional wooden keel. Upon further design refinement, this outside ballast was determined to be optimum at approximately 20 tons. (There would also be 43 tons of inside ballast, in the form of cast lead pigs, loaded in the hold after launching.) The external ballast was to be set into the long configuration of the keel without disrupting the continuity of its line from stempost to after end. In doing this, a slight rocker (downward, rocker-like curvature) was given to the keel profile in order to work in the quantity of outside ballast; otherwise, the fact that there is outside ballast is not apparent, either visually or hydrodynamically.

Keel *rocker* is a term well known among sailors and is a factor in sailing-hull design that adds particularly to the windward performance of the vessel, whether it contains outside ballast or not. The keel ballast works silently and invisibly.

In attaching this much lead, in such a restricted location, to hang at the very lowest level on the outside of the structure, one needs to give serious consideration to the type of attachment. When a vessel is afloat, much of her motion is random, vertical, and semi-rotational. Therefore, the forces involved, which are neither constant nor simply linear in nature, must be introduced into the hull's structure in dispersed uniformity. The attachment of the lead ballast must not be localized.

Small wooden sailboats, before the advent of plastic hulls, have traditionally carried outside ballast in a similar manner. In smaller craft, the ballast is simply bolted through the keel from below with adequately sized bolts. In a larger vessel, the difficulty is mainly a matter of size and multiple components. With 20 tons of lead hanging only on a few long metal rods, sudden changes in direction of motion, together with localized concentration of forces, would soon result in movement between wood and metal. Such motion, increasing over time, results in hull leaks and loosening of fastenings, shock forces, etc. These problems must not be introduced.

In view of these structural considerations, I developed a new bracket arrangement (Figure 5-8) to reinforce the entire hanging structure for the ballast. It is difficult to name the resulting system inasmuch as it is something of a new idea, so I will simply describe it. The bracket is not complex and consists of a series of bronze weldments (or welded assemblies), the lower face of each being oriented on the top of the wooden keel. Each weldment is made up of $1/2$-inch-thick bronze plate and is held down with long, bronze through-bolts $1 1/4$ inch in diameter which reach down into the lead ballast casting at the keel's bottom. The forward and after vertical end pieces of each weldment are horizontally connected through each adjoining floor frame by six symmetrically distributed bronze bolts. In the keel length over which the ballast extends, this bolted assembly of weldments between each frame resolves itself into a continuous bridge structure. The resulting dynamic forces can be dispersed uniformly throughout the skeleton and the skin of the ship's hull. I believe the bracket assembly is a rather unique design feature that will, among other refinements, improve the ship's monocellular structure.

In addition to integrating the keel assembly into the whole structure, I also gave early consideration to the creation of watertight compartments—not as a series of independent, watertight cells, but as an intercommunicating, subdivided whole. First, I needed to determine how many and/or how few compartments could be used for the purpose of watertight integrity. In naval architecture, there is a procedure of computations and resulting overlay of a plotted curve to show the distribution of flooded ship's volumes longitudinally that will bring the vessel down to a pre-selected location called the *margin line*, generally 3 to 4 inches below the main weather deck edge. The line of variation of these flooding amounts along the ship's length is called

The Investigation, and a
Replacement Ship

the *floodable length curve*. Using this tool, the designer can determine the locations of interior flood barriers or watertight bulkheads. In smaller oceangoing vessels such as our Baltimore Clipper, the definition *one-compartment ship* can be applied and permitted. This means that the vessel will not sink with any one compartment flooded — although it was later determined by analysis that this vessel, with her five main (six in all) watertight bulkheads, would not allow sinkage below the margin line if any two adjacent compartments were flooded.

The design was now completed to the extent of hull configuration and rigging plans, the ship's structural plan (both longitudinal and sectional), the flooding plans, the machinery and propulsive system. The time to begin construction had arrived, and the shipyard was ready. The keel was laid on May 3, 1987.

Figure 5-5. Midship framing and drilling deadwood for drift bolts.

Construction (Figures 5-5 through 5-12) was completed with no more than average problems. The design concept was strictly adhered to, and there were no more than two notable deviations from the design drawings, the second of which was caused by failure to read a detail design blueprint properly, and as a result the new *Pride* has one minor ill-fitting fuel tank out of four.

The first deviation, however, caused a bit of discussion—to put it mildly! It was the decision to steer by wheel instead of by tiller. I was mildly overwhelmed by subtle suggestions that the future captain did not like to use a large tiller and that it wearied the helmsmen. This question enlarged itself to the point that the Coast Guard became involved. They agreed to the tiller, providing there were always two helmsmen on watch at sea. This meant four more crew members, a crew increased by 33 percent. This was unacceptable, and the logic was incorrect. Nevertheless, the wheel replaced the historic and conventional tiller that was an inherent part of a Baltimore Clipper. It was an expensive change, involving a finely machined bronze worm-gear mechanism that requires regular maintenance and lubrication,

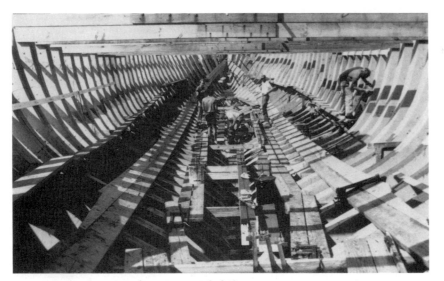

Figure 5-6. Interior framing with bilge stringers incomplete.

and the addition of several hundred built-in pounds of weight above deck, with an additional $5,000 cost.

That is all forgotten now, as is much of the skilled craftsmanship that fitted together the framing (Figures 5-5 and 5-6) on centers measured precisely so that the bronze weldments on the keel's inner surface would fit exactly, without accumulated error in frame spacing. Such error, whether diminishing or increasing over 35 frames, would decrease or increase the designed length of the ship: her hull configuration would not agree with hydrostatic calculations, etc. It did not happen, thanks to the skill and persistence of Lester Twigg, the ship's metalsmith and laboratory metallurgist at Johns Hopkins University.

Figure 5-7. Port side keel and frames, starting first strake of planking (garboard).

Forgotten also (or unknown to most) is the space between frames where these costly bronze weldments rest (Figure 5-8). These spaces were filled with additional ballast lead, sealed in place by cement, and covered with hot pitch (long cooled). Most of the time-consuming fitting and cutting and fastening of parts and pieces which so smoothly rest in their places are pretty much forgotten, even by the shipwrights who worked and sweated and often bled over them. As the heavy timbers of various species were reduced to necessary dimensions, they revealed tones of color and gradations of grain worthy of the finest furniture. A cabinetmaker would have cried at the way preservative paints and creosote-laden pitch were slapped on, covering the natural beauty of the rare woods. This is all largely buried now, too. The interior of the transverse framing itself (Figure 5-6) is covered over by an inner skin of planking called the ceiling, almost as heavy as the exterior planking, which covers the visible evidence of the ship's skeleton.

On the interior ceiling are attached the cabin soles: the standing

Figure 5-8. Bronze inter-frame keel bracket assembly; a strengthening bridge above keel and ballast suspension.

Figure 5-9. Planking progresses below the counter of the stern. This is the structure that forms the distinctive round tuck stern.

Figure 5-10. The "tuck" planking completed. This planking is Maryland white oak 2¹/₄" thick.

and walking surfaces. Bulkheads, the transverse vertical barriers, are built up in heavy plank laminations, tongue-and-groove, with a waterproof membrane between. These watertight bulkheads account for six watertight compartments that are calculated to keep the ship afloat should she flood with seawater into any one of them. And this, of course, is a federal regulation for certification, as were several other elements in the new design.

As the new *Pride* was being built, she was inspected regularly by Coast Guard officers from the Baltimore Office of Marine Inspection. This was as much a trial for them as it was for the builders. It was a situation where every shipwright, every dedicated worker on a new and unique job, was trying to do his best while at the same time having someone watch over his shoulder. Nearly every piece and every technique was questioned. It was understandable; the history that produced this replacement ship made the inspectors superconscious of the day-by-day construction and growth of a wooden ship. There was little to guide them; the only source used in the past was the American Bureau of Ships publication *Rules For the Construction of Wooden Ships*, last published in 1942 and long since out of print. Also, these guidelines were written for the building of larger vessels, for different purposes, according to late-19th-century standards. So

Figure 5-11. Profile of the double transom stern.

the marine inspectors, while of good conscience, had to be convinced that our procedures were sound. We were successful in this, but it frequently slowed progress. Inspectors were present from keel laying, to launching, to commissioning.

The launch

Launching was carried out in the same way that it had been for the original *Pride*, at the same location, by the same great floating crane, "Big Red." This event occurred on April 30, 1988. The new *Pride* was lifted from the building stocks, a few inches from the keel blocks, early that morning before the visitors and audience began to assemble; then she was eased back into the "at rest" position, with most of the tension remaining on the lifting cables, while the site was cleared of scaffolding and last-minute paint touches were applied at previously unreachable spots where blocks and shores had supported her. All the underwater openings, sea valves, intakes for machinery—all were checked. Water in the bilge, which had been there for some days to keep the planking from drying out, was removed. It was a busy morning for the crew.

Figure 5-12. Builder Peter Boudreau inspects sheer wale before the gunwale is planked.

At last, after the speeches were over, the order came to launch, and the *Pride of Baltimore II* was lifted, very slowly, above the treetops (Figure 5-13) and to the edge of the esplanade, where she descended and paused for a few minutes for a champagne bottle to be smashed on her stem. She moved out and down and settled most gracefully into the harbor water at the foot of the steps of the southwest landing.

Differences

From the beginning of the *Pride II* project and also since, the questions asked most frequently by many of the interested public have been: "How is this new ship different from the first?" and "How is she safer?"

The second question, sometimes asked first, is easily dealt with. None of us who were close to the original *Pride*'s building, design, or operation have ever believed she was an unsafe ship, as is implied by

Figure 5-13. Launching Pride of Baltimore II, *April 30, 1988.*

the question. This answer is pretty well confirmed by the findings of facts and conclusions of the official investigation into the tragedy.

The answer to the other question is more involved, as to her design and construction. Very basically, the *Pride II* is larger than the first *Pride* by approximately 50 percent. This comparison is derived from the difference in displacements, or weights, of the two vessels. The new *Pride* is operating at close to 189 tons, while the last record of drafts on the original *Pride* indicated she was 123 tons, just about her designed load waterline displacement. So the *Pride II* is a bit more than half again as large, and this difference is significant in her operation, response, resistance to heeling, her speed, and many other things. Her skippers, two of whom have sailed both ships, remark about her ease in handling and her passagemaking ability.

Further obvious differences are her watertight compartments—six, counting the forepeak and the lazarette—and the fact that she has about one-third of her total ballast outside, below her keel.

She has, proportionately, about the same sail area. Her sails are not made of cotton, but of an appropriate synthetic material—Dura-don—whose appearance and texture is much like cotton sailcloth. It does not rot or mildew or shrink or stretch, and the sails set almost wrinkle-free.

The similarities, of course, are many. The two vessels have the same rig, proportionately, in most sails. Their nonlinear dimensionless coefficients are very close. The table below indicates a numerical comparison of the two.

	Pride II	Pride
LOA	108 ft.	89' 9"
LWL	91 ft.	76' 8"
Beam (extreme)	26' 5"	23' 0"
Beam (WL)	24' 6"	22' 0"
Draft	10' 8"	8' 5"
Draft (extreme)	12' 6"	9' 9"
Draft (molded)	10' 6"	8' 5"
Displ. (full load)	190 long tons	121.2 long tons
Sail area (total)	9707.8 sq. ft.	9523.0 sq. ft.
Sail area (working)	6812.7 sq. ft.	N/A
$B/\Delta = \frac{(Ballast)}{(Displacement)}$	32%	35%
Tonnage (measure)	197	140

After launching, the summer was occupied by the sparmaking and rigging. The spars came from Oregon and were roughed out of Douglas fir to basic dimensions. Two of the upper spars, for some reason, were not in the original shipment; they did not come until mid-July, and so the rigging was delayed, as were the *Pride II*'s sail trials and commissioning.

The necessary ballasting—one of the critical procedures in the building of sailing ships—proceeded almost at once after launching. The quantity of ballast depends upon very careful calculations of weight as well as of stability. Most of the weight calculations depend on manufacturer's weights of large items that are too cumbersome to weigh on the site, nor are there usually large-weight scales to conveniently handle these items: heavy machinery, stainless-steel galley stove, bronze feathering propellers, etc. With structural items— wood, lag bolts, forgings, masts, rope, chain—it is more direct to weigh the material specimen for specific weights (pounds per foot) and extrapolate the totals. As a matter of fact, the record of weight items for the *Pride II* made up a looseleaf binder of 151 pages. My weight master (Francis Taylor) diligently maintained this running record of weights in order that, for that last day of reckoning, when she was ready to sail away (or for the Coast Guard-supervised inclining tests for certification), she would float at the predetermined waterline. It is desirable to ballast with the optimum amount as low as possible to achieve a predetermined condition of stability and at the same time maintain the prescribed load line / freeboard markings. With the help of Archimedes and a diligent weight accountant, the *Pride II* managed this.

Copies of key pages from the stability analysis (Figures 5-14 and 5-15), with the static stability curve determined and approved by the U.S. Coast Guard for certification, are shown here for full load conditions, 190.09 long tons in salt water.

After launching, some 43 tons of lead weights (cast pigs of 40 pounds each) were loaded in the ballast hold. With the external fixed ballast on the bottom of her keel, the total ballast was close to 62.3 tons.

Upon launching, the draft marks (Figure 5-16) showed 10 feet 7 inches aft and 9 feet 7 inches forward, which indicated that she

182 ▶

Pride of Baltimore

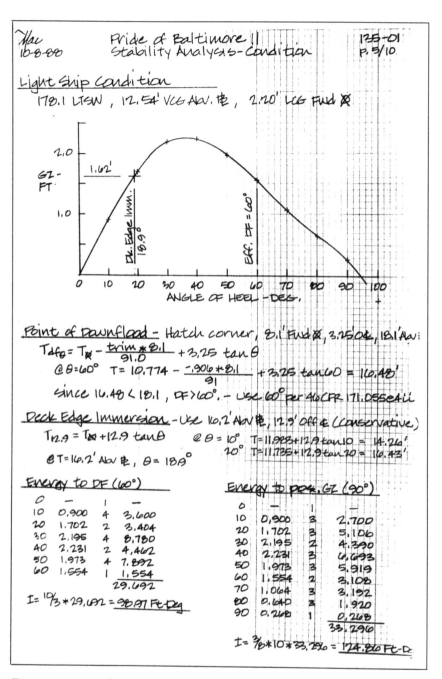

Figure 5-14. Stability analysis condition, light ship.

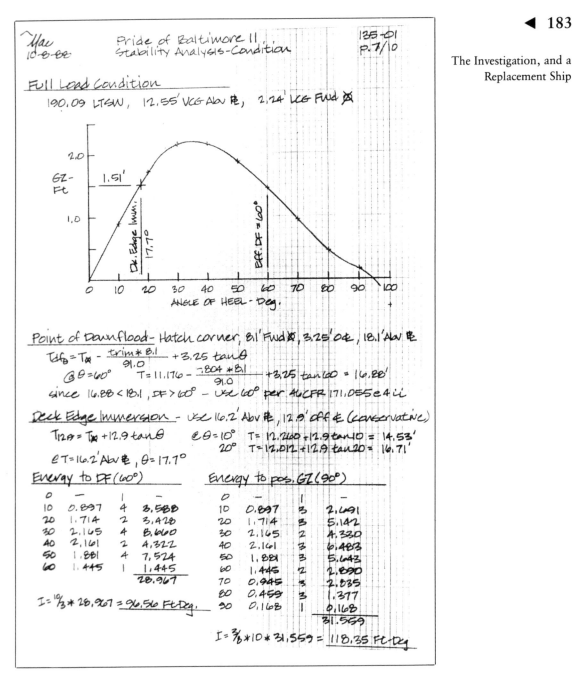

Mac
10-8-88

Pride of Baltimore II
Stability Analysis-Condition

135-01
p.7/10

Full Load Condition

190.09 LTSW, 12.55' VCG Abv ₵, 2.24' LCG Fwd ⊗

GZ-Ft (vertical axis): 2.0, 1.51', 1.0

1.51'

Dk. Edge Imm.
17.7°

Eff. DF = 60°

ANGLE OF HEEL - Deg. (horizontal axis): 0, 10, 20, 30, 40, 50, 60, 70, 80, 90, 100

Point of Downflood - Hatch corner, 8.1' Fwd ⊗, 3.25' O₵, 18.1' Abv ₵

$T_{df_\theta} = T_\otimes - \frac{trim * 8.1}{91.0} + 3.25 \tan\theta$

@ θ = 60° $T = 11.176 - \frac{-.804 * 8.1}{91.0} + 3.25 \tan 60 = 16.88'$

since 16.88 < 18.1, DF > 60° - use 60° per 46CFR 171.055 e 4 ii

Deck Edge Immersion - use 16.2' Abv ₵, 12.9' off ₵ (conservative)

$T_{12\theta} = T_\otimes + 12.9 \tan\theta$ @ θ = 10°   T = 12.260 + 12.9 tan 10 = 14.53'
                                                20°   T = 12.012 + 12.9 tan 20 = 16.71'

@ T = 16.2' Abv ₵, θ = 17.7°

Energy to DF (60°)				Energy to pos. GZ (90°)			
0	—		—	0	—	1	—
10	0.897	4	3.588	10	0.897	3	2.691
20	1.714	2	3.428	20	1.714	3	5.142
30	2.165	4	8.660	30	2.165	2	4.330
40	2.161	2	4.322	40	2.161	3	6.483
50	1.881	4	7.524	50	1.881	3	5.643
60	1.445	1	1.445	60	1.445	2	2.890
			28.967	70	0.945	3	2.835
				80	0.459	3	1.377
				90	0.168	1	0.168
							31.559

$I = \frac{10}{3} * 28.967 = 96.56$ Ft-Deg.

$I = \frac{3}{8} * 10 * 31.559 = 118.35$ Ft-Deg

Figure 5-15. Stability analysis condition, full load.

weighed, at that time, 102 tons. She subsequently took aboard (including the 43 tons of inside ballast) 76 more tons of equipment to reach her commissioning-date weight of 178.1 tons at "light ship condition." This is the basic condition for a ship upon delivery: it is complete, ready for sea, but without fuel, water, crew or their effects.

After ballasting, the masts could be stepped, the engines installed, the fuel and water tanks fitted, the watertight doors put in the watertight bulkheads (only three doors were needed for horizontal access below)—all of the many items that make a floating hull a mobile, waterborne habitat that is reasonably self-sufficient.

Back at sea

The *Pride II* was commissioned October 23, 1988 (Figure 5-17), and sailed at once for Bermuda, repeating her predecessor's maiden voyage; she was sailed primarily by her building crew and Captain Peter Boudreau, her builder. Changing crew and captain in Bermuda, she

Figure 5-16. Draft marks at bow when launched.

continued on to the Caribbean for the winter season and a thorough shaking down. In the spring of 1990 she returned to Baltimore, where she was refitted and provisioned for a summer cruise through the Great Lakes.

The Orient, including Japan and China, was actively planned as a destination to be undertaken in 1990 after her Caribbean winter. However, the world political climate was rapidly changing, and these plans were modified. The *Pride II* returned to Baltimore on March 7,

Figure 5-17. Pride II *under sail, first voyage, early on.*

1990, with just less than 30 days for drydocking, refitting, inclining tests, and provisioning with a new crew and an itinerary for two years in Europe.

On April 7, the *Pride II* sailed from Baltimore, headed for Europe (Figure 5-18). Just 17 days later, she arrived in Baltimore, Ireland — a relatively quick crossing that included fair weather with southwesterly winds, days of calm and fog and sailing off her Great Circle rhumb line to avoid icebergs. In the fog, with good sailing breeze, there were indeed icebergs, identified by radar and avoided. The crew prudently vacated the forecastle, moved their bedding and gear aft to the crew's lounge, and dogged down the watertight door behind them.

The sailing record for crossing the Atlantic, east to west, has been

Figure 5-18. Pride II's departure for Europe, April 8, 1990.

in recent years a confused thing, with the entry of multihulls into the ocean sailing and racing scene. I have addressed this in an earlier chapter, in the context of clipper ship records. However, the west-to-east record of the *Pride II* is among the recorded passages of the great sailing packets of the mid-19th century. The clipper ship *Red Jacket* of the Black Ball Line out of Liverpool, England, sailed from Boston to Liverpool in 14 days, a passage covering a course of some 3,000 miles. For comparison, the *Pride II*'s course from Baltimore, Maryland, to Baltimore, Ireland, was 3,270 miles. So far, there has been no research of passages from the Chesapeake Bay to Ireland, but it may well stand examining, and the west-to-east record may be broadened. At least for now, the sailing record between the two ports named Baltimore may temporarily rest as unchallenged at 17 days.

In Chapter Four, I briefly detailed the sailing performance of the *Pride of Baltimore*; it is appropriate, for the sake of comparison and for the record, to say something of the sailing performance of the *Pride of Baltimore II*.

On this first transatlantic passage, in addition to the respectable crossing time, she had some rough-weather sailing—flat weather, fog, North Atlantic spring gales. The mix of weather and sea state kept the crew on their highly strung best! But I shall mention, with some pride in the *Pride II*, that during gale conditions (Force 10) under single-reefed foresail and staysail for 48 hours logged time, she sailed 480 nautical miles (fix to fix, on course). In full storm conditions, she averaged 10 knots for two days among high seas and 30 percent of sail plan. But comfortable sailing under plain sail plan in Force 2 to 3 winds is 8 to 9 knots. The maximum speed yet recorded is slightly above 13 knots; her theoretical hull speed is 12.9 knots.

Going to windward, she can sail, according to Captain Miles, about 4 degrees closer to the wind than her predecessor and has no trouble tacking through 90 degrees' change of course from port to starboard or reverse. She is very maneuverable under sail in tight quarters, and the crew, properly trained in sail handling, can use the square foretopsail as a brake to stop short in docking or to assist in making tight turns.

All of this is satisfactory confirmation of the tactics that led her predecessors, nearly 190 years ago, in their strategy to confound the British and discourage them from continuing the War of 1812. Baltimore Clippers were, in that time, examples of the highest state of the art in high-performance sailing vessels for ocean sailing.

As a final word in this modern (late-20th-century) treatment of antique sailing machines, they can fairly be said to have proved themselves able to stand among fast ocean sailing vessels. They need no apologies: they are still able. More important, they stand alone as the great ancestors to a remarkable lineage of American sailing vessels.

Appendices

Appendix 1. Terminology

Builders describing their vessels for official documentation used terms and abbreviations that are generally meaningless to people unfamiliar with shipyard terminology. With Baltimore Clippers being of unusual configuration, such terms become important.

Most significant in a vessel's dimensions are those required for standard forms of measurement determining tonnage. Tonnage is a historic term and should not be confused with a measurement of weight. It refers to volume, and over many centuries the mathematics for obtaining it has changed by usage, by laws governing tariffs, and by international agreements. It all began sometime in the Middle Ages for rating ship's capacity for carrying wine casks called "tuns." This measurement became refined and standard and was called the "tons burthen." The official registration measurement was obtained as follows: the length of the ship's keel as a base multiplied by the ship's extreme width and multiplied again by the interior vertical dimension called depth (of hold), and the whole divided by a constant. The value of this factor varied over the years, but at the turn of the nineteenth century the measurement rule in Baltimore, based on the English rule, stipulated the divisor to be 95. For contracting and for designation on carpenter's certificates, the tonnage measurement became simplified to length of hull multiplied by the breadth and by the half-breadth divided by 95. This equation resulted in the commonly called carpenter's measure.

Length for tonnage was not always keel length. It was often a designated length "between perpendiculars." The perpendiculars were at the extreme forward face of the stem and the aftermost face of the sternpost.

Other terms commonly used both officially and noted on descriptions of ship's identity are: "round tuck," "no head," "sharp-built," "full built," "privateer style," "pilot boat style," and "flush deck." These are most significant in Baltimore Clipper identification.

Round Tuck: A type of stern, as opposed to square tuck. It is a stern that is formed by the turning up of the after planking to meet and be fastened to a heavy cross timber called the transom beam.

Square Tuck: An older type of stern with a broad, flat transom historically common on many European vessels and on Chesapeake schooners before 1800. The planking on this type of stern runs out to a transom often of a "wineglass" profile. The transom in this type of stern extends from deck to waterline or perhaps slightly below.

No Head: Lack of figurehead on stem and when so designated shows no headboards or trailboards or stem knees and no decoration but a simple curving knee: the prototype "Clipper bow."

Sharp built: This description is generally applied to a vessel with sharp waterline forward in the narrow angle on each side of the stem, usually less than twenty-eight degrees. It is opposite of full built, and was the usual designation for a fast sailing vessel.

Full built: Describes the traditional vessel of commerce and the historic shape used for most large seagoing vessels of the 17th and 18th century style. Bluff bows with rounded sections and square or round tuck sterns—such ships stood out in sharp contrast to the Chesapeake sharp-built schooners.

Privateer Style: This descriptive term leaves no doubt about the type of vessel it was. When such a term was used on a carpenter's certificate for Baltimore or the Chesapeake Bay region in the first decade and a half of the 19th century, it was surely a Baltimore Clipper for aggressive sea service.

Pilot Boat Style: This description is generally applicable for a fast sailing schooner type and, for a privateer, perhaps to disguise its purpose or to keep it tentative. A genuine pilot boat for the lower bay and Virginia capes was a very substantial vessel of a size slightly smaller or similar to a privateer style schooner. They were of the same hull configuration as Baltimore-built privateer style, often with partial or no closed bulwarks or gunwales.

Flush Deck: A deck that has no break in its continuity from stem to stern. This was the end result of deck configuration development from the late Middle Ages when stern castles and forecastles were piled on up through the middle 16th century and when a gradual reduction of vertical levels began. There were some fast Chesapeake schooners at the 18th century's end that still carried the semblance of a quarter deck with a rise of less than twelve inches aft—or just enough to trip over, but necessary to provide accommodations below deck aft. A flush deck was a feature, among others, that exhibited naval architectural progress in added hull strength.

No Galleries: Some ships at the turn of the 19th century still retained vestiges of the baroque or rococo styles of the 18th century when stern galleries and carved decorations were fashionable. Baltimore-built ships were probably among the first to eliminate these things which also included head boards, trail boards, head knees with scrolls, and figureheads. The term "galleries" probably included the quarter decorations (quarter galleries and quarter badges) on each side of the upper transom. In any case, these stern decorations were noted (or noted in their absence) in descriptions on registrations and carpenter's certificates.

Letter of Marque (and Reprisal): The story of this ominous-sounding term is very old and confusing. Very generally, it is a grant or permission to engage in combat with any vessel flying the flag of a country with whom the grantor is at war. It originated in very early naval history and was useful for Elizabethan England in the years before the Spanish Armada. It is a means of enhancing naval power at no cost to the citizenry and at a profitable risk to the vessels granted this permit. In the War of 1812 (as well as the American Revolution), this practice was prevalent. A ship's captain who is granted a letter of marque for his ship does not necessarily engage in privateering. Very often, Baltimore Clippers carrying such permits were engaged only in commerce and trade. If they were exclusively engaged in privateering, they were identified as privateers — a trading vessel with a letter of marque was identified as a letter-of-marque vessel. The permit (Letter of Marque) was authorized by the President of the United States and sometimes carried his signature. They were issued generally for each voyage by the port captain or customs inspector of the vessel's port of departure.

Appendix 2. Ship identities sailing from The Chesapeake Bay immediately prior to the War of 1812

Key to abbreviations of Maryland county names:

BC: Baltimore County
DO: Dorchester County
QA: Queen Anne's County
SO: Somerset County
TA: Talbot County

Record group 41 of Bureau of Marine Inspection and Navigation Vessel Registration issued at Baltimore, Maryland Chesapeake-built vessels only

Alexander	Ship 1D3M: 100′ L, 28′ B, 12′7″ D, 308 42/95 T
	Round tuck, no galleries, "a bust of a *man* head"

Pride of Baltimore

Built BC 1809 as per master carpenter certificate
Owner: Joseph Despause of BC
Master Wilson Jacobs
Reg. 22 Sept 1810, No. 159

Amphion

Schooner 1D2M: 92′6″ L, 23′10″ B, 9′10″ D, 192
72/95 T
Round tuck, no galleries, no head
Build BC 1807, Reg. BC 18 Sept. 1809, No. 187
Property in part transferred
Owners: John Smith Hollins, John Hollins, Michael
McBlair, Lemuel Taylor—all of BC, merchants;
Master James Knowles
Reg. 8 Mar 1810, No. 31

Ann Maria

Schooner 1D2M: 49′ L, 15′6″ B, 4′10″ D, 30 24/95 T
No galleries, no head
Built TA 1803, enrolled Oxford 16 June 1807, No. 30
Property transferred
Owner: Ichabod Glover of Salem, Massachusetts;
Master Elijah Bevin
Reg. 27 Nov 1810, No. 196

Ann Maria

Schooner 1D2M: 73′3″ L, 22′9″ B, 9′ D, 128 40/95 T
Round tuck, no galleries, no head
Built SO 1808, Reg. BC 13 Oct 1809, No. 203
Property transferred
Owner: John Williams Jr. of BC, merchant;
Master Samuel Silvestor
Reg. 10 Mar 1810, No. 33

Atlas

Schooner "sharpbuilt"* 1D2M: 199′9″ L, 25′3″ B,
10′9″ D, 144 51/95 T
Round tuck, no galleries, no head
Built TA 1808 as per master carpenter certificate
Owner: Thomas Tenant of BC, merchant;
Master James Forbes
Reg. 27 Jul 1810, No. 132
Registration 19 Oct 1811, new owners

Baltimore

Brig 1D2M: 80′ L, 23′6″ B, 11′5″ D, 186 14/95 T
Round tuck, no galleries, no head
Built Mathews County VA 1808,
Reg. BC 27 May 1808, No. 99
Owners: James Ogleby, David Winchester, James
Phillips of BC;

*This is the first time in 1810 this term is used.

Master Herman Perry
Reg. 9 May 1810, No. 78

Bee McFadon Schooner 1D2M: 51′ L, 15′9″ B, 5′6″ D, 37 87/95 T
Square tuck, no galleries, no head
Built BC 1810 as per master carpenter certificate
Owner: John A. McFadon of BC, merchant;
Master Purnell Austin
Reg. 16 Nov 1810, No. 190
Captured by the "Haytians" 1811

B. Franklin Schooner 1D2M: 91′ L, 23′ B, 9′4″ D, 175 35/95 T
Round tuck, no galleries, no head
Built St. Michaels TA 1809 as per master carpenter
certificate
Owners: William Flannigain and James Owings of BC;
Master March M. Duvall
Reg. 20 Oct 1810, No. 172
Surrendered 7 Oct 1811, new owners reside in New
York

Brazillian Brig 1D2M: 76′9″ L, 21′5″ B, 11′8″ D, 168 5/95 T
Round tuck, no galleries, no head
Built Gosport VA 1808, Reg. N&P 25 Oct 1809, No.
73
Property transferred
Owner: Daniel McClean of Alexandria;
Master Fielder Luckett
Reg. 4 Jun 1810, No. 98

Breeze Schooner 1D2M: 68′ L, 18′8″ B, 8′2″ D, 91 29/95 T
Round tuck, no galleries, no head
Built TA 1810 as per master carpenter certificate
Owner: Alexander Mitchell of BC, merchant;
Master John Theobold
Reg. 14 Sept 1810, No. 157
Registration surrendered 20 Feb 1811;
sold in a foreign port

Brothers Schooner 1D2M: 46′7″ L, 15′ B, 5′6″ D, 32 12/95 T
No galleries, no badges, no figurehead
Built DO 1807, enrolled Vienna 7 Aug 1809, No. 31
Change of property
Owner and master: John Payton of Kinsall VA
Reg. 31 Aug 1810, No. 147

Buckskin Schooner 1D2M: 60′ L, 18′ B, 6′ D, 56 T
No galleries, no figurehead

Pride of Baltimore

Built Annapolis 1807, enrolled Annapolis
3 Nov 1807, No.17
Property transferred
Owner and master: John Cole of Charleston SC
Reg. 30 Oct 1810, No. 177

Caroline

Schooner 1D2M: 78′ L, 21′2″ B, 8′11″ D, 129 60/95 T
Round tuck, no galleries, no head
Built TA 1809
Owner: Jonathan Judson of BC, merchant;
Master Hamlet Fairchild
Reg. 15 Jan 1810, No. 9
Registration surrendered 19 Jan 1811, new owner

Caroline

Schooner 1D2M: 86′6″ L, 21′7″ B, 7′9″ D, 157 40/95 T
Round tuck, no galleries, no head
Built QA 1809 as per master carpenter certificate
Owners: Robert Williams and Joseph Patterson of BC,
merchants;
Master Nathanial Sherman
Reg. 10 Jul 1810, No. 119
Registration surrendered at New Orleans 14 Aug 1812,
new owners

Cassius

Brig 1D2M: 97′ L, 23′3″ B, 9′9″ D, 193 16/95 T
Square tuck, no galleries, no head
Built at Baltimore 1809 as per master carpenter
certificate
Owner: Bernard Salenave of BC
Master John M. White
Reg. 5 May 1810, No. 71
Registration surrendered 17 Apr 1812, vessel sold

*Catherine
Augusta*

Brig 1D2M: 95′6″ L, 25′3″ B, 12′ D, 256 22/95 T
Round tuck, no galleries, no head
Built Baltimore 1809 as per master carpenter
certificate
Owners: Jacob LeRoy, Rosewell L. Colt, Herman
LeRoy, William Bayard, James McEvers, John S.
Rouler;
Master Thomas C. Howe
Reg. 8 Mar 1810, No. 30
Registration surrendered at New York 12 May 1810

Charlotte	Brig 1D2M: 92′ L, 23′3″ B, 10′6″ D, 200 62/95 T Round tuck, no galleries, no head Built at Baltimore 1809 as per master carpenter certificate Owner: William Gretham of BC Master Pasqual V. Kelley Reg. 15 Mar 1810, No. 36 Vessel lost 7 May 1811
Ciota	Schooner 1D2M: 64′4″ L, 20′6″ B, 7′10″ D, 88 75/95 T No galleries, no badges, no head Built SO 1809, enrolled Vienna 1 Jun 1810, No. 30 Vessel bound on a foreign voyage Owner and master: Marcelous Jones of SO, mariner Reg. 3 Jul 1810, No. 112 Registration surrendered 4 Jun 1811, new owner in part
Comet	Schooner 1D2M: 43′ L, 14′ B, 5′ D, 25 51/95 T No galleries, no badges, no figure head Built SO 1809, enrolled Vienna 4 Jan 1810, No. 1 Property transferred Owner and master: Robert Gaddy of Smithfield VA Reg. 29 Oct 1810, No. 176 Registration surrendered Norfolk 8 Nov 1810
Despatch (of Annapolis)	Schooner 1D2M: 52′ L, 16′3″ B, 5′ D, 35 12/95 T No galleries, no head Built DO 1808, enrolled BC 22 Jun 1809, No. 47 Property transferred Owners: Benjamin Hancock of Anne Arundel County and Nathaniel Hancock Master Benjamin Hancock Reg. 7 Sept 1810, No. 148 Registration surrendered Annapolis 8 Sept 1810
Dolphin	Schooner 1D2M: 66′3″ L, 18′10″ B, 7′2″ D, 78 13/95 T Round tuck, no galleries, no head Built Baltimore 1810 as per master carpenter certificate Owners: Israel Navarro and Thomas Williams of New York Master Israel Navarro Reg. 11 Sept 1810, No. 151 Registration surrendered 31 Mar 1811

Eliza

"Sharp built schooner" 1D2M: 69' L, 21' B, 8' D, 99 65/95 T
Round tuck, no galleries, "a woman head"
Built on Sassafrass River, Cecil County 1803, enrolled BC 24 Jun 1803, No. 39
Property transferred
Owners: Lemuel Warfield and William Owen of BC; Master William Owen
Reg. 31 Oct 1810, No. 180
Registration surrendered 7 May 1811, new owners in part

Ema

Schooner 1D2M: 85' L, 21'9" B, 9'3" D, 152 454/95 T
Round tuck, no galleries, no head
Built BC 1810 as per master carpenter certificate
Owner: Bernard Salenave of BC, merchant; Master James Watkins
Reg. 21 Nov 1810, No. 192
Registration surrendered 23 May 1811, new owners

Enterprise

Schooner 1D2M: 51'3" L, 15'6" B, 5' D, 34 25/95 T
No galleries, no head
Built DO 1806, enrolled Chester 12 Mar 1808, No. 3
License expired
Owners: James and Thomas Dawson of QA; Master John Alexander of Chester
Reg. 15 Mar 1810, No. 37
Registration surrendered 24 Apr 1810

Experiment

Schooner 1D2M: 80' L, 22' B, 8'6" D, 132 14/95 T
Round stern, no galleries, no head
Built Talbot County 1809, registered Oxford 20 Oct 1809, No. 3
Property transferred
Owner: Thomas Sheppard of BC, merchant; Master Philip Rider
Reg. 18 Apr 1810, No. 61
"Vessel captured by the British 1813"

Express

Schooner 1D2M 91'6" L, 23'6" B, 9'5" D, 180 23/95 T
Round tuck, no galleries, no head
Built Talbot County 1809 as per master carpenter certificate
Owners: John Hollins, Michael McBlair, John Smith Hollins, and Lemuel Taylor of BC, merchants
Master Daniel Chayton

Reg. 5 May 1810, No. 73
Reg. surrendered 3 May 1811, property changed in
part

Fame
Schooner 1D2M: 67'9" L, 19'3" B, 9'6" D, 108 27/95 T
Round tuck, no galleries, "a woman head"
Built Mathews County VA 1805, registered BC
13 Mar 1809, No. 11
Property transferred
Owner and master: Robert Davis of BC, mariner
Reg. 22 Mar 1810, No. 42
Registration surrendered 7 Mar 1811, new owners

Fanny
Schooner 1D2M: 65'3" L, 21' B, 9'9" D, 113 48/95 T
Round tuck, no galleries, no head
Built Mathews County VA 1803, registered BC
12 Apr 1805, No. 49
Property transferred
Owner: Matthew Potter of BC, mariner;
Master John Williams
Reg. 17 Jul 1810, No. 123
Vessel sold at Guadaloupe Sept 1811

Farmers Fancy
Schooner 1D2M: 49'6" L, 16'4" B, 5'5" D, 37 1/95 T
No galleries, no head
Built Talbot County 1810, enrolled Oxford
25 Sept 1810, No. 56
Property transferred
Owner and master: Philip Ryan of Philadelphia
Reg. 3 Oct 1810, No. 164

Felicity
Schooner 1D2M: 73' L, 22' B, 9' D, 124 67/95 T
No galleries, no head
Built Accomack County VA 1804, registered BC
25 Jul 1804, No. 201
Owner: James Biays of BC, merchant;
Master Ezekial C. Wiseham
Reg. 21 Dec 1810, No. 206
Vessel sold to foreigners in Havana, 1811

Female
Brig 1D2M: 89' L, 24' B, 10'6" D, 197 80/95 T
Round tuck, no galleries, no head
Built Talbot County 1807, registered
14 Mar 1809, No. 18
Property transferred in part
Owners: Kennedy Owen, Luke Tiernan, James
Bosley of BC

Pride of Baltimore

Master Wanton Gorton
Reg. 27 Mar 1810, No. 47
Registration surrendered 23 Oct 1811, new owners

Financier

Schooner 1D2M: 87' L, 21'10" B, 9' D, 152 78/95 T
Round tuck, no galleries, no head
Built BC 1808, registered BC 3 Jan 1809, No. 1
Property transferred
Owner: David Easterbrook of BC, merchant
Master Clement Cathell
Reg. 26 Mar 1810, No. 46
"Detained abroad"

Flora

Ship 1D3M: 97'6" L, 26' B, 10'6" D, 235 38/95 T
Round tuck, no galleries, no head
Built SO 1809-10 as per master carpenter certificate
Owner: William Greetham of BC, merchant;
Master Andrew Steuart
Reg. 14 Mar 1810, No. 35
Property transferred (same description)
Owner: Jonathan Hudson of BC, merchant;
Master Robert Dolliver
Reg. 16 May 1810, No. 83

Fly

Schooner 1D2M: 59'3" L, 18'4" B, 7' D, 65 17/95 T
No galleries, no head
Built at Hampton VA 1809
Owner: Peter A. Guestier of BC
Master Henry Yearly
Reg. 11 Jan 1810, No. 7
"Sold to foreigners" 17 Jan 1811

Friendship

Schooner 1D2M: 59'3" L, 18'4" B, 7' D, 65 17/95 T
Square stern, round tuck, no galleries, no head
Built Somerset County 1809 as per master carpenter
certificate
Reg. 5 May 1810, No. 28
Reg. 5 Oct 1810, No. 166 (same description)
Owner: John Wilmot of BC, merchant
Master Freeman Snow
Vessel and papers lost 1810

Greyhound

Schooner 1D2M: 62'6" L, 18'6" B, 6'6" D, 68 22/95 T
No galleries, no head
Built Dorchester County 1807, enrolled Oxford
26 Jun 1808, No. 48
Property transferred
Owner and master: James Lousier of Harford County

Registration surrendered at Havre de Grace 18 Sept
1810
Reg. 31 Oct 1810, No. 178 (same description)
Vessel being bound on a sea voyage
Registration surrendered at Havre de Grace 7 Apr
1811,
enrolled 31 Dec 1811

Harmony   Schooner 1D2M: 61′4″ L, 19′1 1/2″ B, 8′2″ D, 88
22/95 T
Round tuck, no galleries, no head
Built Mathews County VA 1807, enrolled port of
East River 30 Jun 1810, No. 7
Change of property
Owners: Matthew Potter and Thomas Morean of BC;
Master Matthew Potter
Reg. 3 Aug 1810, No. 135
Registration surrendered 13 Mar 1811,
property changed in part

Harriott   Schooner 1D2M: 60′4″ L, 18′10″ B, 8′5″ D, 81 71/95 T
Round tuck, no galleries, no head
Built Somerset County 1803, enrolled Norfolk and
Portsmouth 19 Sept 1809, No. 47
Vessel now bound on foreign voyage
Owners: John and Henry Butler of Norfolk;
Master John O. Butler
Reg. 3 Jan 1810, No. 2, enrolled Norfolk and
Portsmouth 10 Nov 1810, No. 54
Owner and master: John O. Butler of Norfolk,
mariner
Reg. 6 Dec 1810, No. 199
Registration surrendered Norfolk 19 Apr 1811

Hazard   Schooner "sharp-built" 1D2M: 54′6″ L, 16′10″ B, 6′
D, 47 21/95 T
Round tuck, no galleries, no head
Built in Somerset County 1810 as per master carpenter
certificate
Owner: Samuel Grace of BC, merchant
Master Lewis Harrison
Reg. 9 Aug 1810, No. 136

Henry   Brig 1D2M: 73′ L, 22′ 2″ B, 10′ 11″ D, 152 17/95 T
Square tuck, no galleries, no head
Built BC 1801, registered BC 20 Dec 1804, No. 308
Property in part changed

Pride of Baltimore

Owners: William, Robert, and Joseph W. Patterson of BC, merchants
Master Thomas Phipps
Reg. 12 Apr 1810, No. 56
Registration surrendered 10 Jan 1811, "vessel lost"

Herald

Schooner 1D2M: 85' 6" L, 21'10" B, 9'1" D, 151 16/95 T
No galleries, no head
Built BC 1807, registered BC 14 Mar 1809, No. 15
Property transferred
Owner: David Easterbrook of BC, merchant;
Master William Murdock
Reg. 28 Apr 1810. No. 68

Hippomenes

Brig 1D2M: 74' L, 21' B, 10'6" D, 142 52/95 T
Built on East River VA 1807, Reg. BC
15 Mar 1809, No. 19
Property transferred
Owners: James A. Buchanan, Samuel Smith and John McKee of BC
Master William Worthington
Reg. 12 Jul 1810, No. 121
Vessel and papers lost 1811

Hope

Schooner 1D2M: 80'4" L, 20'9" B, 8'6" D, 126 9/95 T
Round tuck, no galleries, no head
Built Talbot County 1808 as per master carpenter certificate
Owners: John McFadon, George Stiles of BC, merchants
Master Baazillui Chase
Reg. 25 Apr 1810, No. 66
Registration surrendered 14 Feb 1811, vessel lost

Humming Bird

Schooner 1D2M: 54' L, 17'6" B, 5'11" D, 47 40/95 T
No galleries, no tuck
Built Dorchester County 1807, enrolled BC
6 May 1808, No. 45
Property transferred
Owner and master: Peter W. Marrenner of New York City
Reg. 13 Apr 1810, No. 58
Registration surrendered at New York 2 Jul 1810

Independence

Schooner 1D2M: 75' L, 22' B, 8' D, 114 38/95 T
No galleries, no figurehead

Built at Havre de Grace, Harford County 1810,
enrolled at Havre de Grace 24 Aug 1810, No. 15
Vessel bound on a foreign voyage
Owner: John Boyd of Havre de Grace;
Master Solomon McCombs
Reg. 15 Oct 1810, No. 168
Registration surrendered 29 Apr 1811, new owners

Jane   Schooner 1D2M: 91'6" L, 23'6" B, 9'6" D, 181 88/95 T
Round tuck, no galleries, no head
Built BC 1809, registered BC 18 May 1809, No. 90
Property transferred
Owner: J.B. Duchamp of Norfolk VA;
Master Lewis Bernard Jr.
Reg. 22 Oct 1810, No. 173
Registration surrendered BC 5 Feb 1812, new owners

Jane Maria   Schooner 1D2M: 67'4" L, 18'10" B, 8'1" D, 89 65/95 T
Round tuck, no galleries, no head
Built BC 1810 as per master carpenter's certificate
Owner: Bernard Salenave of BC
Master Nehemiah Drew
Reg. 10 Jul 1810, No. 120
Registration surrendered BC 5 Feb 1812, new owners

John   Schooner 1D2M: 59'1" L, 19' B, 7'6" D, 70 30/95 T
No galleries, no head
Built Somerset County 1806, enrolled Tappahannock
12 Apr 1810, No. 5
Vessel bound on a foreign voyage
Owner and master: Thomas Jones of Fredericksburg
VA, mariner
Reg. 24 Nov 1810, No. 195
Registration surrendered 16 Mar 1811, property
changed in part

Kemp   Schooner "sharp built" 1D2M: 100' L, 24'2" B, 10'6"
D, 228 36/95 T
Round tuck, no galleries, no head
Built BC as per master carpenter certificate
Owners: Michael McBlair, John Hollins, John Smith
Hollins of BC, merchants
Master Pearl Durkee
Reg. 31 Jul 1810, No. 133
Registration surrendered 23 Oct 1811, new owners

Lancaster   Schooner 1D2M: 61' L, 29' B, 8'3" D, 81 7/95 T

Pride of Baltimore

Round tuck, no galleries, no head
Built Lancaster County VA 1810 as per master
carpenter certificate
Owner: Martin Sherman of Lancaster County VA;
Master Ellis L.B. Tapsicott
Reg. 17 Nov 1810, No. 191
Registration surrendered 31 Mar 1811

Lark
Schooner 1D2M: 70′ L, 18′6″ B, 7′9″ D, 88 87/95 T
Round tuck, no galleries, no head
Owner: Peter A. Guestier of BC, merchant;
Master Henry Thomas
Reg. 5 Nov. 1810, No. 186
Registration surrendered 25 Sept 1811, new owner

Leopard
Schooner 1D2M: 69′ L, 20′ B, 8′3″ D, 98 90/95 T
Round tuck, no galleries, no head
Built Talbot County 1809
Owner: Samuel Grace of BC
Master John Hearn
Reg. 28 Feb 1810, No. 26
Registration surrendered 9 Apr 1811, new owner

Lively Sally
Schooner 1D2M: 43′4″ L, 14′6″ B, 5′ D, 27 25/95 T
No galleries, no head
Built Somerset County 1801, enrolled BC
18 Apr 1810, No. 24
Property transferred
Owner and master: Joseph Jones of Northumberland
County VA
Reg. 16 Jun 1810, No. 105

Loraon
Schooner 1D2M: 56′ L, 17′4″ B, 6′4″ D, 51 45/95 T
No galleries, no head
Built Dorchester County 1802, enrolled Oxford
14 Jul 1809, No. 38
Property transferred
Owners: Manuel Fernandis and Nathaniel Moore of
BC;
Master Abel Smith
Reg. 10 Apr 1810, No. 55
Registration surrendered 20 July, change of property
Reg. 20 Jul 1810, No. 125 (same description)
Owner: Nathaniel Moore of BC
Master George Ellis
Registration surrendered 7 Nov 1810 new owner
Reg. 7 Nov 1810, No. 187 (same description)

Owner: Stephen Gunby of BC
Master John M. White
Registration surrendered 1 Jun 1812 BC, new owners

Luna Schooner 1D2M: 93'3" L, 24'3" B, 10'5" D, 209 16/95 T
Round tuck, no galleries, no head
Built BC 1809, reg. BC 27 Apr 1809, No. 60
Owners: James Williams, Samuel Smith,
James A. Buchanan of BC, merchants
Master James N. Martin
Reg. 22 Mar 1810, No. 43
"vessel and papers lost at sea 1811"

Madiera Brig 1D2M: 77'3" L, 23'10" B, 11'5" D, 180 42/95 T
Round tuck, no galleries, no head
Built St. Mary's County 1806, reg. BC 20 Nov 1809,
No. 233
Property transferred
Owner: Charles Yates of BC, merchant
Master Joseph Hall
Reg. 4 Apr 1810, No. 52
Registration surrendered 12 Sept 1810, new owner
Reg. 14 Sept 1810, No. 155 (same description)
Owner: Jacob Adams of BC, merchant
Master Joseph Hall
Registration surrendered 1 Apr 1811, new owner

Mary Schooner 1D2M: 60'6" L, 18'4" B, 6'6" D, 62 7/95 T
No galleries, no badges, no head
Built Broad Creek, Talbot County 1806, enrolled
port of Yeocomico 21 Apr 1810, No. 7
Vessel bound on a foreign voyage
Owner and master: Joseph Dashields of
Northumberland County VA
Reg. 1 Jun 1810, No. 97
Registration surrendered at Yeocomico 22 Aug 1810

Mary Ann Schooner 1D2M: 60'3" L, 18' B, 6' D, 56 26/95 T
No galleries, no head
Built Dorchester County 1809, enrolled Oxford
12 Dec 1809, No. 65
Property transferred
Owner: Samuel Grace of BC; master Jeremiah Hill
Reg. 13 Jun 1810, No. 100
Registration surrendered 8 Apr 1811, "vessel lost"

Pride of Baltimore

Matilda

Brig 1D2M: 80'6" L, 22'8" B, 10' D, 161 22/95 T
No galleries, no head
Built Accomack County VA 1807, registered BC
30 Mar 1809, No. 39
Property in part transferred
Owner: Joseph White of BC
Master Ralph Porter
Reg. 30 Mar 1810, No. 48
Registration surrendered 3 May 1811, new owner

Matilda

Schooner 1D2M: 93'6" L, 22'7" B, 9'6" D, 180 63/95 T
Round tuck, no galleries, no head
Built Harford County 1809 as per master carpenter
certificate
Owners: Joseph Karrick, Thomas Foulk,
William Burton of BC
Master William Burton
Reg. 7 Jul 1810, No. 115
Registration surrendered New York 15 Jun 1811, new
owners

Matilda

Schooner 1D2M: 81'6" L, 22'3" B, 9'9" D, 155 62/95 T
Round tuck, no galleries, no head
Built Accomack County VA 1809, reg. BC
12 Sept 1809, No. 184
Property transferred
Owner: William Massicot of Philadelphia
Master Louis Bouees
Reg. 17 Jul 1810, No. 122

Merchant

Schooner 1D2M: 77' L, 23' B, 9'3" D, 141 44/95 T
Round tuck, no galleries, no head
Built Somerset County 1809 as per master carpenter
certificate
Owner and master: Robert Hamilton of BC, merchant
Reg. 12 Mar 1810, No. 34
Registration surrendered "this port 20 Apr 1815
pursuant to Act 3, March 1815"

Meteor

Schooner 1D2M: 61'6" L, 17'10" B, 5'6" D, 52 46/95 T
Square tuck, no galleries, no head
Built St. Mary's County 1810 as per master carpenter
certificate
Owner and master: Charles Augustine Chalumeau of
BC
Reg. 14 May 1810, No. 82

Registration surrendered 17 Feb 1811, sold to
foreigners

Milo Brig 1D2M: 105′ L, 25′6″ B, 11′7″ D, 278 75/95 T
Round tuck, no galleries, no head
Built Talbot County 1810 as per master carpenter
certificate
Owners: James Williams, James A. Buchanan, Samuel
Smith of BC, merchants
Master Rinaldo Johnson
Reg. 27 Dec 1810, No. 213
Registration surrendered 7 Dec 1811, new owners

Mira Schooner 1D2M: 49′4″ L, 15′7″ B, 5′5″ D, 35 58/95 T
No galleries, no head
Built Mathews County VA 1804, enrolled BC 4 Jan
1809,
No. 2
Property transferred
Owner and master: George Lee Corgin of
Fredericksburg VA, mariner
Reg. 21 Mar 1810, No. 41
Registration surrendered 10 Mar 1810 at
Tappahannock

Morning Star Schooner 1D2M: 42′ L, 14′ B, 5′ D, 24 65/95 T
No galleries, no head
Built King William County VA 1804, enrolled
Yorktown
5 Apr 1807, No. 53
Property now transferred
Owner: Samuel Sylvester of BC
Reg. 4 Jan 1810, No. 4

Nancy Schooner 1D2M: 53′8″ L, 18′3″ B, 6′ D, 49 44/95 T
No galleries, no head
Built Talbot County 1802, enrolled Oxford
4 Sept 1802, No. 36
Owner: Wesley Hyatt of BC; master John M. White
Reg. 10 May 1810, No. 79
Registration surrendered 10 Oct 1810,
enrollment issued

New Mary Schooner 1D2M: 79′ L, 22′ B, 8′2″ D, 124 48/95 T
Round tuck, no galleries, no head
Built Talbot County 1810 as per master carpenter
certificate

Pride of Baltimore

Owner and master: Joseph Almida of BC, mariner
Reg. 16 Aug 1810, No. 139
Registration surrendered "at this port 27 Apr 1812,
vessel sold at Havana to foreigners"

Nimble

Schooner 1D2M: 63'3" L, 18'6" B, 7'8" D, 80 76/95 T
Round tuck, no galleries, no head
Built BC 1810 as per master carpenter certificate
Owners: Bernard Salenave and John Okely of BC;
Master John Joseph Rey
Reg. 27 Jun 1810, No. 108
"vessel and papers lost 1810"

Ocean

Schooner 1D2M: 65' L, 20'5" B, 9'7" D, 108 57/95 T
Round tuck, no galleries, no head
Built Mathews County VA 1809, registered Norfolk
and Portsmouth 20 May 1809, No. 33
Property transferred
Owners: Joseph Watts and John Firns of BC, mariners;
Master John Firns
Reg. 5 May 1810, No. 74
Registration surrendered 9 Aug 1811, property
changed in part

Phoebe

Brig 1D2M: 73' L, 22'10" B, 10'6" D, 147 34/95 T
Round tuck, no galleries, no head
Built Mathews County VA 1802, reg. BC 1 Dec 1809,
No. 238
Property transferred in part
Owners: Samuel Smith, James A. Buchanan, John
Hollins, Michael McBlair, John S. Hollins, George J.
Brown of BC, merchants
Master Bernard Foley
Reg. 19 Oct 1810, No. 170

Pilgrim

Schooner 1D2M: 45'6" L, 17'2" B, 5'8" D, 45 29/95 T
Square tuck, no head
Built Dorchester County 1802, enrolled Nottingham
11 Apr 1809, No. 3
Vessel bound on foreign voyage
Owners: Thomas Morton and Alexander Edwards of
Charles County
Master Philip Key of Charles County
Reg. 27 Jan 1810, No. 21
Registration surrendered 2 Mar 1810, change of
property

Pilot
Schooner 1D2M: 94′ L, 23′2″ B, 9′7″ D, 187 14/95 T
Round tuck, no galleries, no head
Built Queen Anne's County 1809 as per master
carpenter certificate
Owners: Michael McBlair, Lemuel Taylor, John Smith
Hollins and John Hollins of BC, merchants
Master Patrick Cunningham
Reg. 1 May 1810, No. 69
Registration surrendered 9 Aug 1811,
property changed in part

Providence
Schooner 1D2M: 60′ L, 19′10″ B, 7′ D, 70 42/95 T
No galleries, no head
Built Dorchester County 1804, reg. Alexandria
12 Jun 1809, No. 19
Property transferred
Owner and master: Thomas Jones of BC, mariner
Reg. 15 Jan 1810, No. 10
Registration surrendered 19 Jan 1810, new owner
Reg. 19 Jan 1810, No. 12 (same description)
Owner and master: Robert Smith of BC
Registration surrendered 2 Nov 1810, new owner
Reg. 2 Nov 1810, No. 184 (same description)
Owners: Eaton R. Partridge and Nathan W. Chase of
BC
Master Nathan W. Chase
Registration surrendered Norfolk 2 May 1811, new
owners

Purse
Schooner 1D2M: 94′ L, 23′2″ B, 9′4″ D, 182 26/95 T
Round tuck, no galleries, no head
Built Baltimore 1809 as per master carpenter certificate
Owner and master: Henry Richards of New York City
Reg. 21 Apr 1810, No. 63

Revenge
Schooner 1D2M: 80′9″ L, 20′10″ B, 9′2″ D, 139
19/95 T
Round tuck, no galleries, no head
Built Queen Anne's County 1809 as per master
carpenter certificate
Owner: Samuel Grace of BC
Master Thomas Knappe
Reg. 9 May 1810, No. 76 1/2 (sic)

Rewastico
Schooner 1D2M: 60′6″ L, 17′6″ B, 8′6″ D, 78 27/95 T
No galleries, no head

Pride of Baltimore

Built Somerset County, reg. BC 28 May 1808, No. 26
Property transferred
Owner and master: James Hollis of BC
Reg. 29 Jun 1810, No. 111
Registration surrendered 14 Dec 1810, sold at
"Havanna"

Rumney

Schooner 1D2M: 67' L, 26'6" B, 8' D, 94 49/95 T
No galleries, no head
Built Somerset County 1808
Owner: Samuel G. Griffith of BC
Master Solomon Rathall
Reg. 12 Jan 1810, No. 8
Registration surrendered 7 Sept 1810
Reg 7 Sept 1810, No. 149 (same description)
Owner: John Randall of BC
Master Solomon Rathall

Sally

Schooner 1D2M: 56'6" L, 19' B, 7'9" D, 70 T
No galleries, no head
Built Mathews County VA 1804, enrolled BC 20 Oct
1809, No. 70
Property transferred
Owner and master: John Johnson of Alexandria D.C.
Reg. 9 Jan 1810, No. 5

Sally

Schooner 1D2M: 63'6" L, 19'6" B, 7'1" D, 75 35/95 T
Round tuck, no galleries, no head
Built Talbot County 1807, enrolled BC 14 Sept 1809,
No. 63
Owner: Samuel G. Griffith of BC, merchant
Master John Porter
Reg. 22 Mar 1810, No. 40

Sarah Ladson

Schooner 1D2M: 95'6" L, 24' B, 10'2" D, 208 24/95 T
Round tuck, no galleries, no head
Built Talbot County 1809 as per master carpenter
certificate
Owners: Robert Gilmor Jr., William Gilmor and
Richard Dorsey of BC, merchants, and Washington
Bowie of Georgetown D.C.
Master Christopher Child
Reg. 13 Apr 1810, No. 57
Registration surrendered 12 Dec 1811, new owners

Severn

Schooner 1D2M 58' L, 17'6" B, 6'3" D, 54 65/95 T

No galleries, square tuck, no head
Built Dorchester County VA (sic) 1809, enrolled BC
3 Nov 1809, No. 75
Property transferred
Owners: John McFadon and George C. Muller of BC,
merchants
Master Clement Cathell
Reg. 26 Sept 1810, No. 161
Registration surrendered 19 Feb 1811, new owners

Speedwell   Schooner 1D2M: 77′ L, 22′6″ B, 9′ D, 135 34/95 T
Square tuck, no galleries, no head
Built Dorchester County 1807, reg. BC 12 Sept 1809,
No. 182
Property in part transferred
Owners: George F. Warfield and Joseph White of BC
Master William Atkinson
Reg. 24 Mar 1810, No. 45
Registration surrendered Oct 1811, new owner

Spy   Schooner 1D2M: 90′ L, 22′10″ B, 9′10″ D, 180 39/95 T
Round tuck, no galleries, no head
Built Talbot County 1808, reg. BC 23 Sept 1809, No.
190
Property changed in part
Owners: Michael McBlair, John Hollins, John Smith
Hollins, Samuel Smith, James A. Buchanan, James
Purviance of BC, merchants
Master James W. Mortimer
Reg. 18 May 1810, No. 88
"captured by the British 1810"

Squirrel   Schooner "sharp built" 1D2M: 63′ L, 17′9″ B, 5′11″
D, 57 81/95 T
Round tuck, no galleries, no head
Built St. Mary's County 1810 as per master carpenter
certificate
Owner and master: John Peterson of BC, mariner
Reg. 10 Aug 1810, No. 137
Registration surrendered 9 Jan 1811, sold in a foreign
port

Superior   Brig 1D2M 87′ L, 23′ B, 9′11″ D, 175 82/95 T
Square tuck, no galleries, no head
Built Accomac County VA 1809 as per master
carpenter certificate

Pride of Baltimore

Owner: Matthew Keene of Dorchester County, merchant
Master William Darnell
Reg. 6 Apr 1810, No. 54

Susanna

Brig 1D2M: 74′6″ L, 24′ B, 10′9″ D, 163 16/95 T
No galleries, no head
Built Talbot County 1804, reg. BC 14 Jun 1809, No. 116
Property in part transferred
Owners: James A. Buchanan and Samuel Smith of BC, merchants
Master James Wright
Reg. 17 Dec 1810, No. 202

Thomas

Schooner 1D2M: 62′10″ L, 19′6″ B, 7′6″ D, 79 T
No galleries, no badges, no head
Built Dorchester County 1808, enrolled BC 1 Nov 1809, No. 74
Vessel bound on a foreign voyage
Owner and master: Samuel Dunwick of BC, mariner
Reg. 9 Jul 1810, No. 117
Registration surrendered 4 Sept 1810

Three Friends

Schooner 1D2M: 77′ L, 23′ B, 9′9″ D, 149 28/95 T
No galleries, no head
Built Somerset County 1805, reg. BC 12 Jun 1809, No. 111
Property transferred
Owner: John Laurens of BC
Reg. 2 Feb 1810, No. 22
Reg. 2 Mar 1810, No. 27
Owner: Peter A. Guestier of BC, merchant
Master Peter Coursell
Registration surrendered at Philadelphia 29 May 1810

Tigress

Brig "sharp built" 1D2M: 98′ L, 24′ B, 10′8″ D, 225 23/95 T
Round tuck, no galleries, "a tigress head"
Built Baltimore 1810 as per master carpenter certificate
Owners: Samuel G. Griffith, Samuel Briscoe, James Partridge and John Randall of BC;
Master Thomas C. Horne
Reg. 23 Aug 1810, No. 142

Two Brothers

Schooner 1D2M: 60′ L, 18′ B, 6′ D, 55 94/95 T
No galleries, no figurehead

Built 1809 (no place given), enrolled Oxford 15 Jul 1809, No. 40
Property transferred
Owners: Henry Hubbard and Aaron North of Dorchester County
Master Aaron North
Reg. 1 Nov 1810, No. 181
Registration surrendered 14 Nov 1810, new owner
Reg. 14 Nov 1810, No. 189 (same description)
Owner: William Neilson of BC, merchant
Master Alexander Knott
Registration surrendered 1 May 1811, new owner

Union
Schooner 1D2M: 45′ L, 15′ B, 6′4″ D, 36 T
No galleries, no head
Built Somerset County 1797, enrolled Norfolk and Portsmouth 3 May 1809, No. 26
Property transferred
Owner and master: Gustavus Muschett
Reg. 22 Jan 1810, No. 18

Victory
Schooner 1D2M: 55′ L, 17′3″ B, 5′7″ D, 46 3/95 T
No galleries, no head
Built on Little Choptank River 1805, reg. 22 Jul 1809, No. 148
Property transferred
Owner and master: Peter Collard of BC, merchant
Reg. 12 Sept 1810, No. 152
Registration surrendered 27 Dec 1810, sold to foreigners

Vivid
Brig 1D2M: 87′ L, 23′9″ B, 10′3″ D, 186 40/95 T
Round tuck, no galleries, no head
Built Somerset County 1810 as per master carpenter certificate
Owner: Charles Wirgman of BC, merchant
Master John Hill
Reg. 18 Jul 1810, No. 124

Wasp
Schooner 1D2M: 59′ L, 17′3″ B, 6′3″ D, 55 22/95 T
Round tuck, no galleries, no head
Built BC 1810, enrolled BC 29 Sept 1810, No. 69
Owners: Richard H. Johns and Mark Carroll of BC, mariners
Master Matthew Potter
Reg. 9 Nov. 1810, No. 188

Wigwam	Brig 1D2M: 74'6" L, 21'6" B, 12' D, 167 23/95 T Round tuck, no galleries, no head Built Somerset County 1809 as per master carpenter certificate Owners: James Biays and John Hanna of BC, merchants Master George C. Reed Reg. 2 Nov 1810, No. 182 Vessel and papers lost 1810
William	Schooner 1D2M: 46' L, 15' B, 5' D, 29 20/95 T No galleries, no head Built Smithfield VA 1800, enrolled Norfolk and Portsmouth 29 May 1806, No. 28 Owner: Benjamin Drew of Smithfield Master William Shelby Reg. 18 May 1810, No. 86 Registration surrendered at Norfolk 7 Jun 1810
William & John	Schooner 1D2M: 55' L, 15'8" B, 5'11" D, 45 12/95 T No galleries, no head Built Mathews County VA 1804, enrolled BC 23 May 1804, No. 30 Property transferred Owner: Mathias Rich of BC Master John Marr Reg. 23 Feb 1810, No. 24 "Sold to foreigners" 21 May 1810
William & John	Schooner 1D2M: 50'9" L, 15'5" B, 5'11' D, 39 80/95 T No galleries, no head Built Talbot County 1809, enrolled BC 20 Aug 1809, No. 59 Vessel bound on foreign voyage Owner and master: John Dameron of BC, mariner Reg. 26 Jun 1810, No. 109
William & Susan (of Hunger River)	Schooner 1D2M: 68'10" L, 20' B, 7' D, 83 71/95 T No galleries, no badges, no head Built Dorchester County 1805, enrolled Vienna 22 Aug 1809, No. 38 Vessel bound on foreign voyage Owner: Solomon Firwan of Dorchester County Master Solomon Tyler

Reg. 19 May 1810, No. 87
Registration surrendered at Vienna 3 Aug 1810

Wolf   Schooner 1D2M: 77′ L, 23′7″ B, 9′8″ D, 150 74/95 T
No galleries, no head
Built Accomack County VA 1805, enrolled BC 29 Jan 1807
Owner: Leven Jones of BC, mariner
Master Frederick Travers
Reg. 8 Mar 1810, No. 29
Registration surrendered 18 Aug 1812 at this port
"vessel sold to a Spainard"

Zephyr   Schooner 1D2M: 85′6″ L, 22′5″ B, 8′8″ D, 147 40/95 T
Round tuck, no galleries, no head
Built on West River 1808, reg. 2 Jun 1809, No. 104
Property transferred
Owners: John and Robert Oliver and Hugh Thompson, merchants of BC
Master William Groom
Reg. 26 Feb 1810, No. 25

Appendix 3. Typical ship construction equipment and tools for building vessels in the War years of 1812–1815

"An inventory of all the estate, real, personal and mixed, of James Cordery, lunatic, returned by his Trustees under order of the court dated January 7, 1820."

Inventory of Property of James Cordery, Shipbuilder, Fells Point, Baltimore

"MATERIALS OF TRADE"

63 small spars
16 floor timbers
66 root knees
11 cedar posts
 3 pieces pine timber
 3 pieces oake timber

2 negro servants
3 negro slaves
6 flitch oak timber
4 oak plank 1 1/4 inch
2 wooden capt & 1 cross tree
1 set of shipwright's drawings,
    naval architecture, etc.

Pride of Baltimore

"Carpenter's utensils"

1 case clipsticks
a moddle and draft of a team boat*
32 timber moulds
4 whip saws
2 broken whip saws
1 cross cut saw
1 broken cross cut saw
10 augers
1 adze
1 axe
1 crowbar
1 tiller for whip saw
4 pitch kettles & 2 stands
1 pitch ladle
1 pair timber hooks
3 tar mops
35 bircth brooms
1 pair oyster tongs
1 grind stone & bench
1 gin with fall blocks
3 float stages
1 ladder
1 takle, fall & blocks
1 ship scraper

2 slice irons
1 caulkers box
18 caulking irons
7 caulking mallets
3 horse irons
1 cant hook
2 sets gin irons
4 timber chains
1 pair steelyards
2 prop irons
3 clamps
2 pin malls
1 frow
1 bell & belfry
6 gin benches
2 crabs
1 batteau ⅔ oars
16 perchace blocks
small parcel old rope
200 lbs old spikes &
ribbon nails
2 trussell benches
2 cog wheels

"Blacksmith's made work"

176 hooks & thimbles
451 single thimbles
53 single hooks
198 staples
44 port rings & 16 hatch startss
105 small rings

185 rivets
26 Hencoob hooks
52 round nails
116 forelocks
22 bushes for sheaves
10 pump bolts

"Blacksmith work"

36 dogs for sheave holes
8 pump box staples
15 pair can hooks
13 burs
9 marling spikes

1 fish hook for anchor
1 iron & cross trees
7 ring bolts
1 martingale
2 cap bands

* Most likely mistaken to be steamboat.

7 boat hooks
5 boat chains
2 stantions
1 chain plate
16 hinges
6 pump box straps
7 preventre plates
2 straps for harnes casks
2 windlass hoops
1 boom crutch
1 flat scraper

1 hatch bar
1 pump spear & box & 2 breakes
1 ded eye and strap
2 bake oven doors
1 pump hoop
3 bars iron
5 bars steel
8 bolt rods
1 small stove
2 pair blacksmith bellows complete

"BLACKSMITH UTENSILS"

2 anvils
10 hammers
1 poker
2 shovels
2 gauges
2 wrenches
2 porter bars
12 nail tools
10 cold chizles
small quantity nail rods

2 vices
2 hooks
1 swedge
22 tongs
2 punch handles
1 beck iron
59 punches
2 thimble tools
1 file

Debts of over $887 due the estate including $37.00 owed Cordery "for Board" and $20.90 owed him for "a new ship built by Jas. Inloes".

(Signed by) Maria Cordery
Joseph Zane
Trustee

"James Corderey died 7th April 1820"

The expenses of his illness and the support of his family until 2 August 1820 was paid through the rent of warehouse and wharf, the sale of a few items in the inventory above, the hire of other items such as the stage and kettle, and mostly by the labor of Harry, Charles, Abram, and Lydia, who were hired out. Harry and Charles were negro servants with five and four years (respectivly) to serve. Abraham, or Abram, was a slave as was Lydia. The third slave of the family, Sophie, was not "hired out." Harry, Charles, and Abram worked at least once for Gardner and Robinson.

Citation for this material: Baltimore Chancy Papers .519
Maryland State Archives

Appendix 4. The great galleys

The great galleys of Venice and Genoa gradually gave way together with the political fortunes of their city states. They were replaced by even greater and faster sailing galleys of southern France. These warship galleys became popular as far north as Denmark and Sweden because of their speed and maneuverability. But those of France established the pattern and advanced them to their highest development.

We should not lower the curtain on these fine ships before briefly describing the great *La Reale*. The name of course indicates that it belonged to the king of France. It was originally the ship's name; later the name of any galley commander's flagship, and ultimately (in small letters) a *reale* if it was of the largest class of galleys. As such, it had a total of 462 oarsmen as compared to an "ordinary" galley of 260. This ship measured about 170 feet on the waterline: it was 21 feet in the beam of hull (not including the platform for the oars and holes); it had 33 pairs of thwarts or rowing benches with seven rowers on each. For sailing, the *reale* had two masts with lateen sails (one on each), but together totalling 8,000 square feet. There were five large guns: a 36 pounder and two each of 24 and 18 pounds, all mounted facing forward ahead of the masts and rowers.* This indicates that the vessel had to be pointed directly at its target, for the guns were mounted on fixed supports allowing for recoil only. There was a bronze-headed ram extending some 25 feet beyond the bow and mortised to the extended stem head. One feature below decks that might interest etymologists was the location or room that housed, among things other than reserve sails, the ship's supply of wine which was *sold* to the crew. This place was called the *taverne*. It was adjacent to the powder room that serviced the guns.

The last naval battle in which galleys were used was at the encounter off Matapan in 1717. The last *reale* was built in 1720. They were impressive seacraft and several examples can be studied in Paris at the Musee Marine Nationalle.

Progressing among these European fast rowing and sailing hulls, it might again be stressed that the profits, whether they were naval victories or monetary advantage, went to the ship with the fastest and most maneuverable hull form. Sail could be piled on yard after yard, but it was only the slim, light, fast hull that could make the optimum speeds. Long sharp waterlines with hollow rising sections and flattening quarters for the relative motion of the water as it streaked aft toward an essentially flat and closing wake with minimum wave generation . . . these were the everlasting characteristics.

---

*The size of naval guns during this and later periods was given according to the weight of its projectile (iron ball). Thus an 18-pound gun would throw an 18 pound cannonball.

Appendix 5. Notes from M. Marestier's Correspondence and Treatise, "Memoire sur Les Bateaux a Vapeur des Etats-Unis d'Amerique", 1820

The gentleman from France, a distinguished engineer named M. Jean Baptiste Marestier, traveled to the United States some time around 1814-15 to study the American application of steam engines to marine propulsion. How much of value this study is is not now important, but his attraction to Baltimore Clippers and his recording of them from a technical eye is considerably important toward authenticating them in history.

These dimensional data were of considerable help as were the hull profiles in synthesizing and conceptualizing the Pride of Baltimore in 1975-76. There was also valuable carryover in designing the Pride of Baltimore II in 1986.

In accumulating his numerical data and drafts, Marestier was observing and obviously measuring the vessels himself. He admits, however, referring to the masting and sail profiles, that he was sketching at some distance; therefore, the rig proportions were not altogether reliable.

Principal Dimensions of Some Sharp Baltimore Schooners by M. Marestier

	(1)	(2)	(3)	(4)	(5)	(6)	(7)
Length	102'9"	92'9"	89'11"	72'3"	59'3"	57'3"	54'6"
Beam	25'7"	24'0"	22'7"	21'0"	17'6"	18'3"	16'11"
Hold Depth	11'9"	10'0"	8'2"	--	--	--	--
Stern post rake	12'8"	9'8"	6'6"	7'2"	3'4"	6'0"	3'6"
Maximum section forward of midlength	13'6"	5'4"	7'7"	5'0"	5'5"	5'6"	10'2"
Length of mast (main)	83'11"	72'2"	--	57'(?)	--	--	--
Length of mast (fore)	82'2"	68'10"	--	55'	--	--	--
Diameter mainmast	20"	--	--	--	--	--	--
Diameter foremast	21"	--	--	--	--	--	--

These examples are not sufficient enough in number to establish an average or standard, but they are genuine in themselves. There are but five that are seemingly large enough to have been effective privateer size. The smaller four are likely sharp working schooners more suitable to be coastwise or work boats on the bay.

The profiles from Marestier's collection are typical of his work. The hulls are incomplete in line with the waterline plans; not wholly consistent with the sheer plan. However, they are descriptively of value.

Marestier also measured and recorded such items as the placement of masts with relation to the keel as well as mast rake.

Endnotes

Chapter One

1. *Short History of the United States Navy*, by C. S. Alden. J. B. Lippincott Company, Philadephia.

2. The carpenter's certificates, official recordings of new ships, many of which still exist in the National Archives, do not identify the vessels as to mission or designate that they may be Baltimore Clippers. This identifying popular name came much later. However, each master carpenter had common descriptive terms that made his vessel's identity fairly obvious. The style of the vessel was often noted as "sharp-built," "privateer finish," "privateer service."

Chapter Two

1. Appendix 2 contains alphabetical listings of carpenter's certificates for Baltimore Clippers built in Maryland from 1807 to 1815. These are not complete listings, because many vessels, some built for foreign accounts, were never documented, and an unaccountable number of certificates have been lost. The best estimate of Baltimore Clippers built during the years 1810-1815 is near 300, with 30 to 40 percent of the listings missing.

2. The *ton* as a unit of measure is derived from the medieval unit *tunne*, which was a large wine cask and accounts for the volumetric relationship.

3. It was, and still is, customary for local artists to paint new foreign ships entering Naples with Vesuvius in the background. The artist's work was accurate but sterotyped.

4. There is a registration listing in Maryland records of a schooner whose dimensions are close to this one of the same name. Her deck length was 80 feet, beam 22 feet, and depth of hold 8 1/2 feet. She was built in Talbot County in 1809, registered in Oxford, and captured by the British in 1813.

Chapter Three

1. The cost of most privateers was between $8,000 and $12,000, so she multiplied her initial investment tenfold at least.

2. Howard Chapelle in *The Search for Speed Under Sail* refers to the Ann McKim as the first clipper ship of the pre-Clipper Ship Era.

3. Brass cannons are not practical and became obsolete after the 17th century with the development of better techniques in casting iron. Brass is a great conductor of heat, and after a few rounds brass cannons must be allowed to cool, or they will ignite fresh powder charges.

Chapter Four

1. Her measured tonnage for the old common rule was 176 tons burthen.

2. SA/ ≪ ≧ 2/3 SA = sail area in sq. ft. ≪ ≧ = displacement volume in cu. ft. ≪ ≧/.01L3 ≪ ≧ = displacement in tons

3. Excerpts from letters and the *Pride*'s log, as noted in *Sailing With Pride*, by Greg Pease. Baumgartner Publishing Company, Baltimore, MD; 1990.

Chapter Five

1. *The Downburst*, by T. T. Fujita, University of Chicago, 1985, as quoted in "Sailing Vessel Stability: With Particular Reference to the *Pride of Baltimore* Casualty," by Chatterton and Maxham. SNAME Journal, 1988.

2. Reference Item No. 2, "Conclusions," of the U.S. Coast Guard official report, page 25.

Illustration Credits

Chapter One

Figures 1-1 through 1-4: H.R. Hollyday Collection, Historical Society of Talbot County, Maryland; Figures 1-5 and 1-6: Tom Price; Figures 1-7 and 1-8: Thomas C. Gillmer; Figure 1-9: Peabody Museum of Salem, Massachusetts; Figure 1-10 *Sailing Ships of the Romantic Era*, Edita-Lausanne, 1968; Figures 1-11 and 1-12: Thomas C. Gillmer photos, Marine Museum, Paris; Figure 1-13: Sim Comfort, London; Figure 1-14: Smithsonian Institution, National Museum of American History; Figure 1-15: National Maritime Museum, Greenwich, England; Figure 1-16: Maryland Historical Society of Baltimore; Figure 1-17: Tom Price; Figure 1-18: National Archives, Washington, D.C.; Figure 1-19: Tom Price; Figure 1-20: National Maritime Museum, Greenwich, England; Figure 1-21 and Figure 1-22: Chesapeake Bay Maritime Museum, St. Michaels, Maryland; Figure 1-23: Peabody Museum of Salem.

Chapter Two

Figure 2-1: National Archives, Washington, D.C.; Figures 2-2 and 2-3: Thomas C. Gillmer; Figures 2-4 and 2-5: Edita-Lausanne, 1968; Figures 2-6, 2-7, and 2-8: National Maritime Museum, Greenwich, England; Figure 2-9: Edita-Lausanne, 1968; Figure 2-10: Mariners' Museum, Newport News, Virginia; Figure 2-11: Maryland Historical Society, Baltimore; Figure 2-12: Smithsonian Institution, National Museum of American History; Figure 2-13: Peabody Museum, Salem; Figure 2-14: Mariners' Museum, Newport News, Virginia.

Chapter Three

Figure 3-1: Maryland Historical Society, Baltimore; Figure 3-2: Tom Price; Figure 3-3: Peabody Museum, Salem; Figure 3-4: Tom Price; Figure 3-5: Handels og Sofarts Museet, Denmark; Figure 3-6: Maryland Historical Society, Baltimore; Figure 3-7: Thomas C. Gillmer; Figure 3-8: Naval Historical Center, Washington, D.C.; Figure 3-9: Parker Gallery, London; Figure 3-10: Tom Price.

Chapter Four

Figure 4-1: Baltimore Sunpapers; Figures 4-2 through 4-11: Thomas C. Gillmer; Figure 4-12: William Gilkerson; Figure 4-13: Jan Miles; Figure 4-14: Pride of Baltimore, Inc.; Figure 4-15: Thomas C. Gillmer; Figure 4-16: Jan Miles; Figure 4-17: Pride of Baltimore, Inc.; Figure 4-18: Michael Kozma; Figure 4-19: Jennifer Lamb; Figure 4-20: Thomas C. Gillmer; Figure 4-21: Pride of Baltimore, Inc.; Figure 4-22: Thomas C. Gillmer.

Chapter Five

Figures 5-1 through 5-16: Thomas C. Gillmer; Figure 5-17: Ivar Franzen; Figure 5-18: Thomas C. Gillmer.

Index

A

Aberdeen Clipper, 95, 114
adze, 4, 124, 127
aerodynamics, 59-60, 108, 135, 141. *See also* sailing performance
Alerta (*Hornet*), 87
Alexander, 110-13, 191-92
Alexander, Mark, 24
Amelia, 85
America, 105, 107-08
American Revolution, 18-19, 40-43, 191
Amistad, 89
Amphion, 192
Andromache (HMS), 36-37
Ann Maria (1803), 192
Ann Maria (1808), 192
Ann McKim, 97-102
apparent wind, 141-43
Arab, 26
armament (guns), 9, 21, 46
Atlas, 192
Auld, Hugh, 26

B

backbone. *See* keel
Bailey, James, 113
Baker, William, 1
ballast, 170-71; for *Pride of Baltimore*, 132-33; for *Pride of Baltimore II*, 170, 180-84; hanging bracket, 171, 175
Baltimore, 192
Baltimore: early settlement, 23-26; as shipbuilding and shipping port, 47, 84-91; City of, 1, 115-17, 131, 153. *See also* Chesapeake Bay shipbuilders, Fells Point

Baltimore Flyers, 19, 27, 49
Barbary pirates, 19, 41, 43-44, 74
Barney, Joshua, 39
Bee McFadon, 193
Berbice (HMS), 10
Bermuda sloops, 11-12
B. Franklin, 193
Biedinger, Richard, 157
Black Joke, 113
blockade runners/running, in American Revolution and War of 1812, 18-19, 23, 26-27, 77, 88; in Civil War, 105, 108; in South American revolution, 86-88
Bois, deClair, 106
bolts. *See* fastenings and fittings
Bond, Thomas, 61
Bonne Homme Richard, x
Bordeaux Packet, 39, 67
Boudreau, Peter, 126-27, 152, 160, 167, 178, 184
Bounty (HMS), 1
bow profiles, 51-53, 56
Boyle, Captain Thomas, xiv, 28-30
Brazillian, 193
Breeze, 193
brig, 74-76
Brothers, 193
Buckskin, 193-94
bugeye. *See* Chesapeake Bay bugeye
bulkheads. *See* watertight bulkheads
Buttersworth, Thomas, 80-81

C

California Clippers, 103
California Gold Rush, 104

Caribbean, 91-94
Caroline (1809, 78′), 194
Caroline (1809, 86′6″), 194
carpenter's certificates, 50-54, 219
carpenter's measure, 50, 61-62
carrying capacity, of clippers, 100-03
Cassius, 194
Cathera, 32
Catherine Augusta, 194
Chapelle, Howard, 21-23, 73, 220
Charlotte, 195
chasse-marée (French channel lugger), 16-17
Chasseur, xiv, 23, 28-30, 50-51, 53, 67, 85, 102
Chesapeake, 43
Chesapeake Bay log canoe (dugout), 3-7
Chesapeake Bay shipbuilders (1700s-1800s): x, 2-6, 12, 18-19, 23-28, 47, 54, 57-58, 68-73, 96, 105-06, 118, 213-15; influence on French shipbuilders, 62-68. *See also* carpenter's certificates, shipwrights' tools
Chesapeake Bugeye, 3-4
Chesney, James, 150-52
China trade, 101, 109, 114
Ciota, 195
clipper bow, 53, 56, 190
clipper schooner, British (fruit schooner), 110-14
Clipper Ship Era (1850s-1860s), xv, 97, 100-03
clipper ships, defined, 100-03; earliest, 97-102; extreme (maximum), 102-03; speed records of, 102-03

10/94³
1/97⁹
8/05¹²